Application Interoperability:

Microsoft .NET and J2EE

patterns & practices

Peter Laudati, Microsoft Corporation
William Loeffler, Microsoft Corporation
David Aiken, Arkitec
Keith Organ, Arkitec
Anthony Steven, Content Master Ltd.
Mike Preradovic, Intrinsyc Software
Wayne Citrin, JNBridge, Inc.
Peter Clift, VMC Consulting

ISBN 0-7356-1847-X

Contents

Chapter 7

Integrating .NET in the Presentation Tier   203

Chapter 8

Integrating .NET in the Business Tier   235

Appendix B
Installing XBikes on .NET   317

Index   341

Contributors   361

1

Introduction

Welcome

Welcome to *Application Interoperability: Microsoft .NET and J2EE*. This book gives you the best information available about how to ensure that enterprise applications based on Java 2 Platform, Enterprise Edition (J2EE) work in harmony with components based on Microsoft® .NET and vice versa. If you are developer with responsibility for implementing interoperability between these two platforms in an enterprise environment, this book is for you.

The information in this book is both practical and prescriptive. Rather than discuss every possible interoperability technique in detail, it focuses on the three most likely scenarios and shows how to solve those specific challenges. If you want more in-depth discussions of the concepts behind this material, refer to resources such as Simon Guest's book *Microsoft .NET and J2EE Interoperability Toolkit*, Microsoft Press, ISBN 0-7356-1922-0.

The focus is very much on enterprise or data center environments, where scalability, throughput, reliability, and security are the main operating requirements. It is not intended as a manual for how to write .NET or J2EE applications, but how to get these components to work together while minimizing any compromises to operational effectiveness.

This book includes material from consultants working in the field and from early implementers of interoperability solutions. It contains current best practices for running Microsoft .NET applications alongside J2EE components. We hope you enjoy reading this book and that you find the material contained in it helpful, informative, and interesting.

Who Should Read This Book

This book is aimed at developers who are responsible for creating and implementing enterprise level business applications based on either Microsoft .NET or on J2EE and where interoperability between the two platforms is a requirement.

Prerequisites

Because of the dual audience for this book, there are different prerequisites for each group:

- The sections targeted at .NET developers assume an understanding of the development process for distributed applications and familiarity with the Microsoft Visual Studio® .NET programming tools. The sample applications are in C# (C Sharp), so development experience in this language is essential. Experience with the .NET Framework SDK and the MSDN® Library are also of benefit.

- The sections targeted at Java developers assume a familiarity with Java programming methods and tools, in particular Enterprise Java Beans (EJB) and Java APIs such as Java Naming and Directory Interface (JNDI) and the Java Messaging Service (JMS).

Note: Whether you are a .NET developer or a Java developer, an appreciation of the other platform would be beneficial so that you can understand the interoperability techniques between the two platforms.

Both audiences need to be familiar with cross-platform open standards, such as eXtensible Markup Language (XML) syntax and methods, SOAP, Web Services Description Language (WSDL) and TCP/IP. This book also assumes knowledge of distributed enterprise application concepts, such as multi-tiered architectures, caching, asynchronous messaging, request routing, and buffering. For .NET developers, you can find this information in *Application Architecture for .NET: Designing Applications and Services* on MSDN; and for Java developers, the equivalent information is available on the Sun Web Site. See the References section at the end of the chapter for further details.

Document Conventions

This book uses the style conventions and terminology shown in Table 1.1.

Table 1.1: Document Conventions

Element	Meaning
bold font	Characters that you type exactly as shown, including commands and switches. Programming elements, such as methods, functions, data types, and data structures appear in bold font (except when part of a code sample, in which case they appear in monospace font). User interface elements are also bold.
Italic font	Variables for which you supply a specific value. For example, *Filename.ext* could refer to any valid file name for the case in question. New terminology also appears in italic on first use.
`Monospace font`	Code samples.
%SystemRoot%	The folder in which Windows is installed.

How to Use This Book

This book consists of nine chapters. The eight other chapters are:

- Chapter 2: "Understanding Enterprise Platforms"
- Chapter 3: "Interoperability Fundamentals"
- Chapter 4: "Interoperability Technologies: Point to Point"
- Chapter 5: "Interoperability Technologies: Data Tier"
- Chapter 6: "Implementing Interoperability Design Elements"
- Chapter 7: "Integrating .NET in the Presentation Tier"
- Chapter 8: "Integrating .NET in the Business Tier"
- Chapter 9: "Implementing Asynchronous Interoperability"

The following sections describe the contents of each chapter.

Chapter 2: "Understanding Enterprise Platforms"

Chapter 2 consists of two parts. The first part looks at .NET from the perspective of an experienced J2EE developer. It links .NET concepts to principles that you already understand, showing where the two platforms differ and where they are similar. The second part of this chapter is the mirror image, providing equivalent information but for the experienced .NET developer. It introduces you to the enterprise features of J2EE and explains how Java applications work in distributed environments.

Chapter 3: "Interoperability Fundamentals"

Chapter 3 looks at the fundamentals of connecting .NET and Java-based applications, concentrating on the exchange of data between the two technologies. The main focus is on ensuring that both platforms agree on data types, particularly with complex data types.

Chapter 4: "Interoperability Technologies: Point to Point"

Chapter 4 concentrates on the point to point communication methods of XML Web services and .NET Remoting. Topics include binary communication and routing, together with the use of third-party runtime bridges for integrating Java and .NET.

Chapter 5: "Interoperability Technologies: Data Tier"

This chapter continues on from Chapter 4 to concentrate on techniques that apply to the Data or Resource tier. Techniques covered include shared databases and asynchronous message queuing. Finally, this chapter briefly covers other asynchronous techniques such as using the MSMQ-MQSeries Bridge in Microsoft Host Integration Server.

Chapter 6: "Implementing Interoperability Design Elements"

Chapter 6 takes the concepts from Chapters 4 and 5 and describes how you can implement these ideas in an enterprise-class application. It looks at best practices in both J2EE and .NET programming, emphasizing the role of abstraction layers in applications. The chapter moves on to show how you would implement abstraction layers such as service interfaces and interoperability adapters in your design. Finally, it details how the sample application implements interoperability using these elements.

Chapter 7: "Integrating .NET in the Presentation Tier"

Chapter 7 uses the XBikes example to illustrate the scenario where you want to integrate ASP.NET Presentation tier components while keeping the existing J2EE Business tier. This allows an organization to preserve its existing investment in J2EE and take advantage of the enriched client experience that ASP.NET provides.

Chapter 8: "Integrating .NET in the Business Tier"

Chapter 8 shows how the XBikes example can integrate new .NET Business tier components, while preserving the same JavaServer Pages (JSP)-based front end. This solution is appropriate for companies that want to maintain the same client experience but modify the Business tier. Adding .NET components allows for rapid development of business logic components or allows the use of third-party .NET Framework applications.

Chapter 9: "Implementing Asynchronous Interoperability"

The final chapter looks at interoperability using messaging components in the Data tier. Using the XBikes sample code, it shows how you can use Messaging components such as Microsoft Message Queuing or Java Messaging Service implementations to connect to message queues, providing asynchronous operation and support for transactions and long running operations.

What Is Microsoft .NET?

Microsoft .NET is the term that covers Microsoft's latest programming and development environment for creating distributed enterprise applications. The main component of this is the .NET Framework, which consists of an array of elements designed to simplify and strengthen this process. The .NET Framework includes components such as the common language runtime (CLR), ASP.NET, ADO.NET, enterprise services, and .NET Remoting.

Other components of Microsoft .NET include:

- Visual Studio .NET development system
- Windows Server™ 2003 family of operating systems
- Active Directory® directory services
- Windows Server system components such as SQL Server 2000 and Exchange Server 2003

Microsoft .NET supports open standards, such as SOAP, Web Services Description Language (WSDL), Universal Description Discovery and Integration (UDDI), and XML. Microsoft provides full support for the .NET Framework and there are versions of the Framework that run on most versions of Windows. Chapter 2 provides an introduction to Microsoft .NET for the experienced J2EE programmer.

What Is Java 2 Enterprise Edition?

The J2EE specification describes a multi-tiered application model together with a set of APIs that you can use to create distributed enterprise applications. With J2EE, you can build multi-tiered applications consisting of reusable elements within a unified security model.

The J2EE standard is the intellectual property of Sun Microsystems. A consortium of vendors and manufacturers endorse this standard, with Sun taking the preeminent role in promoting J2EE. Additionally, a number of vendors and enthusiasts provide support for J2EE. J2EE runs on a range of operating systems, including Windows, Sun Solaris, UNIX, and Linux.

The elements making up J2EE include:

- JavaServer Pages (JSP) and servlets
- Enterprise JavaBeans (EJB)
- J2EE containers and modules
- J2EE Software Development Kit
- Java Naming and Directory Interface (JDNI), Java Message Service (JMS), and Java Database Connectivity (JDBC) APIs

The current version of J2EE (v1.3) supports open standards such as SOAP, WSDL, UDDI, and XML through third party implementations. J2EE v1.4 (currently at Beta 2) supports these protocols natively. Chapter 2 provides an introduction to J2EE for the experienced .NET programmer.

Identifying the Business Need for Interoperability

Many organizations already operate large enterprise environments based on either Java or Microsoft .NET. Hence if the company perceives a need for a new application or addition to their current architecture, the automatic tendency is to start thinking in terms of the currently implemented environment. This is sometimes referred to as Technology Aligned Environment, where decisions about enhancing the current environment are more closely attuned to what you already have running rather than on the basis of which provides the best platform.

Designing enterprise systems using either J2EE or Microsoft .NET is an expensive business, but there are often sound business reasons for organizations to implement a mixed environment that has elements of each platform. This section looks at these factors.

Interoperability is a key requirement for many enterprises, allowing internal systems to work together and enabling businesses to connect to customers, external partners, and suppliers. With ever increasing requirements for efficiency, responsiveness, and cost cutting, interoperability is a key demand for the modern IT environment.

Effective interoperability projects take the approach that an organization should use the best technology for the job at hand. If a company creates the majority of its applications in-house, there may be more factors pushing in the direction of staying with the current environment. However, if you need to implement a third-party solution or want to make use of features that, for example, only .NET offers, interoperability offers an effective mechanism for ensuring that the two environments work together.

Delving further into the business needs for interoperability produces the following areas where interoperability is a major factor:

- Achieving reuse of existing systems.
- Implementing proof of concept studies.
- Migration to Microsoft .NET.
- Achieving lower project costs.

Achieving Reuse of Existing Systems

Reusing existing systems is usually highest on the list of considerations for why you might want to implement an interoperability project. Organizations often have large investments in their current infrastructure and want to preserve this investment. However, changing requirements may highlight areas within the current system that cannot adapt to cope with new demands. In this scenario, you might be able to implement the new functionality using an alternative technology, and use interoperability to integrate it with the current infrastructure.

For example, you might want to add a new ASP.NET Web tier to existing J2EE-based Business and Data tiers. Rather than replace the functioning tiers, you can integrate the J2EE environment with the new Presentation tier components. The new .NET components can then increase and extend the value of the existing systems, providing integration between the original applications and newer additions in a changing network environment.

Interoperability techniques can also extend the life and value of software assets, such as Business tier applications running on proprietary hardware. Again, if the application and the hardware function acceptably, there is no immediate need to replace it. Simply adding a Web service interface can extend the operational life of this equipment and give the flexibility to integrate it with newer applications.

Many organizations see retaining and using current skill sets as one of the most important factors. Investment in staff training and development is likely to reflect the money put into the application infrastructure. .NET offers competitive development times compared to Java, but you still need to provide continuing support for the current architecture. Because you are likely to have skilled staff trained on your current environment, you can continue to support those areas.

Implementing Proof of Concept Studies

Proof of concept or pilot studies allow the dynamic company to try out new business approaches and technologies at minimal risk. For example, if you want to implement a new cell phone-based interface, you can use .NET to prototype this very rapidly. You can then enable the new interface to operate alongside your existing environment with no changes to the original code. Hence adding new functionality does not entail ripping out and replacing everything that you worked so hard to create.

The language-neutral development environment in Microsoft .NET provides companies with increased technical agility and the ability to get solutions to market very rapidly. Interoperability techniques ensure that these newly deployed additions operate seamlessly with your current infrastructure.

Migrating to Microsoft .NET

If your organization is considering migration from J2EE to Microsoft .NET, interoperability significantly reduces the risk inherent in any such migration project and can smooth the transition between one environment and the other. A migration plan that exploits interoperability allows you to migrate each application tier independently, which can reduce project dependencies, cope with scheduling constraints and minimize downtime.

Migration is rarely an overnight process, so an interoperability migration plan might consist of creating a new .NET Presentation tier and switching over to that tier. After you are happy that this new component functions correctly, you then start replacing individual components in the Business tier. Finally, you migrate the back-end database to SQL Server.

Using interoperability techniques lets you plan, implement, and correctly execute a migration from J2EE to Microsoft .NET. Even just planning migration can have business value, because it can put you in a stronger negotiating position with your current vendors. It also enables you to react more quickly in a situation where your current vendor no longer meets your requirements.

Achieving Lower Project Costs

Labor costs are the dominant factor in overall project costs involving custom line-of-business applications. .NET has the potential to deliver lower overall project costs, primarily based on higher productivity reducing the labor factor. The sources of higher productivity from using .NET are the following:

- High productivity development tools such as Visual Studio .NET, which allow developers to rapidly translate ideas into applications.

- A broad, well factored, easy to use, class library in the .NET Framework. This class library encapsulates a wide range of programming tasks and techniques that have historically been difficult for many developers to achieve.

- Multi-language support, allowing developers to use the skills they already have. You can write .NET-based applications in any language supported by the .NET Framework, such as Visual Basic® .NET, C++, C# or, for Java programmers, the syntactically identical J#. .NET also supports a number of third-party programming languages, such as COBOL and FORTRAN. The chances are that if you now program in a mainstream development language, there is a .NET version either published or nearing readiness.

Reduced application development time combined with multi-language compatibility help to minimize the cost of developing applications. Developers can write in whichever .NET language they know best, and the ease of creating components such as Web services in Visual Studio .NET increase productivity and reduce deployment time. However, multi-language support must be balanced against the potential risk of higher maintenance costs.

Presentation tier applications particularly benefit from the features in ASP.NET, allowing programmers to create fully-featured Web sites from a minimum of code using the language of their choice. Separation of the scripting elements from the HTML code makes for more efficient debugging, removing the requirement to scroll through HTML to identify coding errors.

Note: The JavaServer Faces specification should allow the J2EE platform to provide similar facilities to ASP.NET, although it is not part of the current release of J2EE. For more information about JavaServer Faces, see the JavaServer Faces Web page at *http://java.sun.com/j2ee/javaserverfaces/*.

Reducing development time significantly improves the chance of your organization being the first to get its solution into the marketplace. Careful selection of the right environment and use of appropriate interoperability techniques can accelerate the successful deployment of enterprise applications and new features, reducing the time to market and cutting development costs.

Defining Interoperability

This book defines Interoperability as follows:

The ability to communicate or transfer data between functional units running on different platforms, implemented in different technologies, using industry standard or widely accepted data description and communication protocols.

For.NET/J2EE interoperability, this process consists of ensuring that applications built on one platform connect to those created on the other. Figure 1.1 shows the J2EE and .NET equivalent components in an enterprise application environment, and highlights the opportunity and need for interoperability at different tiers in the architecture.

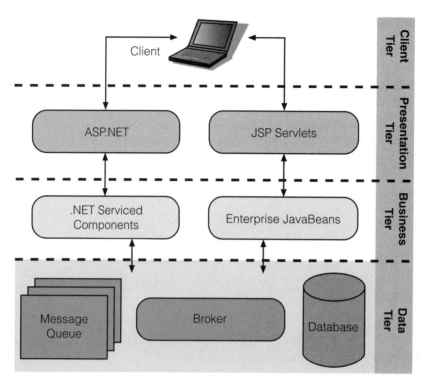

Figure 1.1
J2EE and.NET equivalent components in an enterprise application environment

Organizations benefit from the greater flexibility of being able to choose the best from either enterprise application environment to suit their business needs. However, this interoperability should come with minimal performance overhead or reduction in functionality.

Understanding Interoperability Scenarios

Interoperability comes in a range of guises, with certain scenarios more likely than others, and some combinations either not possible or highly unlikely. This book concentrates on three main interoperability scenarios. These are the following:

- Integrating .NET components at the Presentation tier.
- Integrating .NET components at the Business tier.
- Implementing asynchronous interoperability.

Chapters 4 and 5 show the interoperability techniques you can use in these scenarios. Chapter 6 describes how to apply these techniques in an enterprise class application and summarizes the implementation strategies used in the XBikes sample application. Chapters 7, 8, and 9 work through each interoperability technique at the code level.

Integrating .NET Components in the Presentation Tier

Presentation tier to Business tier interoperability is a very common scenario, accounting for a large slice of all .NET/J2EE interoperability projects. Usually, interoperability between these two tiers involves replacing JSP elements with an ASP.NET-based front end to achieve a richer client experience. Figure 1.2 shows how such an implementation would look.

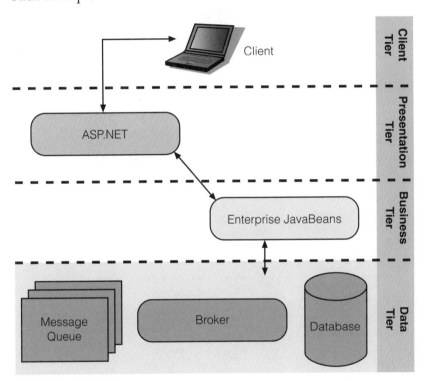

Figure 1.2
.NET Presentation tier linked to J2EE Business tier

The challenge with this first scenario is in getting the ASP.NET components to interact with the J2EE middle tier elements, as Figure 1.2 shows.

Integrating .NET Components in the Business Tier

The next scenario preserves the existing JSP front end but integrates .NET components in the Business tier. This approach allows developers to create programs and assemblies in .NET using any language that the .NET Framework supports. Reasons for implementing .NET Business tier components might include the need to respond to rapid changes in business practice or to make use of third party products. Figure 1.3 shows how such an implementation would look.

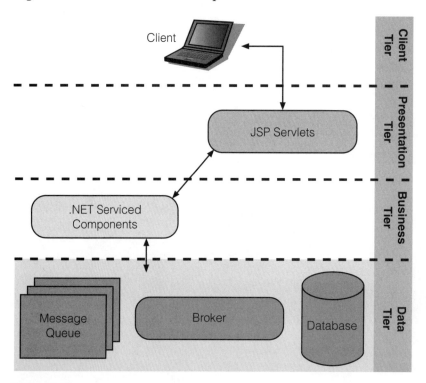

Figure 1.3

Integrating .NET Business tier components into a J2EE architecture

Here you have the challenge of two interfaces between .NET and J2EE—one from Presentation tier to Business tier and one from Business tier to Data tier. Chapter 8 gives a detailed example of how to do this.

Implementing Asynchronous Interoperability

This last major interoperability scenario covers the situation where you need to use transactional support, cope with long running transactions, or provide resilience to network outages. You provide these services by addressing an asynchronous resource or message queue component, such as Microsoft Message Queuing (also known as MSMQ) or IBM WebSphere MQ. Figure 1.4 shows this implementation.

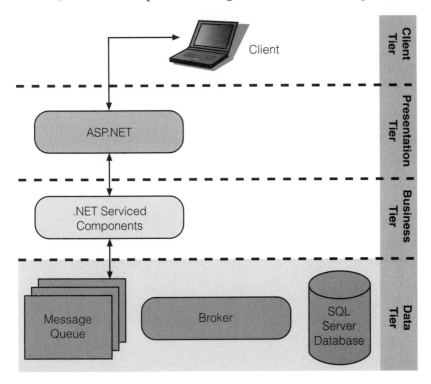

Figure 1.4
Business tier to Data tier interoperability

An example of this scenario might be a link to an order queue that manages and monitors the production of a bespoke bicycle. The application can check items in the queue or can receive notification when a particular operation finishes. After the bicycle is complete, a message can go to the purchaser telling him or her that it is on its way.

Chapter 9 covers this scenario in detail.

Listing Interoperability Technologies

There are a number of ways in which you can implement J2EE to .NET interoperability. Each has particular advantages and disadvantages, and each works in some circumstances but not others. These technologies are the following:

- XML Web services.
- Runtime bridges.
- Message orientated middleware.
- Shared database.
- Integration brokers.

Web services define applications that deliver a service (usually by exposing a programmatic interface) where you can either fulfill client requests directly or integrate the provider service with other Web services using Internet standards. External consumers or applications communicate with Web services by means of XML formatted messages, usually using XML over HTTP. Both .NET-based and J2EE-based applications can implement XML Web services.

Runtime bridges are third-party solutions that provide interoperability between J2EE and .NET, so that Java classes appear as .NET classes and vice-versa. This allows you to use .NET Remoting as a communication method, with the Runtime Bridge handling the calls to the Java side. This book looks at two products in this area, JNBridgePro from JNBridge and Ja.NET from Intrinsyc. Chapter 4 provides more information about these products.

Messaging offers an asynchronous mechanism for communicating between tiers, often based on MSMQ or IBM MQSeries. Messaging enables loosely coupled operation, particularly where you need more than just a one-to-one linkage between application components and Web services are not suitable. Messaging also supports transactions, security (encryption and authentication), tolerance for network outages, and recorded message delivery. However, messaging does not offer any form of synchronous operation and can cause issues with port assignments and firewall operation.

Shared database techniques often involve using some form of database independent connectivity API, such as Open Database Connectivity (ODBC) or Java Database Connectivity (JDBC) to provide a level of abstraction from the database itself (usually SQL Server or Oracle). However, challenges with this technique involve generating an appropriate database schema that all applications can address.

Integration brokers go beyond point-to-point connections to provide end-to-end integration of applications, enabling the automation of critical business processes across an entire distributed application or enterprise. Typically built on a messaging framework, integration brokers are particularly important in environments that use trading partners within the application solution. Integration brokers also provide prefabricated application adapters, allowing multiple external components such as mainframe or third-party applications to interact with the integration broker as either provider or consumer or both. Some leading integration broker products include IBM MQSeries Integrator, CommerceBroker, and Microsoft BizTalk® Server 2004.

Note: Chapters 4 and 5 expand on all of these technologies except for integration brokers.

Linking Interoperability Technologies to Business Scenarios

Table 1.2 shows the possible interoperability permutations along with technologies that can provide solutions for each combination. The check marks indicate which techniques are appropriate for each scenario.

Table 1.2: Interoperability Scenarios

	Presentation to Presentation	Presentation to Business	Business to Business	Business to Data
XML Web Services		✓	✓	✓
Runtime Bridges	✓	✓	✓	
Messaging		✓	✓	
Shared Database	✓			✓
Integration Brokers			✓	✓

The recommended procedure wherever possible is to implement your interoperability solution using XML Web services. For a detailed discussion of the advantages and disadvantages of each interoperability technology, see Chapters 4 and 5 later in this book.

Introducing the Sample Application

This book uses a sample application to illustrate the three interoperability scenarios that Chapters 7 to 9 describe. This application is *XBikes*, an e-commerce application through which you can simulate ordering fantastically expensive bicycles in a variety of "go faster" colors. There are two separate implementations of XBikes, one for the .NET platform and the other version on J2EE.

> **Note:** XBikes is *not* a demonstration of how to write a perfect application in either architecture. It is also not how you would write a secure Web site to sell bikes, but it provides a framework for demonstrating how to get J2EE and .NET applications to interoperate.

XBikes provides a framework and sample code for you to understand the following approaches to interoperability:

- Replace individual parts of the J2EE architecture with the equivalent .NET elements one at a time.
- Show how J2EE components can co-exist with .NET elements indefinitely.
- Demonstrate a migration path for the entire environment from J2EE to .NET.

Chapter 6 explains the XBikes application architecture in detail. The XBikes sample code is on the companion CD to this book.

Summary

This chapter introduced the structure of this book and the contents of the chapters. It looked at J2EE and .NET interoperability from a broad perspective, and then it covered the various interoperability scenarios. It reviewed several interoperability techniques and introduced the XBikes sample application.

To ensure developers familiar with either .NET or J2EE are at the same technical level of understanding, you should now read the relevant section of Chapter 2.

References

Guest, Simon, Microsoft .NET and J2EE Interoperability Toolkit, Microsoft Press, ISBN 0-7356-1922-0

For information about distributed enterprise application concepts, such as Presentation, Business, and Data tiers on .NET:
Application Architecture for .NET: Designing Applications and Services
http://msdn.microsoft.com/library/default.asp?url=/library/en-us/dnbda/html/distapp.asp

For the equivalent information about Java, see the Sun J2EE Web site:
http://java.sun.com/j2ee/

For general information about XML Web services, see the following Web sites:

- .NET XML Web Services Repertory, at *http://www.xmlwebservices.cc/*
- Web Services Developer Home, at *http://msdn.microsoft.com/webservices*

2

Understanding Enterprise Platforms

Introduction

This chapter provides background briefings for developers experienced on one platform who have not had exposure to the alternate technology. It is not a training manual, but it should help you understand the fundamental concepts of one environment by linking them into what you already know about the other.

The rivalry between the Microsoft and Sun platforms is as entrenched as that between supporters of the Apple user interface and proponents of Windows. However, the growing reality of corporate operations is that organizations implement components using the platform that best suits their needs, rather than remain wedded to one particular ideology or another.

It is increasingly rare that as a J2EE developer, you have no exposure to Microsoft .NET during your career. Indeed, the ability to work both with .NET and J2EE is an attractive proposition for employers. Similarly, if you are a .NET developer and have not worked with Java, the second part of the chapter helps you understand the functionality and capabilities of the J2EE platform. Again, this is not intended as a reference book but attempts to correlate concepts from the J2EE world to what you already know about .NET.

Note: If you are an experienced Microsoft .NET developer, go to the section on "J2EE Fundamentals for .NET Developers."

At the end of this chapter is a summary table that lists the equivalent components from .NET and J2EE.

Microsoft .NET Fundamentals for J2EE Developers

Microsoft .NET is a designation that reflects Microsoft's realignment towards Internet operation and distributed applications. Microsoft .NET consists of three main components:

- A language-independent application environment optimized for distributed operations—the .NET Framework.
- A development environment for programming in several Microsoft languages—Visual Studio .NET.
- The operating system that supports distributed environments and the .NET Framework—the Windows Server System.

The unifying vision behind the .NET initiative comprises the following:

- Language-independent programming.
- Enterprise-level scalability and reliability.
- Integrated security.
- Ease of implementation.
- Distributed operation.
- Support for open standards.
- Robust operation and manageability.
- Powerful debugging facilities.

Comparing .NET to J2EE

To seasoned Java developers, .NET may seem similar to the J2EE platform; both provide a structured way to create applications, both have languages that compile to intermediate code, and both provide a large library of APIs for application development. Indeed, many commentators from the Java world have noted that the conceptual jump from J2EE to .NET seems less than that from Windows DNA to .NET. However, .NET has at its core a different set of goals than the J2EE platform.

Java comprises the Java platform (runtime and APIs) and the Java language. The purpose of the Java platform is to support applications written in the Java language and compiled to Java bytecode. Although there have been attempts to compile other languages to Java bytecode, these have largely been academic exercises. The idea of Java has always been a *single language on multiple operating systems*.

.NET comprises the .NET Framework (runtime and APIs) and multiple supported programming languages. The purpose of the .NET Framework is to support applications written in any language and compiled to Microsoft Intermediate Language (MSIL). The goal of .NET is *a single platform shared by multiple languages*.

Investigating the .NET Framework

It is fundamental that you understand the .NET Framework and the services it provides for .NET-based applications.

Note: .NET-based applications or .NET Framework-based applications are applications that use the .NET Framework. This book uses .NET-based applications for brevity.

The .NET Framework includes class libraries that provide support for a wide range of tasks, including data access, security, file I/O, XML manipulation, messaging, class reflection, XML Web services, ASP.NET, and Microsoft Windows services.

Note: There are occasional comparisons between the .NET Framework and the Java 2 SDK, but the two are not directly equivalent.

A central part to this is the support for XML Web services. This technology is both a methodology and transport layer for passing information between components on different computers, different networks, and different operating systems.

Figure 2.1 shows the key features of the .NET Framework.

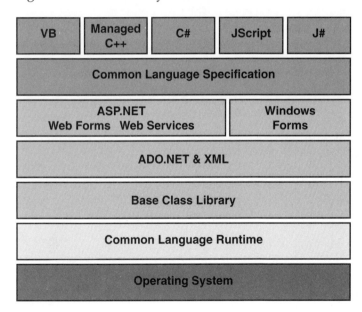

Figure 2.1
.NET Framework components showing reliance on CLR

The .NET Framework is available as a freely redistributable component containing the tools, classes, and API support to run .NET-based applications. You must install the .NET Framework on any computer on which you want .NET-based applications to run.

Windows XP Service Pack 1 includes the .NET Framework version 1.0 and Windows Server 2003 comes with .NET Framework 1.1 as part of the operating system. For earlier versions of Windows, you can download the .NET Framework from the MSDN Web site. You can also install the .NET Framework from the Windows Update Service.

Note: The .NET Framework SDK includes the .NET Framework redistributable package.

There are multiple ways of installing the .NET Framework onto client computers. You can extract the .NET Framework redistributable package as an .msi file, so you (or your network administrator) can then distribute it using Active Directory Group Policy. Alternatively, larger enterprises can use Systems Management Server to deliver the package. Smaller organizations can opt for Software Update Services (SUS) to deploy the .NET Framework onto Windows 2000 clients. Developers can include the redistributable package in a build output from Visual Studio .NET, adding routines that detect for the presence of the framework on the client and installing or updating it if necessary.

Common Language Runtime

The common language runtime (CLR) is the core component of the .NET Framework. The CLR provides central functions for the hosting and operation of .NET-based applications. The main functions of the CLR are the following:

- Just-in-time (JIT) compilation to native code.
- Cross language integration.
- Memory management and garbage collection.
- Managed code operation.
- JIT debugging.
- Exception handling.
- Security.
- Runtime type safety checks.
- Thread management.

Note: Although there are some differences, you can compare the CLR to the role of a Java Virtual Machine (JVM).

JIT Compilation to Native Code

When you deploy and run your application, the JIT complier carries out a quick check of the platform specification. For example, it will look at areas like processor type and numbers, memory, and so on. The JIT compiler then compiles the application to generate the machine code *for that execution environment*. This is the JIT compilation process.

Note: The JIT process in the .NET Framework is similar to the JVM runtime compiler.

Versions of Windows later than Windows NT 4.0 support only the x86 environment, which often leads people to wonder why they need to bother with the MSIL step and just compile directly for the x86 platform. However, not all x86-based computers are the same, and the MSIL route gives the maximum flexibility for future operating system developments.

JIT compilation takes into account the fact that an application may not call all the program code during execution. Rather than use processor time and memory to convert all the MSIL in a portable executable (PE) file to native code, it converts the MSIL as needed during execution and stores the resulting native code so that subsequent calls can access it. The loader creates and attaches a stub to each of a type's methods when the type is loaded. On the initial call to the method, the stub passes control to the JIT compiler, which converts the MSIL for that method into native code and modifies the stub to direct execution to the location of the native code. Subsequent calls of the JIT-compiled method proceed directly to the native code that was previously generated, reducing the time it takes to JIT compile and run the code.

The effect of the JIT operation is that the first time an application executes, it takes marginally longer to start up. However, second and subsequent executions that call the JIT method are faster than a pre-compiled application, because the JIT component returns the previously generated native code, properly optimized for that computer.

The runtime supplies another mode of compilation called install-time code generation. The install-time code generation mode converts MSIL to native code just as the regular JIT compiler does, but it converts larger units of code at a time, storing the resulting native code for use when the assembly subsequently loads and runs. With install-time code generation, installing the application converts the entire assembly into native code, taking into account what is known about any currently installed assemblies. The resulting file loads and starts more quickly than it would have if it were being converted to native code by the standard JIT option.

Cross Language Integration

You might be surprised to learn that the CLR works with only one type of code. What, you may say, of the claim for language independence on the previous page? The answer is that the CLR works only with MSIL. The clever bit is that any programming language that supports .NET can create output in MSIL. This is where the language independence comes from. You can create .NET-based applications in one or more of the following languages:

- Managed C++ (no surprises here)
- C# (C Sharp—similarities to Java and C++)
- Visual Basic .NET
- J# (J Sharp—allows you write Java code for the .NET platform)
- FORTRAN
- Pascal
- COBOL
- PERL
- Python
- Eiffel

C# has proved a popular choice for both experienced Java developers and those new to the .NET platform, because it has many similarities to the Java programming language. J# provides a subset of the Java language that you can compile into MSIL and run on the CLR. However, regardless of the language you use, after you write your code, the compiler turns it into MSIL.

Note: If you are a glutton for punishment (or if you simply enjoy programming in machine code), you can write directly in MSIL. However, because MSIL is a pseudo-machine code, this is not an entirely intuitive process.

Memory Management and Garbage Collection

Memory management in the CLR centers on the process of *garbage collection*, which is similar to the equivalent process in Java. Garbage collection is a background operation that reviews objects committed to memory and recovers those that are no longer needed. Garbage collection acts on three generations, recovering short, medium, and long duration objects, known as *Gen 0, Gen 1,* and *Gen 2* respectively.

All new objects start in the Gen 0 heap. The garbage collection algorithm works by checking to see if there are any objects in the heap that applications are not using.

Note: Many classes create temporary objects for their return values, temporary strings, and assorted other utility classes like enumerators and the like.

If there is not enough free memory in the heap to allocate to a new object, a garbage collection cycle commences on Gen 0 objects. If there is still not enough memory, a garbage collection cycle occurs on the Gen 1 objects, and then on Gen 2. A full pass garbage collection cycle is when the garbage collection processes all generations.

When a garbage collection cycle runs, it promotes all surviving objects to the next generation. Objects survive a garbage collection cycle because they are either still in use (reachable) or awaiting finalization. Surviving objects from Gen 0 go to Gen 1, and surviving objects from Gen 1 move to Gen 2. The garbage collection process then compacts and moves any freed memory to preserve contiguous space and to minimize memory fragmentation. Each generation garbage collection cycle typically occurs on a 1:10 ratio compared to the generation below it, for example, 10 Gen 0 collections occur to every Gen 1, and 10 Gen 1 to every Gen 2.

Note: Higher level garbage collections are more expensive in terms of system resources — the garbage collectors expect a bigger tip.

Managed Code Operation

The forth major function of the .NET Framework is managed code operation. The definition of managed code is fairly simple — managed code uses the CLR, unmanaged code does not. To tighten up on this definition, managed code executes *completely* within the CLR. Calls to unmanaged components (serviced components, COM, or DCOM objects) come outside the remit of the CLR. Hence CLR garbage collection and other functions do not operate against unmanaged code or unmanaged code components.

Just-In-Time Debugging

Just-in-time (JIT) debugging is a technique for debugging a program that you start outside Visual Studio. If you have enabled JIT debugging, the program brings up a dialog box when a crash occurs. This dialog box asks if you want to debug the program and which debugger you want to use.

JIT debugging gives you the flexibility of choosing a debugger when an exception occurs. It also lets you debug on clones of your production computers, which helps identify programming issues more quickly.

Exception Handling

The CLR handles exceptions in .NET Framework applications, but it also provides functions for exception management. The main ones of these are the Try/Catch/__Finally blocks you can use to catch both managed and unmanaged exceptions. The basic approach is to use a **Try** clause when you are about to carry out a risky operation paired with a **Catch** clause if the function in the **Try** statement causes an exception. The **__Finally** clause should run whether the exception occurred or not.

Security

The CLR enforces security with executing applications either through the use of XML formatted configuration files or through the Runtime Security Policy node of the .NET Framework 1.1 Configuration Tool (Mscorcfg.msc). Security configuration files contain information about the code group hierarchy and permission sets associated with a policy level.

The .NET Framework Configuration tool shows the three main security configuration levels of Enterprise, Machine, or User. These levels correspond to the three security configuration files (Enterprisesec.config, and two separate Security.config files for the computer and user levels).

The .NET Framework Configuration tool lets you manage permission sets (for example, FullTrust, LocalIntranet, Everything, and so on) and code groups, such as My_Computer_Zone, LocalIntranet_Zone, Trusted_Zone, and so on. Each code group has a related permission set, for example, the Trusted_Zone maps to the Internet permission set.

Assemblies that meet the code group's membership condition receive the associated permissions from the permission set. A permission set might include whether the application can access the **File Open** dialog box, whether it can print, or what sort of user interface it can display.

Although you can edit the security configuration files directly, it is strongly recommended that you use the .NET Framework Configuration tool or Code Access Security Policy tool (Caspol.exe) to modify security policy. This ensures that policy changes do not corrupt the security configuration files.

Runtime Type Safety Checks

The .NET Framework also enforces security through runtime type safety checks. With type safe code, the common language runtime can completely isolate assemblies from each other. This isolation helps ensure that assemblies cannot adversely affect each other and it increases application reliability. Type-safe components can execute safely in the same process even if they are trusted at different levels.

Type-safe code accesses only the memory locations it is authorized to access. For example, type-safe code cannot read values from another object's private fields. It accesses types only in well-defined, allowable ways.

Although verification of type safety is not mandatory to run managed code, type safety plays a crucial role in assembly isolation and security enforcement. When code is not type safe, unwanted side effects can occur. For example, the runtime cannot prevent unsafe code from calling into native (unmanaged) code and performing malicious operations. When code is type safe, the runtime's security enforcement mechanism ensures that it does not access native code unless it has permission to do so.

During JIT compilation, an optional verification process examines the metadata and MSIL of a method to be JIT-compiled into native machine code to verify that they are type safe.

Thread Management

The common language runtime provides support for multithreaded applications, mainly through the **ThreadPool** class. **ThreadPool** provides automatic thread creation and management mechanism for most tasks.

Common Type System

The common type system (CTS) defines how applications and the .NET Framework can declare, use, and manage types within the runtime, and is also an important part of the runtime's support for cross-language integration. It is the CTS that allows large teams of developers to work on an application, each programming in any of the many languages that the .NET Framework supports.

The CTS performs the following functions:

- Establishes a framework that enables cross-language integration, type safety, and high performance code execution.
- Provides an object-oriented model that supports the complete implementation of many programming languages.
- Defines rules that languages must follow, which helps ensure that objects written in different languages can interact with each other.

Managed code operation implements type safety through CTS, so the CTS ensures that all .NET-based application components are self-describing. The .NET Framework then handles the references between managed code components.

The Global Assembly Cache

Installing the .NET Framework creates a machine-wide code cache called the global assembly cache. The global assembly cache stores assemblies (executable or library files) specifically designated for sharing by several applications on the computer. In conjunction with the Strong Name Tool, it also enables you to run two or more versions of an assembly with the same name. This gives greater control over assembly selection at runtime than with the **CLASSPATH** statement.

There are two versions of the global assembly cache—**MSCORWKS** is the workstation version that runs on Windows XP and any desktop operating system on which you can install the .NET Framework. **MSCORSVR** is an integral part of the Windows 2003 Server family and installs as a component of the .NET Framework on Microsoft's other server operating systems. **MSCORWKS** functions best with single user .NET-based applications whereas **MSCORSVR** works in large, multiprocessor, multi-user environments.

Normally, you place an application's assemblies in the application installation directory. However, you may want more than one application to use the same assembly, so rather than copy it into two separate directories, you can place the assembly into the global assembly cache.

Note: You must sign assemblies with the Strong Name Tool before placing them in the global assembly cache.

There are several ways to deploy an assembly into the global assembly cache:

- Use an installer designed to work with the global assembly cache. This is the preferred method.
- Use a developer tool called the Global Assembly Cache tool (Gacutil.exe), part of the .NET Framework SDK.
- Use Windows Explorer to drag the assemblies into the cache.

For more information about best practices for deploying assemblies into the global assembly cache, see Deploying .NET Framework-based Applications, on MSDN.

Strong Names

The .NET Framework enhances security by letting you digitally sign each code component with the Strong Name Tool (SN.exe). Strong-named assemblies consists of the assembly's identity—its simple text name, version number, and culture information (if provided)—together with a public key and a digital signature.

By creating strong-named assemblies you can support multiple DLLs with the same name in the global assembly cache. Applications then only use the DLL version that they installed, addressing the common issue of DLL conflicts. The use of strong-named assemblies makes it possible for you to install new versions of an assembly side-by-side with an older version of the assembly without conflicts occurring.

Note: To avoid dependencies on assemblies that do not have strong names, strong-named assemblies can only reference other strong-named assemblies.

.NET Remoting

.NET Remoting is Microsoft's new communication mechanism for distributed applications built on the .NET Framework. NET Remoting is similar in function to Remote Method Invocation (RMI) in J2EE.

.NET Remoting enables you to build widely distributed applications easily, whether application components are all on one computer or spread out across the entire world. With .NET Remoting, you can build client applications that use objects in other processes on the same computer or on any other computer that is reachable over its network. You can also use .NET Remoting to communicate with other application domains in the same process.

.NET Remoting provides an abstract approach to interprocess communication that separates the remotable object from a specific client or server application domain and from a specific mechanism of communication. As a result, it is flexible and easily customizable. You can replace one communication protocol with another or one serialization format with another without recompiling the client or the server. In addition, the remoting system assumes no particular application model. You can communicate from a Web application, a console application, a Windows Service— from almost anything you want to use. Remoting servers can also be any type of application domain. Any application can host remoting objects and provide its services to any client on its computer or network.

To use .NET Remoting to build an application in which two components communicate directly across an application domain boundary, you need to build only the following:

- A remotable object.
- A host application domain to listen for requests for that object.
- A client application domain that makes requests for that object.

You can think of .NET Remoting in this way even in a complex, multiclient/ multiserver application. You must also configure the host and the client application to link into the remoting infrastructure and you must understand the lifetime and activation issues that the remoting infrastructure introduces.

Building a .NET-based Application

There are several ways in which you can write and build .NET-based applications. The main ones are the following:

- Use Visual Studio .NET to write and build the application.
- Use your favorite development environment and the command-line compiler.
- Use a text editor and the command-line compiler.

Using Visual Studio .NET 2003

Visual Studio .NET 2003 is the latest release of Microsoft's application development environment, which installs along with the MSDN Library for Visual Studio .NET. Visual Studio .NET is fully in tune with the language neutral approach, making it very easy to create interoperating projects in different languages. It provides built-in templates for different projects, depending on the language you want to use. Project types include the following:

- Windows Forms-based applications.
- ASP.NET Web applications.
- ASP.NET Web services.
- Class libraries.
- Console applications.
- Windows services.

Additionally, Visual Studio lets you package applications for distribution, creating Windows Installer packages, CAB files, and setup routines.

Using Command Line Compilers

You may be pleased to know that there is no requirement to use Visual Studio .NET to create .NET-based applications. The alternative is to use the command line compilers in the .NET Framework SDK in a similar fashion to how you would use **JAVAC** and the J2SE SDK.

You can download the English version of the .NET Framework SDK v1.1 from the SDK Web site.

When you install the .NET Framework SDK, this creates the **%WINDIR% \Microsoft.NET\Framework\versionnumber** directory, where *versionnumber* is v1.0.3705 for .NET Framework version 1.0 and v1.1.4322 for version 1.1. Within that directory, you find the following command line compilers:

- CSC.EXE for C# applications.
- VBC.EXE for Visual Basic.
- JSC.EXE for J#.

Running the compiler with the correct command line switches produces one or more assemblies that the CLR can then execute. Assemblies are usually .exe or .dll files.

Note: To examine the contents of an .exe or .dll file, use the Ildasm.exe disassembler tool included with the .NET Framework (SDK).

.NET assemblies include descriptive metadata, such as the Windows Portable Executable Header, assembly dependencies, and version information. However, there is no direct comparison to an assembly in Java. The closest comparison is to a JAR file, which contains classes storing metadata and can cross reference information to other JAR files without requiring a **CLASSPATH** value.

Locating Assemblies with the Global Assembly Cache

The .NET Framework does not use a variable like **CLASSPATH**, but instead uses the global assembly cache mentioned earlier. The global assembly cache exists on each computer and is both a folder and a database of registered components. The folder is under **%WINDIR%\ASSEMBLY**, and you register an assembly with Gacutil.exe.

Note: When you create installation packages in Visual Studio .NET, you include the registration process as part of the installation.

To view the global assembly cache, complete the following steps.

▶ **To inspect the global assembly cache**

1. Click **Start**, point to **All Programs**, point to **Administrative Tools**, and then click **Microsoft .NET Framework 1.1 Configuration** (or 1.0). The .NET Configuration 1.1 (or 1.0) management console appears.

2. Double-click the **Assembly Cache** node in the left pane.

3. In the right pane, click the **View List of Assemblies in the Assembly Cache** link. A list of registered assemblies appears.

4. Right-click an assembly, and then click **Properties**. The **Assemblyname Properties** dialog box appears.

The **Version** value allows multiple versions to coexist and to let a component such as an executable call a specific DLL. Version numbers are of the form:

MajorVersion.MinorVersion.BuildNumber.Revision

For example, 7.0.5000.0 is a common version number for the Microsoft.VSDesigner assembly.

The **Public key token** is a result of the code signing process that uniquely identifies each assembly. This ensures that an application only loads the correct assembly, preventing malicious or unintentional substitution of an application component.

Understanding Attributes

Attributes are a feature of most Microsoft software components, such as Interface Definition Language (IDL) interfaces in COM, so it should not be a surprise that these appear in the .NET Framework. Current versions of the Java 2 SDK do not include support for attributes, although the proposed Java 2 SDK 1.5 declares support for attribute-like structures. For more details see:

- JSR 175: A Metadata Facility for the Java Programming Language
- New Language Features for Ease of Development in the Java 2 Platform, Standard Edition 1.5: A Conversation with Joshua Bloch

An attribute in the .NET Framework has both keyword and tag-like elements to it. You use tags to document types, fields, document classes, and methods at design time. The assembly metadata contains the attribute information. Many of the standard namespaces in the .NET Framework contain attributes, and developers can implement their own custom attributes if necessary.

An example of an attribute is **WebMethod**. This attribute indicates that you can call a method within a class as an XML Web service. If you place the **WebMethod** tag at the start of the method, the compiler then generates additional information that exposes the method as an XML Web service.

The following lines of code show the simplest demonstration of this.

```
[WebMethod]
public String HelloWorld()
{
    ...
}
```

Attributes can accept parameters as part of the tag. This is similar to a constructor class.

```
[WebMethod(Namespace="http://www.microsoft.com/Interoperability")]
```

This assigns the namespace property of the **WebMethod** attribute to the specified URL.

Note: The CLR supports attributes in any language, although the development language syntax controls how you prefix a tag.

Creating Web Applications

In Java, you create Web applications using JSP pages and servlets. In .NET, you use the latest evolution of Active Server Pages (ASP) named ASP.NET. Normally, ASP.NET applications would run on Internet Information Services (IIS), but this is not a strict requirement. For example, you can also run ASP.NET applications on platforms such as Apache 2.0-based Enterprise Ready Server.

ASP.NET provides enhanced functionality over JSP, with features such as code-behind and event driven Web controls. To implement equivalent functionality in JSP, you need both the scripting language and a set of additional tools. The experience of developers familiar with both Java and .NET is that ASP.NET is more powerful than JSP, which is itself better than the earlier ASP. The introduction of JavaServer Faces is expected to level the playing field between ASP.NET and JSP.

ASP.NET applications tend to have graphical front ends, so developers tend to prefer using Visual Studio .NET to create and edit ASP.NET pages. An alternative free integrated development environment (IDE) is Web Matrix, available for download from the ASP.NET Web site.

You can create ASP.NET Web applications in any language that the .NET Framework CLR supports. This gives you the flexibility to work in any programming language, or even create a Web site by combining elements built in different languages by a team of developers.

Hosting Components

The .NET Framework does not have a direct equivalent to EJBs. However, there are three main techniques you can use to provide hosted components for enterprise applications:

- Run as a Windows service.
- Host on IIS.
- Use component services.

Running as a Windows Service

Windows services (or NT services) are system level processes that run on a computer regardless of the logged in user. Typical services include functions of the operating system, schedulers, virus scanners, database engines, and network components.

You can use templates from within Visual Studio .NET to take a .NET assembly and run it as a service. This generates an application that runs as long as the computer is running.

Note: Applications running as a service need to deal with their own networking arrangements. In particular, they should run under a domain account, not the local machine account. This is because the local machine account only has rights on the local computer.

Hosting through IIS

Internet Information Services provides a framework for hosting Presentation and Business tier components. Using a configuration file associated with the assembly, you can configure support within IIS for the following:

- Deploying assemblies.
- Handling incoming connections.
- Supporting protocols.
- Implementing connection pooling.
- Configuring security.

The alternative approach would be to build your own custom framework to host assemblies. However, this would be a time-consuming and cumbersome task.

Using Component Services

Hosting an assembly in IIS is easy and convenient, but it does not provide the full functionality that EJBs enjoy. Component services (or COM+) provide the additional features, such as:

- Recycling
- State management
- Transaction support
- Method-level security
- Logging
- Impersonation
- Message queue support

A .NET developer can address COM+ properties either through the component services administration tool or using programmatic attributes.

Note: There is no equivalent of container managed persistence (CMP), container managed relationships or EJB-QL in .NET, although there are a number of third party implementations. Visual Studio .NET has tools for auto-generating SQL statements and dragging and dropping database tables into the IDE.

Supporting Web Services

One area where Microsoft has invested considerable effort is in supporting Web services. ASP.NET Web services are the preferred technology for implementing Web services based on the .NET Framework.

ASP.NET Web services support service requests using SOAP over HTTP. ASP.NET Web services automatically generate WSDL and discovery (.disco) files for Web services. You can use ASP.NET Web services to implement a Web service listener that accesses a business façade implemented as a COM component or managed class. The .NET Framework SDK also provides tools to generate proxy classes that client applications can use to access Web services.

Connecting to Databases

The .NET Framework provides ADO.NET (formerly ActiveX Data Objects) as a framework for connecting to databases. From an architect's perspective, ADO.NET represents the abstract design concepts that you can use to build the data access classes within the .NET Framework. From a developer's perspective, ADO.NET represents the concrete implementation of classes inside the .NET Framework that the Framework then uses for data access.

Note: ADO.NET provides functions similar to those implemented in JDBC and JDO.

There are several main design goals to ADO.NET:

- **Explicit and factored object model** — ADO.NET is a simple-to-use object model in which the developer has complete control over how to control data source connectivity, command execution, and data manipulation.

- **Disconnected data cache model** — N-tier programming and XML Web service architecture require that applications can participate in a disconnected, loosely coupled manner. ADO.NET provides a comprehensive caching data model for marshalling data between applications or services and then updating the original data sources or source optimistically.

- **XML support** — XML is the key to building interoperable applications and more robust data processing models. XML support is directly included into the .NET Framework and ADO.NET uses this implementation by providing a seamless interaction with XML in either a relational manner or in a native XML manner.

You can divide the ADO.NET architecture into two logical pieces: command execution and caching. Command execution requires features like connectivity, execution, and reading of results and the .NET data providers enable these features. The **DataSet** function handles caching of results.

Implementing Collections

A *collection* is a set of similarly typed objects that you can group together. These are the equivalent of **java.util.collections** on the J2EE platform.

You can group objects of any type into a single collection of the type **Object** to take advantage of constructs inherent in the programming language. For example, the C# **foreach** statement expects all objects in the collection to be of a single type.

However, in a collection of type **Object**, additional processing, such as boxing and unboxing or conversions, affects the performance of the collection. Boxing and unboxing typically occur when storing or retrieving a value type in a collection of type **Object**.

Strongly typed collections, such as **StringCollection**, avoid these performance hits, if the type of the element is the type that the collection is intended for (for example, storing or retrieving strings from a **StringCollection**). In addition, strongly typed collections automatically perform type validation of each element added to the collection.

You can categorize **collections** classes into three types:

- **Generic collections**—The common variations of data collections, such as hash tables, queues, stacks, dictionaries, and lists.

- **Bit collections**—Collections whose elements are bit flags. They behave slightly differently from other collections.

- **Specialized collections**—Collections with highly specific purposes, usually to handle a specific type of element, like the **StringDictionary**.

Accessing Directory Services

Accessing directory services under .NET usually means connecting to Active Directory, either using Lightweight Directory Access Protocol (LDAP) or Active Directory Service Interface (ADSI), the equivalent of JNDI.

Microsoft implements the LDAP API in Wldap32.dll—also referred to as "LDAP C" or "C-binding LDAP." Applications written in LDAP are compatible only with LDAP directory services, although Active Directory also fully supports the LDAP APIs for directory access.

The primary and recommended API for Active Directory is ADSI. ADSI sits on top of LDAP and also provides the easiest access to Active Directory through LDAP. Native ADSI allows access to Active Directory by exposing objects stored in the directory as COM objects. You then manipulate directory objects using the methods on one or more COM interfaces.

ADSI providers contain the implementation of ADSI objects for a particular namespace, with the main one being the ADSI LDAP provider. By implementing the required interfaces, ADSI providers translate these interfaces to the API calls of a particular directory service.

The ADSI LDAP provider operates on the ADSI client to provide access to Active Directory or to other LDAP directory services. The ADSI LDAP provider works with any LDAP server that supports LDAPv2 or later.

For more information about the LDAP API and about programming in LDAP, see the Microsoft Platform SDK link on the Web Resources page.

Reflection

Reflection allows you to write code that can dynamically examine a data type or an object at run time. You can get a list of its methods, its interfaces, and even its class-level variables. Reflection even allows you to interact with an object by calling those dynamically discovered methods or putting values in those dynamically discovered variables.

Using Reflection, you can create object browsers, applications that list and document methods, or even highly configurable metadata driven applications that create objects and invoke methods based on instructions from a table or XML file. These are powerful capabilities that you can use in .NET-based applications.

You should be aware that Reflection also gives you the power to perform potentially dangerous operations. You can use Reflection to call methods that are **Private** in scope. You can also put values directly into an object's variables *without calling any business logic*. Reflection provides you with the tools to misuse objects in very dangerous ways. However, you can use these capabilities to create very powerful code, such as code to load data from a **DataSet** into an object based on metadata that matches the object's variable name to a column name in a table.

J2EE Fundamentals for .NET Developers

This is where you should start if you are a .NET developer and you want to understand the components and functions of the J2EE platform.

Sun Microsystems developed Java as both a platform and a programming language. There are currently three editions of the Java platform:

- J2SE (Java 2 Standard Edition)
- J2EE (Java 2 Enterprise Edition)
- J2ME (Java 2 Micro Edition)

Note: The term "Java" mostly refers to functionality available within J2SE. Areas that require the Enterprise Edition include the term J2EE.

Java 2 Platform, Enterprise Edition or J2EE is a set of linked specifications that allow developers to create multitier server-based applications. Hence unlike Microsoft .NET, J2EE is a standard, not a product. The J2EE specification consists of a series of downloadable Adobe PDF files that describe application agreements and the makeup of the containers in which these applications run.

Like .NET, J2EE makes it easier to write distributed enterprise applications by letting you focus on writing business logic rather than the enterprise framework itself. J2EE provides the "plumbing" that allows the application to run and would otherwise be tedious and time consuming to write.

Note: At the time of publication, J2EE v1.3 is the latest released version and v1.4 is in final draft.

Hence the J2EE platform is similar in vision to Microsoft .NET, with common themes that run through both platforms. However, it is important that you understand the fundamental differences. Java and Microsoft .NET differ in three main ways, which are:

- Operating system support
- Language support
- Execution method

From the beginning, Java was designed to work with as wide a range of operating systems as possible. Hence Java code runs in multiple environments, such as:

- Windows
- UNIX
- Linux
- MacOS
- BeOS

However, Microsoft .NET runs only on Windows.

Note: Rotor is a version of the .NET Framework that runs on FreeBSD. However, this is more of an academic exercise than a practical implementation scenario.

Language support covers the language, syntax, and grammar that you use to create your programs. You write Java applications only in the Java Programming Language. With .NET, you have the choice of any language that supports the .NET Framework.

There is also a major difference between the two platforms at application run time. When you build a project based on a .NET language, the output consists of MSIL code that the JIT compiler compiles at runtime.

To deploy a Java program, you compile the application to create Java *bytecode*. The JVM running on the target operating system then interprets this bytecode to produce the relevant instructions.

Note: There are also Java JIT compilers that work in a similar fashion to the .NET Framework component.

Understanding the Java Platform

There are two main components of the Java platform. These are:

- The Java Runtime Environment (JRE)
- The Java Language and syntax (API)

The main component of the JRE is the Java Virtual Machine or JVM. The role of the JVM is to interpret Java bytecode into native instructions for the operating system. However, the JVM also provides a number of functions that make it similar to the .NET CLR. The JRE also includes the Java class libraries.

Within the J2EE framework there are additional components that have evolved over the past decade. These include:

- Java Server Pages (JSPs)
- Server side APIs or servlets
- Enterprise Java Beans (EJBs)
- Java Naming and Directory Interface (JNDI)
- Java Message Service (JMS)
- Java API for XML-based RPC (JAX-RPC)
- J2EE Connector Architecture
- J2EE Management Model
- J2EE Deployment API
- Java Management Extensions (JMX)
- J2EE Authorization Contract for Containers
- Java API for XML Registries (JAXR)
- Java Transaction API (JTA)
- Common Object Request Broker Architecture (CORBA)
- JDBC data access API

Many of these components map to equivalents within the .NET Framework or in Windows. For example, JMS provides support for message-based transactions, and maps to the **System.Messaging** namespace.

Because J2EE is a specification, rather than a product, numerous vendors have created their own implementations under license from Sun. These vendors include:

- Sun (Sun ONE Application Server)
- IBM (WebSphere)
- BEA (WebLogic)

There are also several open source implementations, with JBoss being the most recognizable. For more information, see the JBoss Web site at *http://www.jboss.org/*

Implementing the Java SDK

Like the .NET Framework, Java has a software development kit to assist you in creating and compiling Java applications. The Java SDK has been through several revisions, and you can download the Java 2 SDK, Standard Edition 1.4 from Sun's Java site.

Other vendors have produced their own implementations of the Java SDK under license. Like the J2EE Application Servers, these vendors include IBM and BEA, together with open source implementations. Up until version 1.1.4, Microsoft also had an implementation.

The Java 2 SDK contains the class libraries you can use when creating your own Java source code as well as the compiler and binaries for building and executing these applications. The bin directory of the SDK contains Javac.exe which you use to compile Java source code (*.java files) into Java Byte Code (*.class files). However, like with .NET applications, only the most die-hard conservatives work entirely from the command line, and most use a GUI-based IDE to create and build Java applications.

Building a Java Application

When you compile Java classes with the Java compiler, each class in Java generates a separate .class file, which is the standard unit of compilation. The JVM can then execute the .class file using the following syntax:

```
java myapp.class
```

However, .class files are not directly equivalent to .NET assemblies, because .NET assemblies are both units of execution and distribution. To create distributable applications containing multiple .class files, Java developers use Java Archive (JAR) files. A basic JAR file is a collection of compiled Java classes, although JAR files can contain files of any type and have an internal directory structure, like a ZIP file. You use Jar.exe, from the \bin directory of the SDK to add, list or extract .class files from a JAR file.

You can execute a JAR file with the JVM Java.exe. The syntax is:

```
java -jar myapp.jar
```

If you really want to, you can build and deploy a complete J2EE application using only native operating system commands and the basic tools supplied with the Java 2 SDK. However, this method can be tedious and prone to errors. Instead, developers often make use of build tools such as ANT, part of the Apache Jakarta project. ANT is a platform independent build tool that automates the compilation, packaging and deployment of applications. It makes use of XML build files to determine the tasks required to compile and deploy a project.

For more information about ANT, see the Apache ANT Web site.

Locating and Sharing Classes

The Java platform does not include an equivalent to the global assembly cache. However, applications may still need to refer to or share other classes. In Java, you do this using an environment variable named **CLASSPATH**. This is similar to the PATH statement in the Autoexec.bat startup file or the **System Profile** property in Windows.

The default class path is the current directory. You can set the **CLASSPATH** environment variable to one or more different directories if you want; when you do this, you must explicitly include the path to the main Java 2 SDK tools JAR and to the current directory. Hence, a simple **CLASSPATH** statement in release 1.3 of the Java SDK running on Windows would look like this:

```
SET CLASSPATH = .;%J2EE_HOME%\LIB\J2EE.JAR;
```

If your application requires other classes or JAR files, you then amend the **CLASSPATH** variable before running the application. You do this by referring to the current **CLASSPATH** variable as follows:

```
SET CLASSPATH = %CLASSPATH%;C:\OTHERAPP\RESOURCES.JAR;C:\OTHERAPP\CLASSES
```

This appends the new directories to the existing **CLASSPATH** so that when a Java application loads and asks for a class, it also searches any class in the directory C:\OtherApp\Classes or the JAR file C:\OtherApp\Resources.jar.

Both the Javac.exe compiler and the Java.exe execution tool can accept parameters to include or modify the **CLASSPATH** variable. Java IDEs also allow you to include **CLASSPATH** statements. You can also add libraries to the class search sequence automatically without setting **CLASSPATH** by installing them as extensions in the JRE.

Note: If a Java application generates a **ClassNotFoundException**, you can almost guarantee that this is because the required libraries are not in the **CLASSPATH** statement.

Implementing Other Environment Variables

Java applications tend to use environmental variables more than .NET-based applications. This is because Java applications can run on multiple operating systems, so they need to be able to cope with differing environments. Environmental variables provide an easy way to ensure consistency for setting and controlling configuration and application execution paths.

Table 2.1: Common Environmental Variables

Variable Name	Function
JAVA_HOME	Installation location of the Sun Java SDK
J2EE_HOME	Installation location of the Sun J2EE SDK
ANT_HOME	The ANT home directory
PATH	As for the Windows PATH statement

Using Java Integrated Design Environments

Several vendors produce IDE packages to assist with creating and editing, ranging from beefed up text editors to full blown packages that resemble Visual Studio .NET. Some are commercial packages, others are free. Examples include:

- Sun One Studio
- JCreator
- Borland JBuilder
- Java GUI Builder
- JPad Pro
- CodeGuide
- NetBeans
- AnyJ

Note: Although you can create and edit Java applications using Visual J# from Visual Studio .NET, J# IntelliSense® technology only works for Java API classes up to release 1.1.4 of the Java SDK and you need to build the application from the command line using Javac.exe.

All the IDE packages allow you to build applications from within the IDE environment. Alternatively, like Visual Studio, you can build applications from the command line.

Creating Web Applications

For Presentation tier components, Java implements JSP where you would use ASP.NET in the .NET architecture. JSP provides a server side technology for developing Web applications and JSP pages are a mixture of HTML and Java code.

Java-based Web applications use the concept of dynamically compiled JSP pages and servlets. A servlet is a Java programming language class that extends the capabilities of computers hosting applications accessed through request-response programming models. You can also think of Java servlets as portable components that provide dynamic content to user requests.

At first glance, JSP and servlets appear very similar, with both producing dynamic content. You create any scripting elements within the JSP pages or the servlets in the Java programming language. Additionally, the JVM compiles JSPs into servlets at run time and therefore both use the same engine. However, developing a servlet entails writing a Java class and therefore requires stronger programming skills than are needed to develop a JSP. You can think of a servlet as Java code wrapping up HTML content.

Like servlets, JSPs provide dynamic content to users but at a higher level abstraction of servlets. You can think of JSPs as static HTML wrapping up dynamic Java code.

You can host both JSP and servlets on a number of environments. These include free offerings such as Apache Tomcat up to the large commercially available and vendor-supported implementations.

To implement a JSP-based application, you design the application using a Java IDE. Several IDEs include facilities for real-time editing of JSP pages, with previews showing the effect of any changes to the graphics or the controls.

Note: The current JSP specification is release v1.2 and the servlet API is v2.3.

To deploy Web applications, you package them up into a single deployable unit called a Web Application Archive (or WAR) file. This is similar to how you package Java applications into JARs. You can then easily deploy the WAR file onto the Web server.

Hosting Components

The main function of JSP pages and servlets is to interact with the user through the browser in the Presentation tier. However, executing business rules in the Business tier uses components called Enterprise Java Beans (EJBs). EJBs are the equivalent of COM+ components or managed code components, and can provide the following services:

- Maintaining state
- Transactional support
- Method level security
- Logging
- Impersonation
- Message queue support

EJBs come in three forms:

- Session beans
- Entity beans
- Message-driven beans.

Session beans host business logic, such as the rules defining the operation of a customer relationship management system. Session beans can be stateless or can maintain state, tying the client to the session bean for the object's lifetime. Typically a session bean provides some sort of service, such as performing a task, such as authentication, for clients.

Entity beans represent an object in persistent storage. Each instance of an entity bean corresponds to a row of data from a database table. There are two types of entity bean: *container managed persistence* (CMP) beans, which are managed by the container; and *bean managed persistence* (BMP) beans, which manage their own persistence.

With CMP entity beans, the container manages the mapping between bean and database fields using a mapping file. This mapping file usually stores these mappings as XML deployment descriptors. The container manages all the communications with the database. CMP has the following advantages compared to BMP:

- Easier to configure
- Easier to maintain
- Requires no database code

The main disadvantage of CMP can be that of performance, due to greater abstraction levels. However, newer features of the J2EE specification have introduced features such as virtual accessors, which have improved the performance of beans using CMP.

With BMP entity beans, the developer is responsible for writing all the JDBC code for transferring data between a bean and the data store. BMPs require the developer to write much more data-related code than CMPs, but nevertheless there are several good reasons for using BMPs:

- Greater flexibility
- Better performance
- Ability to connect to multiple database sources

A Java developer would use CMP for connecting to standard databases such as Oracle or where the number of transactions per second is low. BMP comes into its own with high data access rates or where the developer needs the flexibility to connect to a non-standard database such as an LDAP directory.

You would use *message-driven beans* (MDB) in conjunction with the JMS API to process messages asynchronously. Message-driven beans are JMS message consumers. Clients do not access MDBs directly; they send a JMS message to a destination where there is a listening MDB. This enables reuse of the MDB, and also means that the developer does not have to worry about where to go to get the message.

The two main benefits of using MDBs are that MDBs enable parallel processing of user requests, which provides a faster response compared to serial invocation using non-message based entity Java beans, and that an MDB implementation can guarantee user response times when searching multiple data sources.

Building Enterprise JavaBeans

When building an Enterprise JavaBean, a developer must create the bean's implementation class and a number of interfaces. Clients access session and entity beans through the methods that the developer defined in the bean's interfaces. The interfaces determine how the client can communicate with the EJB. Message-driven beans differ from entity and session beans in that they do not have interfaces; they contain only a bean implementation class.

The interfaces defined on an entity or session bean are dependent on one key factor: Is the bean going to be accessed remotely or locally?

A remote client is:

- An application or component that runs in a separate JVM from the client (although the application does not necessarily have to run in a separate JVM.)
- An application or component executing on a different computer.
- A Web component such as a servlet, a client application, or another EJB.
- Where the client does not know (or need to know) the location of the EJB.

If an EJB services remote clients, the developer must create two interfaces: a *remote interface* and a *home interface*. The remote interface defines the business methods specific to the bean, for example, **AuthenticateCustomer**. The home interface defines methods that manage instances of the bean. For example, session beans have methods to create and remove instances of the beans. Entity beans also include finder methods. Finder methods allow clients to locate entity beans, for example, **findByPrimaryKey**.

A client is local if:

- The client component or application executes in the same JVM as the EJB.
- The client could be a Web component or EJB.
- The location of the EJB is not transparent to the client.

If an EJB is required to service local client, it is also necessary to create two interfaces, a local interface and a *local home* interface. The local interface defines the bean's business methods in a similar fashion to a remote interface. The local home interface is similar to the remote home interface in that it defines methods for manipulating instances of the bean and defining finder methods.

It is usually more efficient for a local client to invoke methods on the local interfaces than through remote invocation. In a typical J2EE application, a session bean provides remote client access, whereas entity beans normally provide local client access. Entity beans that use CMP almost always employ local access.

Deploying Applications

Building and deploying a J2EE application involves a number of steps to ensure that you deploy everything required for the application to function. In addition to JAR files containing EJBs or other classes, your application may need WAR files. WAR files are JARs with the required structure for a Web application. Finally, Enterprise Archive files (EARs) can contain WARs and JARs stuffed with EJBs and other content.

You configure deployment settings using deployment descriptors, which are XML files with a defined structure. Deployment descriptors specify settings such as security, transactional support, and logging that tell the application server how to deploy and support the components in the application. Again, these settings correlate to those in component services. Some deployment descriptor settings are part of the J2EE specification, whereas others relate to the application server and are vendor-specific.

Comparing .NET and J2EE Features

Table 2.2 shows a comparison of features and functions in .NET and J2EE. However, differences in the background makeup of each platform make direct comparisons between .NET and J2EE not always applicable. For example, MSMQ is a product whereas JMS is an API. Therefore you cannot simply rip out one component and replace it with the equivalent from the other platform.

Table 2.2: Comparison Between .NET and J2EE Functionality

Feature or Service	Microsoft .NET Element	J2EE Element	Comments
Technology Type	Product	Standard	
Middleware Vendors	Microsoft and partners	50+ vendors	
Client Side GUI	Windows Forms Environment	AWT/SWING	SWING/AWT are part of J2SE
Web GUI	ASP.NET	JSP	
Web Scripting	ISAPI	Servlet	
	HttpHandler HttpModule	Filter	
Web Application Hosting	Internet Information Server	Multiple (depends on vendor implementation)	J2EE examples include Apache Tomcat
Interpreter	CLR	JRE	
Server Side Business Logic Component	.NET Class or Serviced Component (COM+)	EJB Session Beans	
Server Side Data Components 1	Serviced Component with DB Logic	EJB with Bean Managed Persistence	
Server Side Data Components 2	ADO.NET Data Set	EJB with Container Managed Persistence	Only an approximate equivalence
Directory Access	Active Directory Services Interface (ADSI) through LDAP	Java Naming and Directory Service (JNDI) through LDAP	LDAP compatibility makes switching between directory services very easy.
Remote Invocation	.NET Remoting	RMI-IIOP	
Data Access	ADO.NET	JDBC, SQL/J, JDO	

(continued)

Table 2.2: Comparison Between .NET and J2EE Functionality *(continued)*

Feature or Service	Microsoft .NET Element	J2EE Element	Comments
Messaging	Microsoft Message Queuing	JMS	Microsoft Message Queuing is a product. JMS is a specification, and therefore requires an underlying implementation.
Transactional Support	COM+/Distributed Transaction Controller (DTC)	JTA	

Summary

This chapter provided an overview into .NET for Java developers and an overview of Java for .NET developers. It compared and contrasted the features from each platform and showed the equivalence of components in the different environments. It also showed how the different platforms deal with common programming issues and the solutions that each employ.

References

For information about the.NET Framework
http://msdn.microsoft.com/netframework/

For information about a development environment for programming in any supported language—Visual Studio .NET
http://msdn.microsoft.com/vstudio/

For information about the operating system that supports distributed environments and the .NET Framework—the Windows Server System
http://www.microsoft.com/windowsserversystem/default.mspx

To download version 1.1 of the .NET Framework
http://msdn.microsoft.com/netframework/downloads/howtoget.aspx#section3

- or -

From the Windows Update Service
http://windowsupdate.microsoft.com/

For more details about Java 2 SDK 1.5 support for attribute-like structures
JSR 175: A Metadata Facility for the Java Programming Language
http://www.jcp.org/en/jsr/detail?id=175

- or -

New Language Features for Ease of Development in the Java 2 Platform,
Standard Edition 1.5: A Conversation with Joshua Bloch
http://java.sun.com/features/2003/05/bloch_qa.html

For more information about best practices for deploying assemblies into the global
assembly cache
Deploying .NET Framework-based Applications
*http://msdn.microsoft.com/library/default.asp?url=/library/en-us/dnbda/html
/DALGRoadmap.asp*

To download the English version of the .NET Framework SDK v1.1 from the SDK
Web site
*http://www.microsoft.com/downloads/details.aspx?familyid=9b3a2ca6-3647-4070-9f41
-a333c6b9181d&displaylang=en*

To download Web Matrix, an alternative free integrated development environment
From the ASP.NET Web site
http://www.asp.net/webmatrix

For more information about the LDAP API and about programming in LDAP
Microsoft Platform SDK link on the Web Resources page
http://windows.microsoft.com/windows2000/reskit/webresources

To download the Java 2 SDK, Standard Edition v 1.4
See Sun's Java site
http://java.sun.com/

For more information about ANT
See the Apache ANT Web site
http://ant.apache.org/

3

Interoperability Fundamentals

Introduction

Chapter 2, "Understanding Enterprise Platforms," shows many similarities between Microsoft .NET and J2EE. However, although the two platforms share certain concepts that appear equivalent, a detailed examination shows significant differences. These differences are particularly important when you look at how the two platforms describe data at the most basic level.

This chapter covers the basics of interoperability techniques. It focuses on a discussion of interoperability fundamentals, mainly concerning the exchanging of data types and formats between J2EE and .NET. Without this understanding, you cannot expect either platform to consume data from the other platform.

The chapter then moves on to discuss ways to enable interoperability by standardizing on data types. Finally, it describes recommendations for overcoming the challenge of exchanging data.

Facing Interoperability Challenges

At the most basic level, implementing interoperability between application platforms involves the exchange of data. When implementing a .NET and J2EE interoperability project, you confront three main data exchange challenges. The three challenges are:

- Primitive data type mappings
- Non-existent data types
- Complex data types

Note: Primitive data types are components based on the underlying type system for .NET or Java, for example, Integer, Strings, Doubles, and so on.

All challenges involve type compatibility and have the potential to hinder or prevent data transfer.

These three challenges break down as follows:

- **Primitive data type mappings**—You may know that the type "String" exists in both the CLR and in Java. However, this does not mean that **java.lang.String** in Java maps exactly to **System.String** in .NET. If your sample exposes **java.lang.String**, how do you go about mapping this to its equivalent in the CLR?

- **Non-existent data types**—How do you map data types on one platform that don't exist in the other? For example, **System.Collections.Specialized.HybridDictionary** is a documented data type in the CLR, but nothing in Java resembles it in the slightest. Java contains similar examples that are not in .NET, such as **Java.util.Vector**.

- **Complex data types**—Your application may expose complex data types, made up of numerous or even nested primitive data types. Here you need to expose the complex data type so that the other platform can use it.

Consider the example of integrating an ASP.NET Presentation tier with a J2EE Business tier as Figure 3.1 shows. In this example, an EJB in the J2EE Business tier exposes a method that the ASP.NET Presentation tier then calls. In a production application, this returned data is unlikely to be a simple "Hello World" string, and would probably contain complex elements.

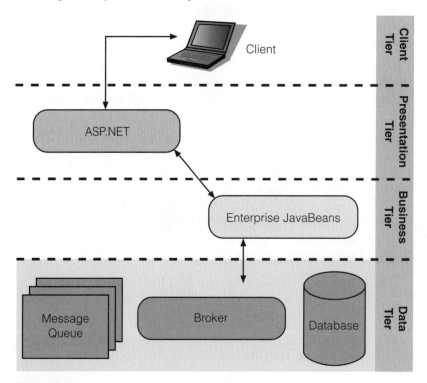

Figure 3.1

ASP.NET Presentation tier linked to J2EE Business tier

Luckily, a number of possibilities exist that allow applications to exchange data types from one platform to the other, and Chapters 4 and 5 cover these options in detail. However, before you can make the connection between the two platforms, you have to ensure that both sides understand a particular data type before they attempt to exchange it, and also that you have a means of making the transfer that both sides can use. This next section looks at how you can use serialization to make the transfer.

Using Serialization

Serialization is the process of encoding an object or class into a persistent or transportable state. This allows you to take a complex data type, then encode, save, transfer, and decode it, with the possibility that a separate process handles the decoding.

There are two main serialization types:

- **Binary serialization**—Takes the data type and converts it into a binary stream.
- **XML serialization**—Converts the data type into an XML stream which you can then convert to an XML document.

You can take the output from either serialization type and store it in memory, place it into a file, or pass it across a network connection. For example, your application may have a defined **CustomerData** complex data type which stores information about a customer (such as name, address, telephone number, and so on). You can use serialization to convert the **CustomerData** data type into a binary or XML stream that you can then transport across process boundaries or save to a file for later use. The object is serialized when it is in the binary or XML format.

De-serialization is the process of converting a serialized object back to its original form. Generally, you de-serialize objects back into their original type. Hence, if you serialize the **CustomerData** data type as a binary stream or as an XML document, you de-serialize it back to the data type **CustomerData** and not to the data type **OrderData**.

Both .NET and J2EE use serialization to exchange data between applications within the same platform. You can also use serialization to exchange data between applications on different platforms by passing serialized objects for de-serialization on the alternate platform. The next sections examine how to implement binary and XML serialization on .NET and Java.

Understanding Binary Serialization

Binary serialization is the process of taking a complex data type (or object) and encoding it into a binary stream, changing to a persistent state, transporting, and then decoding (de-serialize) back into the original complex data type.

Both Java and .NET include a binary serializer that can convert any serializeable data type into a byte stream. The classes that perform this serialization are similar in each platform and simple to implement.

For binary serialization in both .NET and Java, you must first apply a label to indicate that you want to serialize a type. In .NET, you can use the **[Serializable]** attribute or implement the **ISerializable** interface. In Java, the equivalent approach is to make the class implement **java.io.serializable**.

Unfortunately, the .NET and Java serializers are incompatible. Hence, you cannot stream the serialized version of the **CustomerData** object output from the Java serializer straight into the .NET version and vice versa. Even if you could, you would still face the challenge of getting the .NET Framework application to understand the **CustomerData** object that the Java serializer produced. The .NET side may not have an equivalent **CustomerData** data type to accept the de-serialized **CustomerData** object from the Java side.

You *can* use binary serialization for linking .NET to Java as long as the same formatter performs the serialization and de-serialization of an object. The format that creates the byte stream from the data type must match exactly the format that receives the byte stream and reconstructs the object.

There are two approaches that you can use to circumvent the incompatibility of the default J2EE and .NET binary serializers. These are:

- Create a custom serializer sharing the same formatting options on both Java and .NET.
- Use a third-party product that works with the binary formatter in the .NET Framework, such as Ja.NET or JNBridgePro.

For more information about implementing binary serialization with Ja.NET and JNBridgePro, see Chapter 4, "Interoperability Technologies: Point to Point."

Understanding XML Serialization

XML serialization is the process of taking a complex data type (or object) and encoding it into an XML stream. You can then make this XML stream into a persistent state in the form of an XML document, transport it, and then later decode (de-serialize) it back into the original complex data type (or object).

In order to understand the process of XML serialization, you need to have a basic understanding of XML. XML is text-based document markup language that contains structured and extensible data. XML is text-based, so you can read it like normal text and because it is extensible, you can use it to describe almost any type of information. Hence XML documents can contain:

- Text
- Pictures
- Program settings
- Data schemas
- Annotations
- Inserts

XML documents may also contain instructions about how to use the data within the document itself.

For more information about XML, see the Microsoft XML Web site.

In the "Understanding Binary Serialization" section, you saw how the binary serializers of the .NET and Java platforms are not compatible with each other. However, XML is platform independent. If you can serialize an object or data type from one platform into an XML document, it should be relatively easy to read, understand, and de-serialize this document back into an object or data type on the other platform. Unfortunately, this is not always the case, but XML serialization does provide an interoperability route in most situations.

Parsing XML Documents

There are several different ways to read, write, and edit XML documents within .NET and J2EE. This process is XML *parsing* and both platforms have stable and mature XML parsers. Using a parser, you can write code within your application that reads data from an XML document manually and then inserts it into a complex data type object. For example, you could use parsing to read data from an XML document that a J2EE application generates, and then insert the data into a .NET data type. Parsing allows the exchange of data between .NET and J2EE.

Parsers for reading and writing XML documents tend to fall into three main types:

- Document Object Model (DOM) on both platforms
- Simple API for XML (SAX) on Java only
- Pull model parsing on .NET only

DOM XML parsers load the entire document into memory, which has some advantages and disadvantages. With the whole document in memory, you can traverse the XML hierarchy quickly and easily, but large documents affect performance and responsiveness due to memory usage.

SAX reads sections of the XML file as required. This affects performance less due to reading the file on demand, but it reduces flexibility by preventing backwards parsing.

Pull model parsing uses a forward-only, read-only **XmlReader** cursor. **XMLReader** provides fast, non-cached stream access to the input data, allowing you to pull data and to skip records that are of no interest. Because **XmlReader** is pull mode, applications can pull nodes from the reader as necessary. The pull model provides advantages such as state management, multiple input streams, extra string copy avoidance, and selective processing. For more information about using **XmlReader**, see "Reading XML with the XmlReader," on MSDN.

The **System.Xml** namespace provides the **XmlDocument** and **XmlElement** classes to allow you to parse XML in .NET. They also provide methods that let you add to and modify elements within XML documents and to traverse those documents.

In Java, you can use **Document** and **Element** classes to achieve similar results.

Limitations of Parsing XML

There are some limitations to XML parsing that you need to understand. Parsing works well when you access and read distinct data elements from an XML document. However, manipulating information within the document itself can rapidly become unwieldy. Also, there is no intrinsic way of using a parser to map objects in the XML document to classes either in Java or in .NET. Mapping data in an XML document to application objects and classes requires XML serialization.

XML parsing can be considered an inefficient way of implementing XML serialization and is not the recommended way for exchanging XML data between .NET and Java. Both .NET and J2EE have XML serializers that include parsing functionality.

XML serialization provides significant enhancements when creating XML documents. It frees you from the tedium of the XML parsing process, letting you concentrate on developing the application itself and associated data types. XML serialization simplifies the task of taking an object in .NET, converting it to an XML document and enabling a Java application to read it, and vice versa.

Implementing XML Serialization on the .NET Platform

The.NET Framework provides numerous classes and APIs for XML serialization. The main one of these is the *System.Xml.Serialization.XmlSerializer* class. This class allows the serialization of .NET Framework types to an XML document and back again. XML serialization converts (serializes) only the public fields and properties of an object into an XML stream whereas binary serialization converts the object's public and private fields and the name of the class together with the assembly containing the class into a stream of bytes.

You can use the [**Serializable**] attribute to indicate that you want to serialize a type, just like with binary serialization. Alternatively, you can have your data type class implement the **ISerializable** interface.

XML serialization uses different rules from binary serialization. For example, you do not need to label .NET data types with the [**Serializable**] attribute, although this is still recommended practice. However, .NET data types must have a valid default public constructor.

Serializing .NET Objects into XML

The following example demonstrates how you can use **XMLSerializer** in .NET to convert an instance of the **CustomerData** class, called **custData,** into an XML stream. This example assumes your .NET Framework application already has a defined **CustomerData** data type class which you marked as serializable.

```
XmlSerializer serializer = new XmlSerializer(typeof(CustomerData));
serializer.Serialize(fileStream, custData);
```

The **Serialize** method of the **XMLSerializer** class serializes the contents of the **CustomerData** object, **custData,** and generates the output as a file stream. This stream points to a file, which is an XML document representing the serialized version of the **CustomerData** object, **custData.**

Deserializing Objects from XML to .NET

This next example demonstrates how you can use the **XMLSerializer** in .NET to return an instance of a **CustomerData** object, **custData,** from an XML document stored as a file.

```
XmlSerializer serializer = new XmlSerializer(typeof(CustomerData));
CustomerData custData = (CustomerData)serializer.Deserialize(fileStream);
```

Here you use the **Deserialize** method of the **XmlSerializer** class to return a **CustomerData** object, **custData,** from an XML document passed to the serializer as a stream.

Note: The **Deserialize** method returns an object with a type of **System.Object**. Ensure that you cast the returned object appropriately before assigning it to the target type.

Serialization can fail for a number of reasons:

- The XML document under de-serialization contains fields the serializer cannot process.
- The object cannot be serialized, such as any object that implements the **IDictionary** interface.
- Objects are not declared as *public*.
- Objects do not contain a valid no-argument constructor.

Note: Attempting to serialize an object that fits into one of the previous four categories generates a **System.InvalidOperationException** from **XmlSerializer**. When debugging XML serialization, you should check for and resolve any instances of this exception.

Implementing XML Serialization for the Java Platform

XML serialization of objects is not part of the core specifications for either J2SE or J2EE. Hence, you need to use a third party serializer, of which there are several to choose from:

- Electric XML
- Apache Cocoon
- Open XML Framework (OXF)
- Java Architecture for XML Binding (JAXB)

Many serializers form part of a larger Web services package, although you do not need to be using Web services to use the XML serialization features. Java serializers use a combination of *reflection* and *mapping* to write the object's data into the correct XML format. Reflection is a technique for inspecting the structure of an object, and mapping is like an Extensible Stylesheet Language Transformations (XSLT) document, mapping the fieldnames in the object to elements or attributes in the XML document.

To make a Java class serializable, you need to implement the **Serializable** interface. Hence the class declaration for **CustomerData** would be the following.

```
public class CustomerData implements java.io.Serializable
```

A serializable class must also have a no argument constructor. You can also use the **serialPersistentFields** member to declare explicitly which fields can be serialized, or the transient keyword to indicate fields that cannot be serialized. Examples of non-serializable fields might be ones that include sensitive data.

Classes that you have marked for serialization in Java may also implement the **readObject** and **writeObject** methods for controlling saving, and reading information, together with the **writeReplace** and **readResove** methods to designate replacement objects.

You may also implement **Externalizable** instead of **Serializable** for complete control of class serialization. When using **Externalizable**, you have to implement the **writeExternal** and **readExternal** methods to write, not only the contents of the data, but also the data format and associated metadata.

The next two examples use Electric XML to demonstrate how to serialize and deserialize a Java object. Here you see that Electric XML handles the serialization and deserialization processes in a similar fashion to .NET.

Serializing Java Objects into XML

The following example assumes that your Java application defines a serializable **OrderData** data type class which implements **java.io.serializable**. It demonstrates how you can use the Electric XML serializer in J2EE to convert a named instance of this class, **order**, into an XML document.

```
electric.xml.io.IWriter writer = new LiteralWriter(xmlNameSpace,OrderData);
writer.writeObject(order);
electric.xml.Document document = writer.getDocument();
```

In this example, you first create an instance of type **electric.xml.io.IWriter**, passing in the XML namespace of the XML document you want to create, and the object type (**OrderData**) as parameters. The **writeObject** method of the **IWriter** object serializes the contents of the **OrderData** object, **order**. Finally, the **getDocument** method of the **IWriter** object retrieves the XML document containing the serialized contents of the **OrderData** object. You can then write this document to a stream.

Deserializing Objects from XML to Java

This next example demonstrates how you can use the Electric XML serializer in J2EE to return an instance of an **OrderData** object, **order**, from an XML document named **xmlDocument**.

```
electric.xml.io.IReader reader = new LiteralReader(xmlDocument);
OrderData order = (OrderData)reader.readObject(OrderData.class);
```

Here you use the **readObject** method of the **IReader** class to return an **OrderData** object, **order**, from an XML document which you pass to the reader as a parameter.

Note: The **readObject** method returns a generic object of type **java.lang.Object**. You must cast this returned object appropriately before assigning it to the target type.

For an additional example of XML Serialization on the Java platform, see Chapter 7, "Integrating .NET in the Presentation Tier."

Using XML Schemas to Ensure Type Compatibility

You have now seen how you can use XML serialization to serialize objects into an XML format on one platform, and then de-serialized them back into the original object type in the alternate environment. However, XML serialization alone does not solve the issue of exchanging data between .NET and Java.

A major consideration when using serialization techniques is to ensure that when you generate an XML document from one platform, the document is compatible with the other. You should not take this compatibility for granted. The *XML Schema* provides the interoperability contract that specifies the format for XML documents. It is this component that provides the template for successfully linking .NET and Java.

By itself, an XML document does not define the data types within the document. Hence a value of 4.56 could be a **string**, a **double**, or a **float**. This makes it difficult for the receiving platform to import the value correctly. Similarly, both platforms could implement the type **OrderData**, but the .NET version could be totally unrelated to the identically named type in Java.

For example, if you serialize the **OrderData** object on the .NET platform into an XML document and pass it to the Java application for consumption, you need to answer the following questions:

- How will the Java application know how to de-serialize the **OrderData** object?
- Is there an **OrderData** data type in Java equivalent to the **OrderData** data type in .NET?
- What if the **OrderData** data type in Java has nothing in common with the **OrderData** data type in .NET?

These questions all point to data type compatibility issues that you need to resolve to enable the exchange of data between .NET and J2EE.

Understanding XML Schema Documents

The XML Schema provides a linking framework through the XML Schema Document (XSD) that assists in exchanging data between .NET and J2EE by defining the format of an XML document. An XSD file specifies an XML Schema, and the XSD file itself is simply another XML document with a set structure. Nodes and elements within the XSD define the elements and data types in the related XML document(s). An XSD also contains any constraints for each element with the XML document.

Within the XSD file, you can specify the definition of a data type stored in the XML format. For example, when defining the **OrderData** data type in an XSD, you can specify the names and number of fields within the object, such as **orderID**, **itemDescription**, and **price**. You can also specify that the value of the **price** field (4.56) in your **OrderData** object is of type **double**.

XSDs allow you to define *XML namespaces*. XML namespaces allow you to declare unique types and also let you identify different data types that may have the same name.

One essential component in the XSD is the *common namespace*. This lets you declare elements such as **xs:complexType** as unique for the document. For more information about the XSD namespace, see the W3Consortium Web site.

Visual Studio .NET includes an XML Designer tool that allows you to design XML schemas easily. The XML Designer lets you switch modes between a graphical representation of your schema or the XSD document that represents that XML Schema. XML Designer creates platform independent XSDs that conform to the W3C standards. For more information about generating schemas in Visual Studio .NET, see Visual Studio .NET Help.

IBM Websphere Studio Application Developer 5.0 also contains a tool that allows you to design XML Schemas easily. The XSD designer allows you to switch modes between a graphical representation of the schema you are designing to the actual XSD document representing the XML schema. XSDs designed in IBM WebSphere Studio Application Designer are also platform independent and conform to the W3C organization's XSD standards.

Using XSDs to Ensure Class Compatibility

You saw in the previous section how you can implement an XML Schema in an XSD to define the format of an XML document. You can use this knowledge to complete the final piece of the data exchange puzzle.

The fact is that the .NET and Java platforms are highly unlikely ever to agree on data types. However, using XSDs, the two platforms *can* agree on the format of an XML document. If interoperability was like international diplomacy, this would be hailed as a major milestone toward world peace.

Both .NET and Java have tools that allow you to map a class to a defined XML Schema and vice versa. When you map a class to an XML Schema, the XML document that you generate by serializing an instance of that class matches the XML format that the XSD defines. By mapping classes on each platform to a common XML Schema, you can ensure that each platform can exchange XML data with the other.

For example, you map a **CustomerData** class in both .NET and Java to a common XML Schema file, **CustomerData.xsd**. You should then be able to serialize an instance of the Java **CustomerData** class into an XML document, and de-serialize it back into an instance of the .NET **CustomerData** class.

With the XML Schema mapping tools in .NET and Java, you have two main approaches for developing a common format for exchanging data:

- Start with a common XML Schema, and then generate data type classes on both platforms. This approach guarantees that you build data types and a schema in a platform independent format.

- Start from an existing data type class (from either platform), generate an XML Schema from it, and then generate a corresponding data type class for the other platform from the resulting XML Schema.

Note: The first technique is best if the classes do not already exist on either platform. If they do exist on one or other, then you must use the second method.

For each of these approaches, the technique differs, depending on whether you are working on the Java or .NET platform.

Mapping XSDs and Classes in .NET

The .NET Framework provides an XML Schema Definition tool, Xsd.exe, which you can use to map .NET classes to XML Schemas and back again. Using this tool, you can:

- Generate a .NET class from an XSD.
- Generate an XSD from a .NET class.

For example, if you define an XML Schema document *ProductsData.xsd* for a data type named **ProductsData**, you can use Xsd.exe to generate a serializable .NET class named **ProductsData**. Serializing an instance of the .NET **ProductData** class produces an XML document that matches the XML format defined in the XML Schema document, *ProductsData.xsd*.

Alternatively, if you define a serializable **ProductsData** class in .NET, you can use Xsd.exe to generate an XML Schema, *ProductsData.xsd* defining the format of an XML document containing a serialized version of the **ProductsData** object.

Note: Xsd.exe only allows you to manipulate XML Schemas that follow the World Wide Web Consortium's implementation of the XML Schema definition language.

For more information about the XML Schema Definition tool, see XML Schema Definition Tool on MSDN.

For additional examples of how to use the XML Schema Definition tool, see Chapter 3 of Simon Guest's book *Microsoft .NET and J2EE Interoperability Toolkit*.

Mapping XSDs and Classes in Java

On the Java platform, there are multiple tools you can use to map Java classes to XML Schemas and vice versa. Examples are:

- **schema2java** and **java2schema** from Electric XML
- Java Architecture for XML Binding (JAXB)

Note: Most of the XML serialization tool vendors produce equivalent utilities to **schema2java** and **java2schema**. However, the examples in this book use the Electric XML versions.

The **schema2java** and **java2schema** tools provide functionality very similar to Xsd.exe in .NET. With Electric XML tools you can:

- Use **schema2java** to generate a Java class from an XSD.
- Use **java2schema** to generate an XSD from a Java class.

You can use the **schema2java** tool with the same XML Schema file, *ProductsData.xsd* that you defined for a data type named **ProductsData** in the.NET example to generate a serializable Java class named **ProductsData**. Just as in .NET, serializing an instance of the Java **ProductData** class generates an XML document that exactly matches the XML Schema from the *ProductsData.xsd* document.

The **java2schema** tool allows you to perform the reverse process. If you define a serializeable **ProductsData** class in Java, you can use **java2schema** to generate an XML Schema, *ProductsData.xsd*. This document defines the format of an XML document containing a serialized version of the Java **ProductsData** object.

Note: You can only generate XSDs from compiled classes, not source code.

For more information about **schema2java** and **java2schema**, see Package electric.xml.io.tools in the References section at the end of this chapter.

For an example of how to use the Electric XML tools to map Java classes and XML Schemas, see *Microsoft .NET and J2EE Interoperability Toolkit*, Chapter 3, pages 70–80.

In both the .NET and Java examples in the earlier section, because the same *ProductsData.xsd* is the source for both the Java **ProductsData** class and the .NET **ProductsData** class, both classes serialize into the same XML format. Hence you can serialize an instance of the **ProductsData** class on one platform into an XML document, then de-serialize it back into an instance of the **ProductData** class on the other platform.

Generating types using XSDs is very powerful, and it goes a long way to providing cross-platform interoperability. XSDs are also a foundation element in WSDL. Understanding the structure of XSDs is very helpful when looking at data type transportation in XML Web services.

Mapping XSD Types

The previous section described how to map classes and XSDs in both .NET and Java. However, there are limitations when using this technique to create a common format for exchanging data. In most cases, the complex data types you use to store data in both .NET and Java consist of primitive types. Unfortunately, not all primitive types have a direct mapping between .NET and Java.

The XSD common namespace defines a set of data types that XML can represent. Both .NET and Java have mappings to the XML data types defined in the XSD common namespace.

Note: When designing complex data types, you are recommended to use only the platform data types that map directly to XML data types.

Table 3.1 shows the mapping between XML data types, .NET data types, and J2EE data types using the serializer in Electric XML.

Table 3.1: XML to .NET and Electric XML Data Type Mappings

XML Data Type	.NET Data Type	Electric XML Data Type
anyURI	System.Uri	java.net.URL
base64Binary	Byte(Array)	byte(Array)
boolean	Boolean	Boolean
byte	SByte	Byte
dateTime	DateTime	Java.util.Date
decimal	Decimal	Java.math.BigDecimal
double	Double	Double
float	Single	Float
hexBinary	Byte(Array)	electric.util.Hex
Int	Int32	Int
long	Int64	Int
negativeInteger	System.Decimal	Int
nonNegativeInteger	System.Decimal	Int
nonPositiveInteger	System.Decimal	Int
short	Int16	short
string	String	java.lang.String
unsignedInt	UInt32	int

Data Exchange Recommendations

You should now understand the techniques for using XML serialization in conjunction with XML Schemas to exchange data between .NET and Java in a common format. This section discusses the recommendations for exchanging data between .NET and J2EE successfully in different enterprise environment scenarios.

In enterprise environments, there are three interoperability scenarios that frequently occur when developing a common format for exchanging data between .NET and J2EE. These are:

- Linking new applications.
- Linking a new application to an existing application.
- Linking two (or more) existing applications.

Unfortunately, the first scenario is the easiest but least common, whereas the last is the most difficult and the most common.

Linking New Applications

In this scenario, you are developing applications on different platforms that need to exchange data with each other. Here the assumption is that you are building each application from scratch and your developers have decided on a common data format for each application before development.

The best practice recommendations for this scenario are:

- Use XSD to define common or shared types and then generate platform-specific code from those shared types.
- Create a central XSD repository for your development teams to provide for consistency in generating types across applications.
- Avoid exposing elements that XSD does not define—always use types that are published in XSD.
- Test data types with test utilities before writing your application.

Linking a New Application to an Existing Application

In this second scenario, you have an existing application on either platform and you need to implement interoperability between this existing application and a new application on the opposite platform.

Note: This scenario assumes you do not have the ability to change the data types in the existing application.

For example, you may have an existing multi-tier J2EE application that uses several defined complex types, such as **CustomerData** or **OrderData**. You now have to develop a new ASP.NET Presentation tier that must interoperate with this existing J2EE application. You need to exchange data in the **CustomerData** and **OrderData** data types with the new .NET Presentation tier application. However, .NET has no corresponding data types to match the Java **CustomerData** and **OrderData** data types.

In this scenario, the best practice recommendations are:

- Generate XSDs from the data types that the existing application exposes.
- Use these XSDs to generate corresponding data type classes in the new application's platform.
- Follow the recommendations from the first scenario.

Linking Existing Applications

This is the most common scenario in enterprise environments, and, unfortunately, the most difficult. Here you have two or more existing applications on different application platforms and you need to implement interoperability between these applications. You also have limited or no ability to change the data types in any of the existing applications. You will have to adapt or convert the data in at least one of the applications into a different format in order to exchange data.

There are several solutions to this scenario. The two most common are:

- Use a common format and a single adapter:
  1. Select one application's data type as a common format for exchanging data.
  2. Implement an adapter layer on the other application to convert its data type to the common format.
- Use a common XML Schema and adapters for each application:
  1. Design a common canonical XML Schema based on the business requirements of the exchanged data.
  2. Generate platform-specific types from the common schema.
  3. Implement adapters on all applications to convert their data types to the common data type.

For example, you have an existing .NET Framework application that needs to talk to an existing J2EE application. The applications need to exchange data about customers. The J2EE application has a **Customer** class and the .NET Framework application also has a **Customer** class. Unfortunately, neither the .NET nor J2EE **Customer** classes derive from the same schema. Interoperability was not a factor when the developers created these applications, so the classes are incompatible.

You could design a common XML Schema for **CustomerData**, and then generate platform-specific **CustomerData** data types for exchanging data based on that common XML Schema. However, you may not have the ability to replace the platform-specific **Customer** class used throughout each application with the new **CustomerData** classes that the common schema generates. This approach would also not be consistent with application best practice.

To resolve this issue, add a new interoperability layer (or adapter) to each application that converts the existing **Customer** type to the new common **CustomerData** data type. This adapter copies the field values of the **Customer** native type into the new **CustomerData** common type (or vice versa, depending on the direction of data exchange). You can then use the new **CustomerData** classes in both .NET and Java to exchange data between the two applications through each application's adapter.

Summary

This chapter described the factors behind implementing interoperability. You saw the importance of ensuring class consistency and methods for implementing serialization. You also looked at basic type mappings between XML data types, .NET data types, and Electric XML data types. Finally, you examined the three most common interoperability scenarios and the best practice recommendations to deal with each of these. With this information, you can now move on to examine the different interoperability mechanisms in detail in Chapters 4 and 5.

References

For more information about XML
See the Microsoft XML Web site
http://msdn.microsoft.com/library/default.asp?url=/nhp/default.asp?contentid=28000438

For more information about using XmlReader
"Reading XML with the XmlReader"
http://msdn.microsoft.com/library/default.asp?url=/library/en-us/cpguide/html /cpconreadingxmlwithxmlreader.asp

For more information about the XSD namespace
http://www.w3.org/2001/XMLSchema

For more information about the XML Schema Definition tool
XML Schema Definition Tool
http://msdn.microsoft.com/library/default.asp?url=/library/en-us/cptools/html /cpconxmlschemadefinitiontoolxsdexe.asp?frame=true

For additional examples of how to use the XML Schema Definition tool, see Chapter 3 of *Microsoft .NET and J2EE Interoperability Toolkit* by Simon Guest, Microsoft Press, 2003, ISBN: 0735619220.

For more information about schema2java and java2schema
Package electric.xml.io.tools
http://www.themindelectric.com/docs/exml/api/electric/xml/io/tools/package-summary.html

For an example of how to use the Electric XML tools to map Java classes and XML Schemas, see *Microsoft .NET and J2EE Interoperability Toolkit*, Chapter 3, pp 70–80.

4

Interoperability Technologies: Point to Point

Designing an effective interoperability solution requires a detailed understanding of the techniques used to connect Java and .NET Framework systems. This chapter looks at the means you can employ to link the two platforms in point to point scenarios, where one application interoperates synchronously with another.

The technologies that allow .NET Framework and Java to interoperate on a point to point basis fall into two main categories:

- .NET Remoting
- XML Web services

.NET Remoting is the first technology covered; it provides advantages such as greater performance and easy implementation in a pure .NET Framework environment. However, Java applications cannot connect using .NET Remoting directly; they require the implementation of a runtime bridge. This chapter investigates two of the most popular runtime bridge offerings, Ja.NET and JNBridgePro.

Web services are increasingly fashionable whenever developers and system architects start discussing interoperability. Web services certainly promise ubiquity and the freedom from having to describe methods explicitly, but they are not always the best interoperability solution.

Using .NET Remoting for Connectivity

In Chapter 2, "Understanding Enterprise Platforms," you learned that .NET Remoting is Microsoft's communication and data transfer mechanism for distributed applications built on the .NET Framework. While primarily designed for communication between .NET Framework applications, .NET Remoting provides an extensible communication framework that you can build on and customize to enable connectivity with Java applications.

To use .NET Remoting for interoperability with Java applications, you must implement a runtime bridge, and you look at two of these, Ja.NET from Intrinsyc and JNBridgePro from JNBridge, Inc. later in this chapter. Before you learn about runtime bridges, you need to have a solid understanding of .NET Remoting.

Understanding .NET Remoting

At its fundamental level, .NET Remoting allows two processes within the same or different application domains to communicate with each other in a client-server relationship. In this basic scenario, the server component is a remotable object.

.NET Remoting implements interprocess communication by separating the remotable object from a specific client, server application domain, or particular communication mechanism. As a result, .NET Remoting is flexible and easily customizable.

This abstraction works through the use of two main concepts:

- **Channels**—Channels provide the transport between remote components. The default channels are TCP and HTTP.

- **Formatters**—Formatters convert (serialize) objects into a common format the other process (or, in the case of interoperability, platform) can understand. The default formatters are binary and SOAP.

Note: Later sections in this chapter discuss SOAP.

In Chapter 3, "Interoperability Fundamentals," you learned about binary serialization and XML serialization. The binary formatter performs binary serialization on data objects; the SOAP formatter performs XML serialization on data objects. However, the SOAP formatter wraps the serialized XML document with extra SOAP-related XML tags.

By specifying a channel and a formatter, you can define how you establish communications between a remotable object and its client. The channels specify the communication protocol. The formatters then act as serializers, serializing and de-serializing the data objects that pass between the remotable object and the client. The ability to customize these channels and formatters is what allows you to use .NET Remoting for connectivity between .NET Framework applications and Java applications.

.NET Remoting provides more than just communication between processes; you can also use it for links between two or more application components that are in different application domains. To do this, just change the configuration of .NET Remoting to exchange data between the separate application domains. This gives you flexibility to build an application that runs on just one computer but that you can then extend to run in a distributed environment with minimal adjustment to the code.

.NET Remoting also supports two ways for passing data between application components. These are:

- Pass by value (PBV)
- Pass by reference (PBR)

Pass by value involves returning of the data from a remote system call to the client. Pass by reference returns a pointer or reference to the data and the remote server maintains the data's state.

Each method has advantages and disadvantages. The method you choose depends on the type of application you are developing, the data that you want to pass, and the network environment the application must function in.

Passing by reference can offer performance benefits when exchanging large data objects or with distributed systems where network latency slows down pass by value communication. However, if you pass a data object by reference, this makes a remote call to the referenced data object on the server each time the client accesses another field on the object.

For example, if you pass a **CustomerData** object, named **custData**, to a client by reference, each time the client accesses a field, such as **custData.Name** or **custData.Address**, this makes a remote call to the server. This can result a tightly coupled and chatty application.

Note: In service oriented applications, loose coupling between application components is more desirable, and you should use pass by value.

Implementing .NET Remoting

A typical .NET Remoting implementation, in which two components communicate directly, consists of the following items:

- A remotable application object or server component.
- A host application that listens for client requests to the remotable application component.
- A client application component that makes requests to the remotable application component.

Figure 4.1 shows an example of a .NET Remoting framework connection between a client and server.

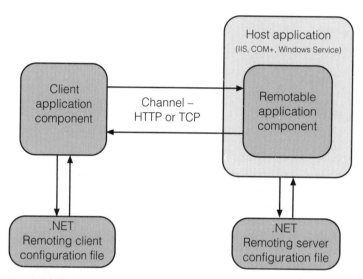

Figure 4.1

A typical .NET Remoting implementation

Implementing .NET Remoting involves the following phases:

- Determining the host application or environment.
- Creating the server component.
- Creating the client.
- Editing the configuration files.

The following sections provide an overview of the steps necessary to implement .NET Remoting. For more information about .NET Remoting, see the References section at the end of this chapter. For coding examples in the XBikes sample application, see Chapters 7 to 9.

Determining the Host Application or Environment

.NET Remoting server components require hosting in an application domain that can listen for incoming requests for that object. You have four choices for hosting a remoting server component:

- ASP.NET on IIS
- Component Services (COM+)
- A Windows system service
- A Windows application (console or Windows forms based)

You can host .NET Remoting objects as ASP.NET components running on IIS. This brings many advantages, including built-in support for security and easy scalability. With this configuration, you can use either the binary or SOAP formatter but you can only use the HTTP channel, which is slower than TCP.

You can host a remoting object in Component Services as a COM+ Serviced Component on either Windows XP Professional SP1 or Windows Server 2003. This configuration provides the enterprise features of Component Services such as integrated security, transactions, pooling, and activation.

You can host remoting objects in any managed Windows service. Hosting a remoting object in a Windows service provides the flexibility to use any channel or formatter configuration you choose, including the highest performing combination of binary over TCP. However, .NET Remoting does not have a built-in security model. Hence if you host a remotable object in a Windows service, you need to build your own authentication and authorization mechanisms.

Finally, you can host a remoting server component in a Windows application. However, applications run in the context of the logged on user, and therefore require user logon to execute. They also run in the security context of that user, which might not be appropriate for your environment. It is preferable to host the remote server component in a Windows service.

Note: When hosting a component in a Windows Forms application, a Windows Service or some other application type, it is up to the programmer to specify the port. For non-ASP.NET hosts, remoting can listen on any unused port.

In general, you should use IIS to host your remoting objects because of the security and performance advantages it provides. For more information about hosting a remotable object in IIS, see the References section at the end of this chapter. For examples of using Ja.NET in conjunction with .NET Remoting in the XBikes sample application, see Chapters 7 and 8.

Creating the Server Component

The server component is the service provider, providing methods that client applications call by reference or data that clients send and receive by value. Server component classes need to inherit from the **MarshalByRefObject** class to communicate over .NET Remoting. Any data that the server component passes by value must be serializable.

Creating the Client Component

To enable .NET Remoting on the client, you do not need to implement any additional interfaces. However, the client must have a reference to the server component or interface. The client uses this reference to interrogate the server component for any methods or data types that the server component exposes. The client also needs to load the remoting configuration, either from its own code or from a configuration file.

Editing the Configuration Files

The following .NET Remoting items are configurable:

- References to remote systems
- Channels
- Formatters

You can configure each of these items through settings that you can either store in the application code or access them at run time from a configuration file. It is recommended that you store your configuration settings in a configuration file so that you can change them without having to recompile the application. This method is much more flexible in production systems, allowing you to implement changes without recompiling and redeploying the application.

Both the server component and the client component in a .NET Remoting scenario must have access to configuration information. Assuming you have stored the configuration settings a file, the contents and locations of these files differ for the server and client.

.NET Remoting configuration files are XML formatted text files. You can edit these in Notepad or the text editor of your choice.

Server Component Configuration

On the server side, you must register all remote objects with the .NET Remoting environment before clients can access them. During this registration process, you must provide the .NET Remoting framework with all the information required to activate and manage the lifetime of the object. The most important pieces of information required for registration are:

- Object type
- Object location (URL)
- Activation requirements for managing the object lifetime
- Channels for connecting to the object

The location of the remoting configuration file for the server depends on the host application you use. For example:

- For IIS-hosted applications, you store the remoting configuration in the Web.config file located in the application virtual root.

- For Component Services hosted applications, the remoting configuration would be in a file that you create named Dllhost.exe.config file in the \System32 directory. This is because the server component runs as part of the COM+ process, Dllhost.exe.

- For a Windows service, the remoting configuration information is in the application configuration file of the Windows service. For example, if the Windows service is named Myservice.exe, the remoting configuration is in the file Myservice.exe.config.

Client Component Configuration

The client side must also have the same configuration settings loaded as the server. You store client configuration settings in a file that you create named, for example, *Remoting.config*. The client application loads this file by calling **RemotingConfiguration.Configure** with the configuration file name as a parameter. The location of the *Remoting.config* file depends on the type of application the client component belongs to. For example:

- For ASP.NET-based clients, the *Remoting.config* file lives in the application's virtual root. These configuration settings must load in the **Application_Start** method of the Global.asax file.

- For COM+ Serviced Components clients, the *Remoting.config* file lives in the \system32 directory.

- With any other client, the *Remoting.config* file should be in the same directory as the client executable file.

Now that you understand the basics of .NET Remoting, the next section looks at how you can use this technology to connect to Java applications.

Implementing Runtime Bridges

There are several vendors that enable interoperability between .NET Framework applications and Java applications with .NET Remoting as the underlying connecting protocol. Runtime bridges expose Java objects and methods in a way that enables you to address them with .NET Remoting and vice versa. Two of the main products in this category are Ja.NET from Intrinsyc and JNBridgePro from JNBridge, Inc.

Note: Ja.NET and JNBridgePro differ in that JNBridgePro allows calls from a .NET Remoting client to Java objects and classes whereas Ja.NET also works in the opposite direction. This difference does not affect the scenarios that this book covers.

Evaluating Ja.NET

Ja.NET provides a two-way implementation of the .NET Remoting stack for Java. Using Ja.NET, you can generate Java proxies that expose or consume components using the .NET Remoting protocol.

Because Ja.NET is a bi-directional bridge, accessing Java from .NET generates a set of C# proxies. Similarly, accessing .NET from Java generates a set of Java proxies.

If you examine the generated proxies, you should notice how the by value class contains all its fields, and the remote by reference class only a shell that defines the class definitions. Ja.NET needs these for compile definitions, and then again at run time for the **_TransparentProxy** class to mimic the remote server. If you attempt to create a local copy of this class, this generates an exception. You can only have a *remote* instance of this class. The proxies use no custom code, just pure .NET Remoting.

If you look at the Java proxies generated when analyzing a .NET assembly, you should see a lot of code for marshalling and un-marshalling the call parameters to the Ja.NET runtime. When accessing .NET from Java, you need custom code to initialize the Ja.NET runtime, as well as any remote send or receive classes. However, the .NET side still does not require any special code, as Ja.NET follows the .NET rules for remotable objects.

Ja.NET enables Java components to appear as CLR components, and CLR components appear as Java components. In addition, the Ja.NET Janetor tool expands upon this functionality by generating the Java proxies within a WAR file. You can then host this WAR file on a Web server, enabling access to EJBs from .NET Framework—again with all of the communication based on .NET Remoting.

Accessing a .NET Framework Server from Java

The simplest implementation is when the Ja.NET runtime lets a Java client access a
.NET Framework server, in this case, implemented in Visual Basic .NET. Figure 4.2
shows how to do this.

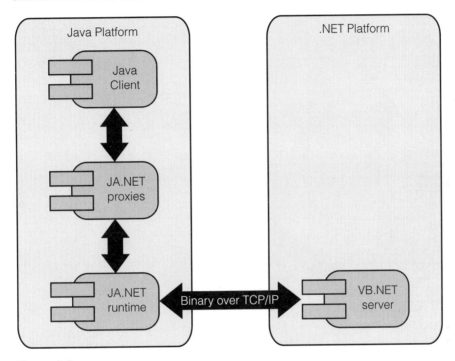

Figure 4.2
Connecting Ja.NET to a VB.NET Server component

Figure 4.2 shows the Java platform hosting the Ja.NET runtime component.

Accessing IIS Components from Java

Java clients can also use the Ja.NET runtime to access a remote CLR component as if it is a local Java component. Figure 4.3 illustrates this method.

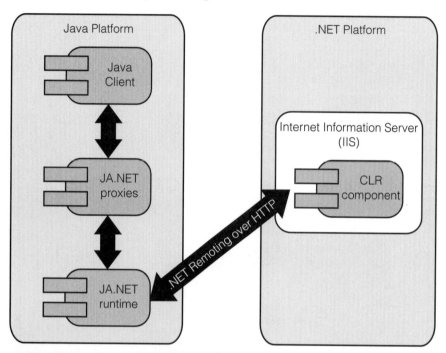

Figure 4.3

Connecting Ja.NET to a .NET component hosted on IIS

Figure 4.3 shows the Ja.NET proxies that handle communication between the Java client and the Ja.NET runtime. In this example, IIS is hosting the .NET Framework application.

Accessing an EJB from .NET Framework

The third method deploys a WAR file containing the Ja.NET runtime onto any Web server that supports servlets. The CLR client (written in any supported .NET Framework language) can access the EJBs as if accessing local CLR components. Figure 4.4 shows an example of this arrangement.

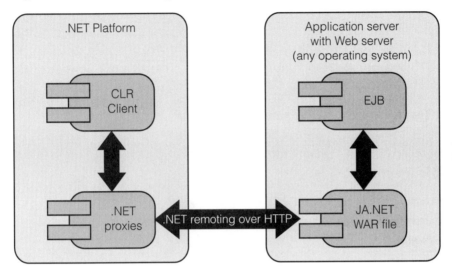

Figure 4.4
Connecting .NET Clients to an EJB using Ja.NET

In addition, the Ja.NET runtime lets you:

- Write clients for EJBs in any language supported by .NET.
- Access .NET Framework components from any Java object or EJB.
- Reuse components from either platform with the other environment.

Note: Because .NET Remoting is an extensible protocol from both the transport and data formatting perspective, Ja.NET supports HTTP and TCP/IP transport protocols together with SOAP and binary data formatting and can support future transports and formatters.

Ja.NET Toolset

There are six main parts that make up the Ja.NET toolset. These are:

- **GenService**—The GenJava and GenNet tools use GenService to provide access to .NET Framework assemblies for development. You require only GenService to generate the proxies, so you do not have to install it in the production environment.
- **GenNet**—GenNet generates the .NET Framework proxies that access the Java classes through the Ja.NET runtime.

- **GenJava**—GetJava generates Java proxies that access .NET Framework assemblies through the Ja.NET runtime.

- **Janetor**—The Janetor tool allows you to view and modify the Ja.NET runtime configuration settings. You can also use the Janetor to generate WAR files to assist with deploying the Ja.NET runtime onto a Web server. Janetor includes licensing for the Ja.NET product, locally shared and remotely accessed objects.

- **Ja.NET TCP server**—Ja.NET TCP server provides standalone hosting for Java classes through the Ja.NET runtime where the classes are not hosted on a J2EE server. The Ja.NET runtime includes this component.

- **Ja.NET runtime**—Ja.NET runtime is the main collection of classes that hosts the tools. The Janet.jar file contains the runtime components.

Linking Types between .NET Framework and Java

When linking .NET Framework to Java using Ja.NET, you need to understand the links between data types in the .NET Framework and data types in Java. Table 4.1 shows this information.

Table 4.1: .NET Framework to Java data type mappings

.NET Framework Data Type	Java Data Type
System.Boolean	boolean
System.Char	char
System.String	java.lang.String
System.Single	float
System.Double	double
System.Int8	byte
System.Int16	short
System.Int32	int
System.Int64	long
System.Byte	byte
System.UInt16	short
System.UInt32	int
System.UInt64	Long
System.Object	java.lang.Object
System.DateTime	Java.util.Date

Table 4.2 shows how you can use Ja.NET to map collections between Java and the .NET Framework.

Table 4.2: Ja.NET Collection Mappings between Java and the .NET Framework

Java Collection Class	.NET Framework Collection Class
java.util.ArrayList	System.Collections.IList
Java.util.LinkedList	System.Collections.IList
Java.util.Vector	System.Collections.IList

Table 4.3 shows the opposite mapping from the .NET Framework to Java.

Table 4.3: Ja.NET Collection Mappings between the .NET Framework and Java

.NET Framework Collection Class	Java Collection Class
System.Collections.ArrayList	java.util.List

For more information about type and collection mappings, see the Ja.NET documentation.

Understanding Ja.NET Events and Exceptions

There are a few more concepts that you need to understand to appreciate the complete range of .NET Remoting options. These include the following:

- **Events**—Ja.NET provides event support through the ability to extend **java.util.EventListener** to system events in the .NET Framework. This provides a major advantage in that the server component can now implement a callback to the client through this event model. Events are particularly useful where you want to implement asynchronous operations or transactions with long run times.

- **Exception handling**—Ja.NET provides exception handling facilities, reporting back exceptions on one platform to the alternative platform. Java server exceptions map back to the **System.Runtime.Remoting.RemotingException** function in .NET Framework and exceptions on .NET Framework map back to **com.instrinsyc.janet.RemoteException**.

  Usually, these derived exceptions contain the text from the original. To deal with these exceptions, trap the resultant exception and then search the text within the embedded exception to obtain more information.

- **Support for strong naming**—Ja.NET supports the use and creation of strong-named assemblies. You can then register these assemblies in the global assembly cache for use with serviced components (COM+).

- **Ease of configuration**—Because Ja.NET is a pure Java implementation of the .NET Remoting protocol, the .NET Framework side requires no special runtime libraries. Configuration on the .NET Framework side is the same as with a normal implementation of .NET Remoting, requiring only a simple DLL that contains class and interface definitions. Anything that you can make remotable in the .NET Framework (derived from **MarshallByRefObject**), you can also make remotable in Ja.NET. You can also send serialized classes by value, as in .NET Framework-only implementation.

Implementing Ja.NET Best Practices

There are several best practices that you should implement when using Ja.NET. These issues include performance, design, and deployment factors. For example:

- Upgrade to version 1.5.
- Use binary protocol for .NET Remoting.
- Deploy WAR packages on the application server to access EJBs and JMS.
- Understand .NET Remoting to facilitate good design practice.
- Comprehend the differences between pass by reference (PBR) and pass by value (PBV).

Upgrade to Version 1.5

You are strongly recommended to upgrade to Ja.NET version 1.5, which is free for users of earlier versions of Ja.NET. Version 1.5 contains many important new features, including some that are necessary to run the examples in this book. Some of the new features include the following:

- Support for strong-named assemblies.
- Improved type mappings between .NET Framework and Java types.
- Significant performance increases.
- Improved serialization capabilities for pass by value classes for both platforms.
- Integral Web server for non-enterprise level remoting access with HTTP.
- Improved SDK.
- Runtime support for .NET Framework versions 1.0 and 1.1.
- Integral .NET Framework proxy for JMS.
- Stability and performance enhancements.

Use Binary Protocol for .NET Remoting

This chapter describes the benefits of using .NET Remoting rather than SOAP. Although Ja.NET also supports SOAP connections, .NET Remoting provides better performance, with TCP/binary providing the fastest connection. However, if you need to traverse firewalls, want to use the security infrastructure of IIS, or easily deploy components inside an application server, HTTP/binary is the preferred protocol.

Note: HTTP/binary is still significantly faster than HTTP/SOAP.

Deploy WAR Packages on the Application Server to Access EJBs and JMS

The fastest way to access an EJB is from within the application server itself. The easiest deployment scenario is to create a WAR file that contains the Ja.NET runtime JAR, the EJB client JARs, and a configuration file. You can use the Ja.NET Janetor tool to create the WAR file easily, which you can then immediately deploy to the application server. Because the WAR file resides in the same process space as the application, access to the EJBs is much faster than accessing it from an external process with RMI.

Understand .NET Remoting to Facilitate Good Design Practice

Because Ja.NET is a pure Java implementation of the .NET Remoting protocol, the same rules for .NET Remoting best practice apply to Ja.NET. Make sure you read the current literature about .NET Remoting to understand how best to employ it in conjunction with Ja.NET.

Comprehend the Differences between PBR and PBV

In a PBR class, every method call results in a request for data. However, if you send a PBV class, this serializes the entire class, including fields of the super class or classes. If you PBV a very large object with numerous fields that contain significant amounts of data, this may generate a sizeable about of network traffic. In this case, it may be better to use PBR. Similarly, if you have a small class, consider using PBV to send a copy of the class, rather than making a call to the network to access each field. Understanding the differences between PBR and PBV reduces network traffic and improves performance.

Evaluating JNBridgePro

JNBridgePro is a point-to-point bridging solution that links Java components to .NET Framework. The Java code runs in an ordinary Java Virtual Machine (JVM) or J2EE application server and the .NET Framework code runs in a normal .NET Framework CLR. JNBridgePro then manages the communication between the two sides.

Proxies make Java classes and objects appear as ordinary .NET Framework classes and objects. .NET Framework components interact with those proxies just like normal local .NET Framework function calls, but the proxy objects transparently redirect the calls to the Java side. The Java components process the method calls and field accesses and return the values or data to the proxies. The proxies then present the results back to the .NET Framework components.

An application using JNBridgePro to perform Java/.NET Framework interoperation contains JNBridgePro's .NET Framework-side and Java-side runtime components, which manage inter-platform communication and object lifecycles, and a .NET Framework assembly (a DLL) containing the proxies for the Java classes exposed to the .NET Framework. Developers generate the proxies using the JNBridgePro toolkit.

Figure 4.5 shows the architecture of JNBridgePro.

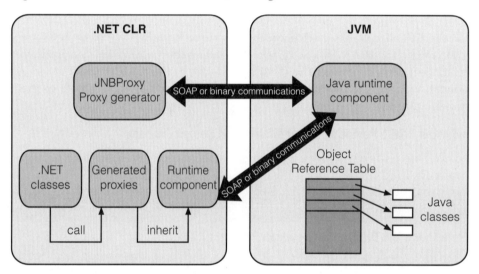

Figure 4.5
Internal architecture of JNBridgePro Runtime Bridge

Figure 4.5 shows the runtime component and proxies on the .NET Framework side. Compare this with Figure 4.3.

Integrating JNBridgePro with .NET Remoting

JNBridgePro employs .NET Remoting to implement the communication between the .NET Framework and Java sides. Because .NET Remoting is an extensible architecture, you can change communications channels as required. JNBridgePro uses this extensible architecture to support both SOAP and binary communications.

.NET Remoting also includes concepts alien to conventional "local" object-oriented development, such as leasing, well-known objects, and client-activated and server-activated objects. JNBridgePro can encapsulate these concepts and conceal them from the user. Hence JNBridgePro interoperation between Java and .NET Framework code appears to the developer as local development.

JNBridgePro builds additional capabilities on top of .NET Remoting. For example, basic .NET Remoting can access members of actual objects, but it cannot access static members of classes that are not members of actual instances of the class. JNBridgePro provides the ability to access those static class members.

Understanding JNBridgePro Features

JNBridgePro allows access to Java classes and objects through calls to the corresponding JNBridgePro proxies. JNBridgePro supports access to both static and instance members, in addition to supporting access requests to fields and calls to methods. You can make explicit calls from .NET Framework to Java by having the .NET Framework code call .NET Framework proxies for Java classes and objects, and you can make implicit calls from Java to .NET Framework by having the .NET Framework code register a callback object and having the Java code access the callback object through its implemented listener interface.

The Java side components can reside in a standalone JVM or in a J2EE application server. Communication between the .NET Framework and Java sides can use either SOAP or the faster binary protocol.

JNBridgePro supports transactions, giving you the ability to make a sequence of calls from .NET Framework to Java as part of the same transaction. If the transaction fails, the entire sequence rolls back to the start point. This prevents application calls from hanging between the .NET Framework and the Java side. JNBridgePro can also create .NET Framework proxies for dynamically generated Java classes at execution time. Such dynamically generated classes frequently appear in J2EE applications, particularly when linking to JNDI and EJB components.

JNBridgePro also supports the following:

- Mapping between .NET Framework and Java primitives.
- Strings.
- Collections.
- Support for pass by value (PBV) and pass by reference (PBR).
- Connections to Java-based messaging servers.

Selecting JNBridgePro

Choose JNBridgePro for J2EE and .NET Framework interoperability if your application requires synchronous, point-to-point communication between .NET Framework and Java objects, and has one or more of the following requirements:

- **High performance**—Your application requires a high performance interoperability mechanism with a very low overhead, where the Java platform and the .NET Framework are located on the same local area network or intranet, or on the same machine.

- **Expose a rich object-oriented Java API to .NET Framework interface**—Your application requires that Java exposes a large number of Java class APIs to .NET Framework applications, or the Java API returns custom Java objects or requires custom Java objects as parameters.

- **"Chatty" interaction**—Your application performs frequent fine-grained calls between Java and the .NET Framework. Web services work better with less frequent and more coarse-grained "chunky" interaction.

- **Desire to stay with "local," object-oriented development model**—Your application architects decide that they will not implement a service-oriented model that exposes the APIs of a few classes as services. Instead, they want the .NET Framework code to construct new Java objects using the new operator, employ cross-platform garbage collection, and provide a conventional "local" object-oriented model.

Implementing JNBridgePro Best Practices

There are a number of best practices that you should implement with JNBridgePro, regardless of the interoperability scenario. Performance-related best practices include increasing the speed of the communications channel, or reducing the number of inter-platform round trips, thereby improving the apparent execution speed of the application.

Upgrade to Version 1.3

If you are using JNBridgePro version 1.2 or earlier, you should consider upgrading to version 1.3, particularly if your .NET Framework and Java components reside on different computers. Version 1.3 or later provides a significant performance enhancement when using binary communications to connect over a network. Some implementations demonstrate a reduction in the time to access an EJB from 200 milliseconds to 2.3 milliseconds.

In addition to the network communications performance improvement, version 1.3 supports value objects and directly mapped collections, both of which can improve performance.

To take advantage of this improvement, download and install version 1.3, and then regenerate your proxies using the version 1.3 proxy generation tool. Replace the old copies of Jnbshare.dll and Jnbcore.jar in your application with the version 1.3 files.

Use the Binary Communications Protocol

Binary/TCP communication is over an order of magnitude faster than SOAP/HTTP. Use SOAP/HTTP only when using the Internet to link the .NET Framework and Java sides and the communication path traverses firewalls.

To use the binary/TCP communications channel, make sure that the setting in the Jnbproxy.config remoting configuration file uses the JTCP: protocol instead of the HTTP: protocol. Also, set the **servertype** property in the Java-side configuration file Jnbcore.properties to TCP, not HTTP.

Place the Java-side Component inside the J2EE Application Server

If you are using JNBridgePro to access EJBs running inside a J2EE application server, deploy the JNBridgePro Java side inside the application server. These components comprise the WAR file containing Jnbcore.jar, the JAR files containing the EJB stubs, and the associated configuration files. Figure 4.6 shows this in place.

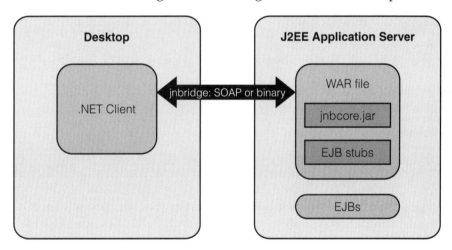

Figure 4.6
Java-side component in J2EE application server

This arrangement ensures that Jnbcore.jar, which performs the EJB calls, bypasses RMI and makes direct calls to the EJBs.

Place Java-side and .NET Framework-side Components on the Same Computer

If a single .NET Framework client accesses the Java classes, place the Java-side component, including the Java classes, on the same computer as the .NET Framework-side component, if possible. This minimizes the communication overhead. Figure 4.7 shows this in operation.

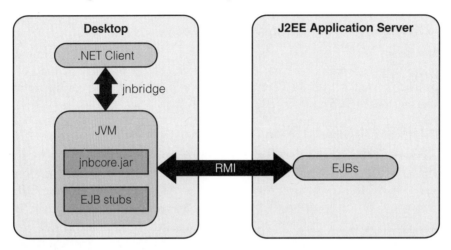

Figure 4.7
Java-side component on the computer running the .NET Framework component

Any increase in round trip time and latency for the communication link affects the overall responsiveness of the platform interface.

Reduce Round Trips

One of the best ways to improve JNBridgePro performance is to reduce the number of round trips from the .NET Framework side to the Java side and back by reducing the number of calls to proxies. One example of how to do this is when a number of proxy calls are necessary to obtain information from which another value is calculated. To reduce the number of proxy calls, create a Java façade class that performs the calls, does the calculation, and returns the value. Then, create a proxy for this class. The value can now be obtained through a single proxy call.

Implement Return Arrays

JNBridgePro offers full access to Java APIs, so there is a great temptation to use the full API functionality. For example, if you have a Java-side **Vector** object, you should extract an array from the vector and return that array by value. .NET Framework then represents that array natively, removing the need for iterations to extract further values from the original **Vector** object.

Some Java APIs support stateful objects that you may want to call repeatedly to obtain additional information. The JDBC class **ResultSet**, for example, represents the results of a query and can contain multiple rows through which you have to scroll. Again, this can result in multiple round trip calls to **ResultSet**.

To improve performance, create a Java wrapper class that returns an array of objects with each containing one row of results. If there is a chance that the results array is very large, and that returning its entire contents will take a long time, modify the wrapper class to return a limited number of results at a time (for example, no more than 50).

Use Value Objects

The default setting for object calls from .NET Framework to Java are as pass by reference (PBR) results. The called object remains on the Java side, and only the reference to that object returns to .NET Framework. References are much smaller than the actual object, helping performance, but they involve a trip back to the Java side to extract any useful information. Even getting a field value requires a round trip to obtain the data. If you are performing multiple queries on an the object's fields for data or using accessor methods to look up data on an EJB, you would be better to designate objects of that class as *value objects*.

A value object is a snapshot of an object from the Java side then copied back to the .NET Framework side. Depending on the kind of value object it is, this copies either the values of its public fields, or in the case of a Java Bean value object, the values of its **accessor** (**get**) methods. This process does not copy the object's methods other than **get** methods for a Java Bean value object, because it is problematic to translate the meanings of Java methods to .NET Framework automatically.

Consider using value objects when the object is really just a large package of data that you want to access in many different ways. For example, an object representing a customer's bank account might have fields for the customer's account number, first name, last name, address, current balance, previous balances, and the date the owner opened the account.

The default setting is that the account object **userAcct** passes by reference, resulting in each field access in **userAcct** generating a round trip. However, if you set up **Account** to pass by value, this copies the data in **userAcct** from the Java side to the .NET Framework side and each subsequent field access is a local call.

Whether it is advisable to pass an object by value or by reference depends on the size of the object and how much of its data you want to access. For example, in the bank account example, if the only data you access in the account is the current balance, it is probably not worthwhile to pass this object by value. In this case, the time taken to copy all the data to the .NET Framework side outweighs the time savings that result by making all field accesses local to .NET Framework.

The code is the same regardless of whether the object is passed by reference or by value; the only difference is whether the object's class is designated as a value object or a reference object. Ideally, the decision on whether to pass the object by value or by reference depends on observed measurements within the pilot environment rather than the developer's judgment.

Note: Individual objects cannot be designated as pass by reference or pass by value; all objects of a given class have the designation.

For more information about value objects and reference objects in JNBridgePro, see the JNBridgePro Users' Guide.

Use Directly Mapped Collections

Directly mapped collections return certain object collections from the Java side and automatically convert them to native .NET Framework collections on the Java side. You can then access these elements quickly after conversion without a round trip.

JNBridgePro supports a variety of directly mapped collections. Java Vectors, array lists, linked lists, and hash sets map directly to .NET Framework array lists. Java hash tables and hash maps map to .NET Framework hash tables. You can also use directly mapped collections to pass parameters from .NET Framework to Java. For more information, see the JNBridge Users' Guide.

As with value objects, directly mapped collections take longer to pass between Java and .NET Framework than reference objects, but you can then access their elements faster. Deciding whether to use a directly mapped collection depends on the size of the collections being transferred, the number and frequency of accesses, and tests in the pilot environment.

Each exposed class results in the generation of a proxy of the same name. The generated proxy's members (including constructors, methods, and fields) correspond to the members of the Java class underlying the proxy.

Generate All Supporting Proxies

When generating proxies, generate all the supporting proxies for each specifically requested proxy class. It is often possible to omit generating supporting proxies (such as proxies for the classes of all parameters, return values, thrown exceptions, implemented interfaces, and superclasses); however, it is never harmful to generate such supporting classes and it may be harmful to leave them out. In addition, creating proxies for supporting classes ensures that you can call methods and access fields requiring proxies for those additional classes without having to regenerate the proxy assemblies.

Note: An additional problem with not generating all supporting proxies is that in some situations, applications throw an exception if you do not do so.

Depending on the side of the original set of seed proxies, generating all supporting proxies adds about 200–300 additional proxy classes to the original set. Typically this takes no more than five minutes to generate the additional proxies.

With care, it is possible, in many cases, to avoid generating supporting classes. However, it is never harmful to generate such classes, and doing so may avoid various issues in the future, even when the lack of supporting classes does not represent a problem now.

Connecting with Web Services

In the previous section, you saw how you can use .NET Remoting to connect the Java platform and .NET Framework with runtime bridges. However, .NET Remoting is closely linked to the .NET Framework and you may need an interoperability solution that is platform neutral.

There is currently a lot of interest in the computer industry around Web services, and Web services offer you additional choices as part of an interoperability solution. It is worth looking at what Web services are and what they offer.

A high-level definition of a Web service would be a programmable application component accessible through standard Internet protocols. Many more detailed definitions of Web services exist, and they all seem to contain the following elements in the description:

- Web services expose useful functionality through standard Internet protocols. In most cases, this protocol is SOAP over HTTP.

- Web services describe their interfaces in enough detail to allow a user to build a client application to talk to them. An XML document named a Web Services Description Language (WSDL) document contains this description.

- Users can search for available Web services in some form of registration database. Universal Description, Discovery and Integration (UDDI) is the most common way to implement this.

Because Web services are standards-based and platform independent, they provide a natural fit when it comes to getting applications in different platforms to interoperate with each other. This partially explains the alacrity with which so many vendors have endorsed the Web services standards. From this book's perspective, Web services can provide a useful mechanism for connecting the .NET Framework and J2EE. Specifically, Web services address three main interoperability issues:

- **Protocol standards**—HTTP and HTTPS are the most common implementations, but Web services have the flexibility to use any transport protocol.

- **Type definitions**—Web services always expose strongly typed data, so if a Web service exposes a type, another Web service can understand and consume that type regardless of the underlying language or platform.

- **Multiple levels of support**—The ability to implement Web services in any language on any platform and using any vendor's toolkit, hence a consumer does not need to be aware of the platform that a particular service runs on.

Both .NET Framework and Java offer implementations of Web services, with varying degrees of integration into the underlying platform. In fact, one of the central tenets of the .NET Framework is its high degree of integration with Web services. Web services are well-suited to providing a wide variety of services over the Internet, and they are a promising technology for enterprise application integration.

However, while Web services provide a very powerful technology, they are not suitable for all applications and interoperability scenarios. Because SOAP is text-based, Web service calls may be too slow for applications that require frequent, fast, and fine-grained communications.

Service-oriented interfaces such as Web services are also unsuited for conventional object-oriented models. Although you can think of a service as a single persistent server activated object, client-activated objects such as ones that the **new** operator constructs, and access requests to static methods are not generally supported. Similarly, if your application needs to access a wide variety of objects and classes, a Web service is not generally suitable. Again, if you need to link to a rich object-oriented set of Java APIs from .NET Framework, Web services are probably not the solution.

In addition to the preceding issues, Web services do not support callbacks in the same manner as local object-oriented architectures. Finally, there may be problems returning rich custom Java objects to .NET Framework through a Web service. In such cases, look at alternatives to Web services such as JNBridgePro and Ja.NET.

Understanding Web Services

In a typical Web services scenario, a client application can learn about what functionality a Web service provides and how to call this functionality by querying the service's WSDL file. Next, the client sends a request to the service at its given URL using the SOAP protocol over HTTP. The service receives the request, processes it, and returns a response. The request and the response are XML formatted using the SOAP protocol.

It is worth examining the protocols and specifications (or stack) that make Web services possible. The Web services stack consists of five layers, as Figure 4.8 illustrates.

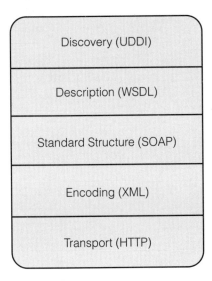

Figure 4.8
The five-layer model of the Web services stack

These layers consist of the following elements:

- Transport (HTTP)
- Encoding (XML)
- Standard structure (SOAP)
- Description (WSDL)
- Discovery (UDDI)

The next sections describe each of these elements.

Transport (HTTP)

At the lowest level, two components in a distributed architecture must agree on a common transport mechanism. Because of the near universal acceptance of port 80 as a less risky route through a firewall, HTTP became the standard for the transport layer. However, Web services implementations can run on other transport protocols such as FTP and SMTP, or even other network stacks, such as Sequenced Packet Exchange (SPX) or non-routable protocols such as NetBEUI. Changing from the dependence on HTTP or HTTPS (for encrypted connections) is possible within the bounds of the current specification.

Encoding (XML)

After agreeing on the transport, components must deliver messages as correctly formatted XML documents. This XML dependence ensures the success of the transfer, because both provider and consumer know to parse and interpret the XML standard.

Standard Structure (SOAP)

Although XML defines message encoding, it does not cover the structure and format of the document itself. To guarantee interoperability, both provider and consumer must know what to send and what to expect. SOAP is a lightweight, message-based protocol built on XML (XSD version 2) and standard Internet protocols, such as HTTP and SMTP. The SOAP protocol specification defines an XML structure for messages (the SOAP envelope), data type definitions, and a set of conventions that implement remote procedure calls and the format of any returned data (the SOAP body).

Description (WSDL)

The description layer provides a mechanism for informing interested parties of the particular bill of fare that a Web service offers. Web Services Description Language (WSDL) provides this contract, setting out for each exposed component:

- Component name
- Data types
- Methods
- Parameters

This WDSL description enables a developer for a remote component to query your Web service and find out what the service can do and how to get it to do it. The WSDL file is an XSD-based XML document that defines the details of your Web service. It also stores your Web service contract. The WSDL file is usually the first point of entry for any client attaching to your Web service so that the client knows how to use it.

Discovery (UDDI)

Discovery attempts to answer the question "Where." If you want to connect to a Web service at an Internet location (for example, www.nwtraders.msft/services /WeatherService.aspx), you can enter the URL manually. However, URLs are somewhat unwieldy and not very user friendly, so it would be better if you could just request the NWTraders Weather Web Service. To do this, NWTraders could publish their weather service on a Universal Description, Discovery and Integration (UDDI) server. Finding their weather service is now just a question of connecting to the UDDI server using an agreed message format to locate the URL for the service.

Figure 4.9 shows the how the basic architectural elements of a typical Web service work together.

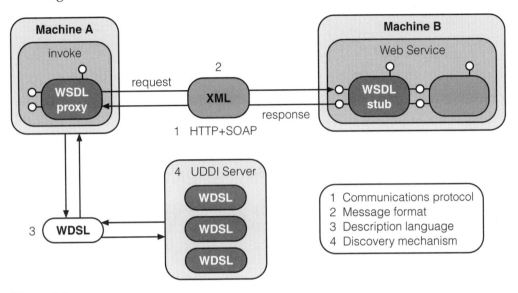

Figure 4.9
Typical architectural elements from a Web service

Now that you understand the individual parts of a Web service, it is easier to create a more precise definition. Hence a Web service is an application component that does the following:

- Communicates using open protocols (such as HTTP and SMTP).
- Processes SOAP framed XML messages.
- Describes its messages through the XML Schema.
- Uses WSDL to provide a service description.
- Enables discovery through UDDI.

Web Services Interoperability Organization

The protocols Web services depend on are platform independent. This suggests that interoperability between Web services on different application platforms should be automatic. Unfortunately, this is not necessarily the case.

While most of these protocols are generally accepted specifications, many of the Web services draft standards have not received full ratification from any of the common Web standards bodies, such as the World Wide Web Consortium (W3C) or Organization for the Advancement of Structured Information Standards (OASIS). Not surprisingly, many vendors have their own implementations of these specifications. As a result, interoperability between different vendors' Web services is not guaranteed.

Because many vendors were so enthusiastic about Web services, it became imperative to start an independent organization dedicated to maintaining standards and providing direction. Without this body, it would be impossible to ensure that Web services implementations were truly interoperable. From this requirement arose the Web Services Interoperability Organization (WS-I). The initial membership was 170, consisting of vendors, enterprise customers, system integrators and independents all working together to define the implementation of Web services.

Any organization or individual who wants to contribute to supporting and furthering the cause of Web services interoperability can join the WS-I. The WS-I targets developers and provides a framework and guidelines for the following areas:

- **Profiles**—These are specifications that define technology standards.
- **Samples**—These highlight interoperability concepts and demonstrate the features of the profiles.
- **Implementation guidelines**—These show a best practices approach to design solutions that require interoperability with Web services.
- **Tools**—These include a sniffer and analyzer to monitor and log interactions with Web services, including identifying errors and warnings for implementations that do not meet the profile guidelines.

For more information about the WS-I, see the Web Services Interoperability Organization Web site (*http://www.ws-i.org/*).

Implementing the Web Services Basic Profile

The most important publication to date from the WS-I is the Basic Profile 1.0. This profile provides a group of named Web services specifications, together with a series of recommendations for implementing each standard. Basic Profile 1.0 covers four areas:

- Messaging (HTTP, XML 1.0, XSD 1.0, SOAP 1.1)
- Description (WSDL 1.1)
- Discovery (UDDI 2.0)
- Security (HTTPS)

Note: WS-I does not control the individual specifications within Basic Profile 1.0, so it acts as a unifying intermediary for Web services. The XBikes sample application does not fully support the WS-I Basic Profile 1.0.

Implementing Web Services

Implementing Web services in .NET Framework and on the J2EE platform are different processes, due to the levels of support that each provides. Because .NET Framework includes built-in support for Web services, you do not require any additional components. Visual Studio .NET lets you create Web services implementations from a project template. With J2EE, you currently need to add a third-party Web services implementation.

Whether you implement your Web service in .NET Framework or in Java, there are certain common architectural elements, as Figure 4.9 shows.

There are two main stages to implementing Web services:

- Creating the Web service.
- Creating the Web service client.

The following two sections look at how you do this on the two platforms.

Creating Web Services in .NET Framework

Web services are tightly integrated into the .NET Framework. This makes it very easy to use the Visual Studio .NET IDE to design and create a Web service in .NET Framework. The .NET Web services implementation uses the same page framework as ASP.NET, consisting of the following:

- An addressable Web service entry point (.asmx file).
- The code that implements the Web service's functionality (typically kept in a .asmx.cs code-behind file).

To create Web services using Visual Studio .NET, your developer workstation needs access to a Web server configured for ASP.NET applications. If your server is running a version of Windows Server 2003, you must install IIS from the Application Server options and include support for ASP.NET applications.

Note: The Windows Server 2003 family does not include IIS in a default installation. This is a change from Windows 2000.

Visual Studio .NET lets you create an ASP.NET Web service project in any of the supported Visual Studio languages using the Web service project templates. After you create the Web service project in Visual Studio, the Component Designer appears. The Component Designer is the design surface for your Web service. You can use the Design view to add components to your Web service, and the Code view to view and edit the associated code.

When you create an ASP.NET Web service project in Visual Studio, it constructs a Web application project structure on the Web server and a Visual Studio solution file on your local computer. The solution file (.sln) contains the configuration and build settings and keeps a list of files associated with the project. In addition, Visual Studio automatically creates the necessary files and references to support a Web service. When completed, Visual Studio displays the .asmx file in Design view.

By default, Visual Studio uses code-behind files, such as Service1.asmx.vb (for Visual Basic) or Service1.asmx.cs (for C#), when you create a Web service using one of the ASP.NET Web service project templates. The code-behind file contains the code that implements the functionality of the Web service. In this file, you implement the methods you want your Web service to expose.

Note: By default, Solution Explorer hides the code-behind file. When you look at the .asmx file in Code view, you see the contents of this code-behind file. The .asmx file itself contains a processing directive, **WebService**, which indicates where to find the implementation of the XML Web service.

You implement the Web service's functionality the same as you would with any other class in the .NET Framework. To make a method available through the Web service, you mark the method with a **[WebMethod]** attribute before its **public** declaration. **Private** methods cannot serve as the entry point for a Web service, although they can be in the same class and the Web service code can call them.

When you build a Web service, ASP.NET automatically provides the infrastructure and handles the processing of Web service requests and responses, including the parsing and creation of SOAP messages. The compiled output is a .dll file in the project's Bin folder.

Chapters 7 and 8 of this book show detailed examples of how to implement Web services in the .NET Framework as part of the XBikes sample application. For additional reading on Web services, see the References section at the end of this chapter.

Exposing an Existing Class as a Web Service

A common scenario is where you want to expose the functionality of an existing .NET Framework class as a Web service so that other applications (such as Java applications) can access it. To do this, you can create a new Web service that acts as a service interface to the existing class. The new Web service should implement the same interface as the existing class, with each of its methods simply calling the methods of the existing class. This solution is known as the *Service Interface* pattern.

For more information about the Service Interface pattern, see the References section at the end of this chapter.

Component Services for Windows Server 2003 can use the built-in SOAP activation feature to expose a **ServicedComponent** through a SOAP endpoint which you can then access through a WSDL document. SOAP activation involves the automatic generation and hosting of a SOAP endpoint through IIS. This SOAP endpoint can then accept SOAP requests over HTTP.

It could be argued that because you can access this SOAP endpoint through a WSDL document, it is a Web service. Unfortunately, this may not always be the case because although you used SOAP, HTTP, and WSDL to build the endpoint, the WSDL document generated from the SOAP activation is not XSD compliant and contains .NET Remoting-specific data types.

Only clients that understand .NET Remoting can access SOAP-activated **ServicedComponents**. Therefore, by default, non-.NET Framework Web service clients cannot connect. To overcome this, you can do the following:

- Use a Java client with a runtime bridge installed to consume any exposed methods from the **ServicedComponent's** SOAP endpoint. This works because the runtime bridges understand .NET Remoting.
- Create a new Web service to accept incoming Web service requests and pass them on to the **ServicedComponent** as in the Service Interface pattern described earlier in this chapter.

Whichever technique you chose, you should now have a functioning Web service and can look at creating a client application.

Creating the Web Services Client

After you create your Web service, you then need to have client applications to access it. There are several ways of doing this, depending on the protocols that your Web service supports.

If your Web service supports the **HTTP-GET** protocol, you can access it from a Web browser. By default, Web services that you create in Visual Studio using the ASP.NET Web service project template support **HTTP-GET**, **HTTP-POST**, and **HTTP-SOAP** commands.

Note: The WS-I Basic Profile 1.0 does not support the **HTTP-GET** and **HTTP-POST** protocols. It is recommended that you disable the use of **HTTP-GET** and **HTTP-POST** to make your Web service WS-I Basic Profile 1.0 compliant.

.NET Framework provides two Help techniques for when you do not know how to address a Web service. Calling the Web service's .asmx file directly from a browser without parameters generates a Help page, as shown in the following example.

```
http://localhost/WebService1/Service1.asmx
```

The other way to discover information about the Web service is to query its WSDL properties. You can do this by calling the Web service's .asmx file directly from a browser with "?WSDL" appended as a parameter.

```
http://localhost/WebService1/Service1.asmx?WSDL
```

These built-in Help systems can assist you both in the design and debugging phases of creating a Web services client.

Implementing a .NET Framework Web Service Client

A Web service client is any component or application that references and uses a Web service. This does not necessarily need to be a client-based application—in many cases your Web service clients might be other Web applications, such as Web Forms or even other Web services.

When accessing Web services in managed code, a proxy class and the .NET Framework handle all of the infrastructure coding. The proxy class implements the interface Web service's interface and handles all communication between the Web service client and the Web service. Figure 4.10 shows the relationship of the proxy class to the Web service client and the Web service itself.

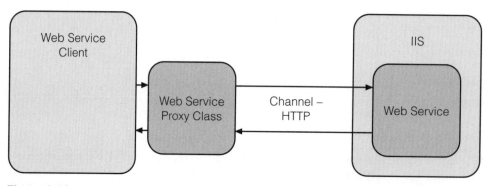

Figure 4.10
Web service client using a proxy class to communicate with a Web service

Note: You can create and manage proxy classes manually, or you can let Visual Studio .NET manage them for you through the automated Web References feature. The recommended approach is to use Web References.

► **To access a Web service from managed code in Visual Studio .NET**

1. Add a Web reference to your project for the Web service you want to access. The Web reference creates a proxy class with methods that serve as proxies for each exposed method of the Web service.

2. Add the namespace for the Web reference.

3. Create an instance of the proxy class, and then access the methods of that class like you access the methods of any other class.

After you build the project, you should then be able to access the referenced Web service.

Locating an XML Web Service and Adding a Web Reference

Sometimes you may be both the provider and consumer of a Web service. In this case, you probably know the location and function of the Web service. At other times, you may be accessing a Web service provided by someone else. When this occurs, you may not even know if a Web service that suits your purposes in fact exists.

To simplify the coding model, applications written in managed code use a Web reference to represent each Web service locally. You add a Web reference to your project by using the **Add Web Reference** dialog box. To access the **Add Web Reference** dialog box, right-click the Web References folder in Visual Studio .NET's Solution Explorer, and then click **Add Web Reference**. This dialog box makes it possible for you to browse your local server, the Microsoft UDDI Directory, and the Internet for Web services.

The **Add Web Reference** dialog box uses the process of Web service discovery to locate eligible Web services on Web sites that you navigate to in the dialog box. For a particular address, it interrogates the Web site using an algorithm designed to locate Discovery of Web service (DISCO) documents and ultimately, Web service description documents that adhere to the grammar of the Web Services Description Language (WSDL).

Generating a Proxy Class

After you locate a Web service for your application to access by using the **Add Web Reference** dialog box, clicking the **Add Reference** button instructs Visual Studio to download a copy of the service description to the local computer and then generate a proxy class for accessing the chosen Web service. The proxy class contains methods for calling each exposed Web service method both synchronously and asynchronously.

Note: This technique works only when the computer running Visual Studio has access to the Web service.

Alternatively, you can manually generate a proxy class using the same tool (Web services Description Language Tool, WSDL.exe) that Visual Studio uses to create a proxy class when adding a Web reference. This is necessary when you cannot access the Web service from the computer that Visual Studio is installed on, such as when the Web service is located on a network that the client is unable to access until run time. To generate a proxy file manually, run WSDL.exe from the command prompt with the URL of the target Web service's WSDL file as a parameter. You then manually add the file that the tool generates to your application project.

Using the Proxy Class

The generated proxy class has its own namespace associated with it, and you must add that namespace to your client application before you can create an instance of the proxy class. As with any other class, you must first create an instance of it before you can call any of its methods. This process does not differ at all from creating an instance of any other class.

When using a proxy class that Visual Studio generated directly from the service description of a Web service, accessing a Web service in managed code is a relatively simple process. To access a Web service method, your client application invokes either the corresponding synchronous method or asynchronous methods of the proxy object. These methods do the necessary work to remote the call over the wire to call the desired Web service method. By default, the proxy class uses SOAP to access the Web service method because SOAP supports the richest set of data types of the three supported protocols (**HTTP-GET**, **HTTP-POST**, and **HTTP-SOAP**).

The proxy class that the Add Web Reference process generates derives from the **System.Web.Service.Protocols.SoapHttpClientProtocol** class, which contains several properties that you can use to control or customize the behavior of how this class accesses a Web service. For more information about the properties available in the **SoapHttpClientProtocol** class, see the .NET Framework SDK.

Note: When you update a Web reference, Visual Studio .NET automatically generates a new proxy file. The new file overwrites the old one, removing any customization you may have added to the original proxy file. Keep a backup copy of any customized proxy files to guard against this possibility. This does not happen if you manually generate a proxy file with the WSDL.exe tool.

Referencing with Dynamic and Static URLs

A Web reference can use either a static URL or a dynamic URL. The **Web Reference URL** property specifies the location of the Web service. By default, this property is the URL of the Web service you selected, which is a static URL.

If you leave the **URL Behavior** property set to the default value of **Static**, a hard-coded URL sets the proxy class's URL property when you create an instance of that class. If you set the **URL Behavior** property of the Web reference to **Dynamic**, the application obtains the URL at run time from the **<appSettings>** section of your application's configuration file.

```
<appSettings>
    <add key="myApplication.myServer.Service1"
         value="http://myServer/myXmlWebService/Service1.asmx"/>
</appSettings>
```

When you create an instance of a proxy object, you can also programmatically set the URL property of the object in your application. Regardless of which URL the proxy uses, it must be for a Web service that conforms to a WSDL that matches the one you used when adding the Web reference. Otherwise, the proxy class that you generated earlier will not work with it.

Calling Web Service Methods

After adding a Web reference to a Web service, you can invoke the exposed methods of that Web service and access the results just as you would any other method of a component.

For examples of how to implement these techniques in the XBikes sample application, see Chapters 7 and 8.

Creating Web Services in J2EE

Implementing Web services in Java is currently not as straightforward as with Microsoft .NET Framework. At the time of this writing, the latest released version of the J2EE specification is version 1.3, and version 1.4 is currently in beta. In version 1.3 there is no native implementation of Web services. For example, there is no **java.webservices** package that you can import and use with the Java syntax.

However, there is considerable drive within the Java community to define and implement Web services. The Java Community Process defines the following Java Specification Requests (JSRs) that cover Web services:

- JSR 109—Implementing Enterprise Web Services
- JSR 93—Java API for XML Registries 1.0 (JAXR)
- JSR 67—Java APIs for XML Messaging
- JSR 101—Java APIs for XML based RPC

JSR 109 defines the Web services for J2EE architecture. It uses the J2EE component architecture to provide a familiar, portable, scalable and interoperable client and server programming model. JSR 109 builds upon JSR 67, JSR 93 and JSR 101.

> **Note:** If a Java vendor's Web services implementation complies with JSR-109, other JSR-109 compliant implementations should be able to interoperate with it.

JSR 93 defines how Java applications connect to XML registries, such as JNDI, ebXML and UDDI. This JSR provides mechanisms so that Web services can publish their interfaces and client applications can then discover these interfaces.

JSR 101 concentrates on XML RPC and the Java language. These include the following:

- Representing XML based interface definitions in Java.
- Defining interfaces with XML based interface definition languages such as SOAP.
- Implementing marshalling.

JSR 67 provides similar definitions for XML messaging.

Java Web Services Stacks

Currently, Web services support on the Java platform requires a Web services stack, of which there are several from which to choose. The most popular implementations are the following:

- Apache Axis is an open source implementation of Web services from the Apache Software Foundation.
- IBM has several Web service stacks available, such as WebSphere Application Server, Web Services Developer Kit (WSDK), and the Emerging Technologies Toolkit (ETTK). IBM also offers a UDDI Registry and Server product.
- WASP from Systinet provides a Web services stack for both C/C++ and Java Environments. Systinet also provide a separate UDDI Server.
- GLUE from The Mind Electric is a popular Web services stack. The Mind Electric (recently aquired by webMethods, Inc.) also provides a UDDI Server.
- WebLogic application server from BEA also has a Web service stack.

The decision on which Web stack you select is likely to reflect organizational preferences as well as technical requirements.

Creating a Web Service in Java

Creating a Web service in Java differs depending on which Web services stack you choose, and to some degree, which Java IDE you use. All vendors provide tutorials on how to build Web services in their documentation. However, the main steps for building a Web service are the same.

First, you need to identify which functionality you want to expose. With that information, you either need to create a new class exposing this functionality or identify an existing class that already does the job. Many Web service stacks allow you to expose an existing class or EJB as a Web service. From an architectural point of view, you should create a new class, even if it simply calls an existing one. This provides some protection against changes in the application.

After you decide the class you want to expose, you have to configure your Web service stack to expose this class. Most Java Web service implementations run as a servlet inside an application server.

Note: Some stacks, such as GLUE and WASP, provide their own container if an application server is not available.

You configure these servlets using various configuration files. To deploy a Web service, you need only modify these configuration files. Many vendors also supply a way of exposing Web services dynamically using an API, but this hard coding should be avoided.

For example, GLUE requires that you create an XML configuration file for your Web service. To expose this Web service, you just add your class to the configuration file. The GLUE servlet parses this file when it loads and creates the appropriate WSDL and schema documents based on the class.

For more information about how to create a Web service using GLUE, see the GLUE documentation. The XBikes sample application provides an example of implementing Web services for interoperability in Chapter 7, "Integrating .NET in the Presentation Tier."

Consuming a Web Service in Java

Despite there being many different Java Web services vendors, consuming a Web service is a fairly simple task in nearly all vendor implementations. You can use a tool named WSDL2Java against a local or remote WSDL document, which then creates a Java proxy implementation. This is similar to the way in which .NET Framework consumes Web services, except the Java tools simply create an interface rather than an actual class. WSDL2Java usually creates a helper class, which creates an object based upon the URL endpoint. This object implements the interface that the WSDL2Java creates, which you can then use in your client application.

Chapters 7 and 8 provide examples of consuming a Web service on the Java platform.

Securing Web Services

Applications running in production environments usually require some form of authentication and authorization. This enables tracking of the users of a service and keeps their data separate from others.

The easiest way to implement authentication is to use the infrastructure built into HTTP to provide user names, passwords, and domains to the Web service. Web services published from .NET Framework can use HTTP authentication. Although this identifies a user, it is not secure, because HTTP packets are not safe from interception. Basic authentication sends user names and passwords in clear text, making it possible for an electronic eavesdropper to identify user names and passwords.

More advanced authentication methods such as Kerberos, NTLM, or Digest provide for encrypted authentication methods but these methods provide encryption for only the authentication process itself. Your Web service implementation may require a completely secure process with encryption applied to all client to server transactions. To do this, you have a choice of approaches:

- Transport level security.
- Application level security.
- Web Services Security (WS-Security).

Transport level security such as Secure Sockets Layer (SSL) encryption over HTTPS works at the protocol level and encrypts all the packets between the start point and endpoint of an individual Web service call. This works fine from the client (for example, an ASP.NET application in the Presentation tier) to a Web service in the Business tier. After the packets arrive at the Business tier, this is the SSL endpoint and the Business tier Web service decrypts the packets.

There is a problem when you want to keep the packets encrypted until they reach the Database tier, which stores the user names and passwords. Because SSL is a point to point encryption method, it is not suitable for keeping your data encrypted across multiple Web service calls in multi-tier environments.

Application level security involves developing some sort of custom security implementation. Although this technique can avoid the point to point issues with SSL by providing end to end encryption, it requires coding that would work only with clients that implement that custom security implementation. In Web services, this is counter to the idea of promoting accessibility.

The third option, WS-Security, provides application level security using a published specification. As long as the clients understand WS-Security, they can connect securely to the Web service.

WS-Security defines XML structures for security tokens, and clients use these security tokens as proof of identity. WS-Security tokens would typically include a user name, binary, and security token reference. WS-Security uses standard components, such as X.509 certificates, to endorse the identity of the client. WS-Security also provides encryption, either for the body of a SOAP message, the header, or both.

You control WS-Security settings through policy files, which are XML files with a .wsse file name extension. Implementing WS-Security involves creating the policy file and associating the file with your Web service. The Web service then checks both incoming and outgoing messages against the policy to ensure that they comply with the settings in force.

To access a secured Web service, you create a security policy file and associate it with the Web service control. The client policy settings must match those on the server.

Although the WS-Security standard is not fully ratified, a number of vendors have produced their own implementations, including the following:

- WSE (Web Services Enhancements) from Microsoft.
- IBM Web Services Toolkit from IBM.
- Weblogic Workshop from BEA Systems.

For more information about implementing WS-Security and WSE, see the References section at the end of this chapter.

Using Universal Description, Discovery, and Integration

UDDI is a standard specification for publishing and locating Web services. To implement UDDI, set up a UDDI server, and then register Web services URLs and descriptions with the service. You can think of UDDI as similar to Internet Locator Services (ILS), but dealing in Web services rather than people. Like ILS, UDDI servers can be public (a UDDI Business Registry or UBR), private (intranet based), or semi-private, for use between business partners. You can also compare UBR servers to telephone directories, with white pages listing businesses by name, yellow pages organizing them by function, and green pages describing the services they provide.

UDDI overcomes the issue that a simple URL is rarely very revealing. For example, it does not tell you very much about the service offering. Also, URLs have a habit of morphing into other URLs, preventing clients from connecting. UDDI uses a publish and subscribe model to enable consistency in connecting to Web services, independent of the vagaries of URL strings.

The UDDI directory database stores URLs or access points, associating them with the service offerings and the businesses involved. Business information can include contact details and the market sector in which the business operates, enabling flexible and efficient searches.

Major IT vendors such as Microsoft, IBM, SAP, Veritas, and NTT UDDI are part of the UDDI initiative, which is now at release 3.0. These five vendors also maintain the public UBR registries. For more information about UDDI, including details on white papers and best practices, see the UDDI Web site (*http://www.uddi.org/*).

Interoperability Benefits Using UDDI

UDDI provides major benefits for interoperability projects that involve Web services. Any Java or .NET Framework client that needs to make dynamic lookups for service offerings can make good use of UDDI. Other benefits include the following:

- **Common Web service publication**—UDDI provides a platform-independent view of Web services.

- **Dynamic configuration**—Any client application can use UDDI to configure a Web service proxy dynamically, removing the need for a hard coded URL. Additionally, dynamic rebinding allows multiple URL instances for a Web service. Similar to round-robin DNS, if one link fails to respond, applications can request another service instance from the same provider through UDDI.

- **Web service re-use**—Large organizations may have multiple departments working on development projects, often resulting in duplicated Web service offerings. UDDI lets development teams browse through a list of already published Web services, preventing departments from wasting time and money on providing a service that is already available.

- **Location specific Web services**—Improves performance and reduces network traffic by allocating a location to a Web service, enabling clients to bind to the closest service instance.

UDDI Registries

The central component of UDDI is the registry, which enables organizations to publish location information on available services. However, you do not have produce Web services for public consumption to benefit from UDDI.

Note: Microsoft, IBM, and SAP host test public registries that allow developers to test registration and publication processes.

Several vendors have implemented UDDI services on the latest operating systems:

- Microsoft includes UDDI as a core service in Windows 2003
- IBM have added a UDDI registry to WebSphere
- The Mind Electric package a UDDI server with GLUE

Note: If implementing UDDI internally, check for support of the 3.0 standard.

UDDI promises to be a major growth area in the future and offers significant benefits when implementing Web services. This next section considers a number of best practice recommendations to assist Web services and interoperability.

Implementing Web Services Interoperability Best Practices

Web services is still an emerging technology. The protocol specifications that Web services are based on are not yet officially ratified standards, so different vendors' implementations may not be interoperable with each other. The WS-I Basic Profile should help improve Web services interoperability in the future. However, to give yourself the best chance of implementing Web services when interoperating between .NET Framework and Java, follow these best practice guidelines:

- **Define data types first**—If you plan to use complex data types over Web services, design your data types from a common XML schema using some of the strategies outlined in Chapter 3, "Interoperability Fundamentals."

- **Test your data types**—Before you start to code your main application, use test applications that simply pass your data types back and forth in a proof of concept pilot that show your interoperability solution working.

- **Use simple data types whenever possible**—If you can implement a simpler data type, do so. Implement complex data types only for sound business reasons, rather than because you enjoy the challenge.

- **Base all data types on XSD data types**—This is especially important if you implement complex data types. As described in Chapter 3, "Interoperability Fundamentals," this ensures that the data types in your complex data objects map to types in .NET Framework and Java.

- **Store all data types centrally**—Separating out the data types from the proxy file and storing them in a separate location is particularly useful when the .NET and Java assemblies require a single XML namespace for all types.

- **Comply with WS-I Basic Profile 1.0**—This is an overriding factor if making your service publicly available. Make sure you keep up to date with revisions and new releases of the WS-I profile.

- **Standardize on document/literal style rather than combinations involving SOAP or RPC encoding**—Implementing SOAP encoding prevents validation against a schema and RPC encoding tends to be tightly coupled into the service and interface-driven.

Note: WS-I Basic Profile 1.0 actively promotes document/literal style.

- **Use the latest Java Web services distribution**—In the fast-moving world of Java distributions and associated tools, using the most recent distribution keeps you working with the latest specifications, improves reliability, and provides consistent interoperability.

- **Use UDDI to discover Web services**—UDDI is a powerful and effective way of discovering Web services either within an organization or as part of a public service offering.

- **Apply abstraction through Interoperability Adapter/Service Interface patterns** —This lets you add functionality to a Web service call without modifying the caller logic. The abstraction layer might be between the business logic and the ASP.NET Presentation tier making the call. Implementing an Interoperability Adapter/Service Interface pattern keeps the ASP.NET code clean of additional overhead, such as working out a URL from the UDDI registry. For more information about Interoperability Adapter/Service Interface patterns and example implementations, see Chapter 6, "Implementing Interoperability Design Elements."

As with all best practice recommendations, there may be occasions when you need to implement a different solution. However, keeping to these guidelines should assist you to enable your applications to work together with the minimum of fuss.

Comparing .NET Remoting to Web Services

.NET Remoting with runtime bridges and Web services provide different approaches to application platform interoperability that provide flexibility in specifying the communication method between application components. Although sharing some similarities, .NET Remoting and Web services differ in a number of details. Table 4.4 summarizes the similarities and differences.

Table 4.4: Feature comparison between .NET Remoting and Web services

Feature	.NET Remoting	Web services
HTTP Channel	✓	✓
SOAP over HTTP	✓	✓
TCP Channel	✓	✗
XML Formatter	✓	✓
Binary Formatter	✓	✗
Pass by Value	✓	✓
Pass by Reference	✓	Difficult to implement
Storing Session State	Easy	More complicated
Invoke single method on a stateless object	✓	✓
Invoke multiple methods on a stateful object	✓	✗

(continued)

Table 4.4: Feature comparison between .NET Remoting and Web services *(continued)*

Feature	.NET Remoting	Web services
All clients can invoke methods on same server side object	✓	✗
Traverse Firewalls	✓	✓
Use IIS as host	✓	✓
Use custom host	✓	✗
Retrieve complete copy of complex object	✓	✗

Because there is considerable industry momentum behind Web services at present, you might be inclined to implement Web services as a matter of course. However, Table 4.4 shows that there are several areas where .NET Remoting shows notable advantages.

Because .NET Remoting incorporates a TCP channel, this removes the need for HTML headers. Combining this with a binary formatter usually provides a significant performance boost for large traffic volumes.

Implementing pass by value and pass by reference are possible for both methods, but they are significantly more difficult to implement in Web services. Also, session state management in .NET Remoting is less complicated than with Web services.

Other advantages of .NET Remoting over Web services include the following:

- Guaranteed interoperability.
- Support for client activation and lifetime control of remote objects (similar to DCOM).
- Support for callbacks and events.
- Support for additional context information specific to .NET Framework. In the future, such information will enable additional features such as distributed transactions and additional security levels.
- Support for type system fidelity, which means that there is a one-to-one mapping between the class and type hierarchy. Web services and SOAP do not support such an object-oriented mechanism for accessing remote objects.

Implement .NET Remoting within a tightly coupled intranet environment where you expect high transaction volumes and you control both sides of the communication. Use Web services for more loosely coupled systems, particularly those connecting across the Internet, or where you do not have control of both ends of the conversation.

Web services have advantages over .NET Remoting, mainly in the following areas:

- **Platform independence**—Web services use open and ubiquitous standards such as XML, SOAP, HTTP, and WSDL. Consequently, Web services offer genuine platform independence; you can invoke a Web service from any client platform, irrespective of the server platform or implementation technology of the Web service.

- **Security**—IIS is the standard host of choice for ASP.NET components, so Web services applications created using ASP.NET can automatically take advantage of the security features in IIS, such as support for Windows authentication, Secure Sockets Layer (SSL) encryption and logging. You can use IIS to host .NET Remoting components, in which case they can make use of the same security mechanisms. However, if you do not host your .NET Remoting components in IIS, you must implement authentication, authorization, and privacy mechanisms yourself.

- **Caching**—Hosting ASP.NET components in IIS also adds IIS caching support for Web services. Effective caching can significantly reduce the performance advantages of .NET Remoting, depending on the type of data that you want to cache. Caching is most effective for repeatedly requested public data, and decreases in effectiveness when caching private data or with dynamic data. .NET Remoting has no built in support for caching, even when IIS hosts the remoting components. Hence, like security, you have to build caching support manually.

- **Ease of creation**—Visual Studio .NET makes it easy to create and consume Web services. To create a Web service, create an ASP.NET Web service project and implement methods decorated with the **[WebMethod]** attribute. To consume a Web service, create any kind of project in Visual Studio .NET and add a Web reference to a Web service of your choice; Visual Studio .NET generates a client-side proxy that simplifies access to the Web service.

If these factors are important to you, Web services might be a better choice than .NET Remoting to achieve point-to-point interoperability.

Summary

This chapter described the methods for providing point to point interoperability between .NET Framework and Java. It covered .NET Remoting and how you can use runtime bridges such as JNBridgePro and Ja.NET to link .NET Framework and Java. It then investigated the rapidly evolving world of Web services and described how emerging standards such as UDDI and XML can simplify the process of linking Java and .NET Framework components. In the next chapter, you examine interoperability techniques based on message queuing.

References

For more information about XML Web Services, see:

Chapters 5 and 6 of Simon Guest's book, *Microsoft .NET and J2EE Interoperability Toolkit*, Microsoft Press, ISBN 0-7356-1922-0

Scott Short's book, *Building XML Web Services for the Microsoft .NET Platform*, Microsoft Press, ISBN 0-7356-1406-7

For more information on JNBridgePro from JNBridge, see
http://www.jnbridge.com

For more information about the JSR specifications
See the Java Community Process Web site
http://www.jcp.org/en/jsr/all

For more information about Apache Axis
http://ws.apache.org/axis/

For information about IBM's Web services implementations
see the developerWorks Web site
http://www-106.ibm.com/developerworks/webservices/

For more information about Systinet's Web services implementation
http://www.systinet.com/products/wasp_jserver/overview

For more information about GLUE from The Mind Electric
http://www.themindelectric.com/

For more information about Web services on the .NET Framework
http://msdn.microsoft.com/webservices/

For more information about how to implement Web services on the .NET Framework
"Creating XML Web Services in Managed Code"
http://msdn.microsoft.com/library/default.asp?url=/library/en-us/vbcon/html/vbconWebServicePublishing.asp

For more information about .NET Remoting
"Microsoft .NET Remoting: A Technical Overview"
http://msdn.microsoft.com/library/default.asp?url=/library/en-us/dndotnet/html/hawkremoting.asp

For more information about .NET Remoting configuration files
"Format for .NET Remoting Configuration Files"
http://msdn.microsoft.com/library/default.asp?url=/library/en-us/dndotnet/html/remotingconfig.asp

For more information about hosting remotable objects in IIS
"Hosting Remote Objects in Internet Information Services (IIS)"
http://msdn.microsoft.com/library/default.asp?url=/library/en-us/cpguide/html/cpconhostingremoteobjectsininternetinformationservicesiis.asp

For more information about security in Web services
"Security" in the Web Services Developer Center
http://msdn.microsoft.com/webservices/building/security/default.aspx

For more information about implementing service interfaces
"Enterprise Solution Patterns: Implementing Service Interface in .NET"
http://msdn.microsoft.com/practices/type/patterns/enterprise/impserviceinterfaceinnetwasp/

For more information about implementing WSE, see the following articles on MSDN:
"Web Service Enhancements 1.0 and Java Interoperability, Part 1"
http://msdn.microsoft.com/webservices/building/wse/default.aspx?pull=/library/en-us/dnwebsrv/html/wsejavainterop.asp

- and -

"Web Service Enhancements 1.0 and Java Interoperability, Part 2"
http://msdn.microsoft.com/webservices/building/wse/default.aspx?pull=/library/en-us/dnwebsrv/html/wsejavainterop2.asp

For more information about UDDI services on the IBM platform
"Understanding UDDI" on the IBM Web site
http://www-106.ibm.com/developerworks/webservices/library/ws-featuddi/#What%20is%20UDDI?

For equivalent information about GLUE
See the GLUE UDDI Web site
http://www.themindelectric.com/docs/glue/guide/uddi/index.html

To install UDDI on Windows Server 2003, see the topic "Using UDDI Services" in Windows Server 2003 Family Help.

5

Interoperability Technologies: Data Tier

Introduction

Chapter 4, "Interoperability Technologies: Point to Point," describes implementing point to point interoperability techniques, such as .NET Remoting and Web services. This chapter covers technologies that can help you implement connectivity between .NET Framework and Java applications at the Data tier such as database connectivity and asynchronous connectivity through message queuing.

One interoperability scenario is where you have an existing data repository that you now want to access from both .NET Framework and Java applications. This chapter considers the implications of such a setup together with best practice recommendations for creating shared databases.

.NET Remoting and Web services provide the ability to link either tightly or loosely coupled systems on intranets or across the Internet. However, these techniques cannot cope with environments that must withstand very high latency levels or non-permanent connections, for example, the increasing use of handheld devices connected through some form of wireless link. Asynchronous methods can overcome issues of non-permanent links.

Linking through a Shared Database

You may have the situation where you have two applications, on different platforms, that you want to share the same underlying database. This configuration addresses the issue of maintaining multiple data stores. Sharing a database between .NET Framework and J2EE applications is a simple and effective means of implementing interoperability between the two environments.

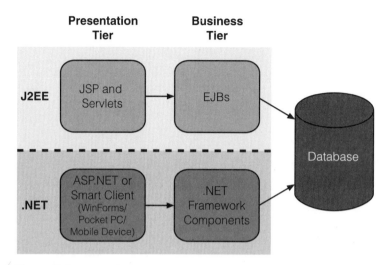

Figure 5.1

.NET Framework and J2EE applications sharing a common database

The technologies that enable you to do this are not new. Both platforms have had mechanisms to implement database connectivity since they started. The existence of database drivers makes it easy for you to link Business tier applications to a common back-end storage and share tables, records, and fields between platforms.

Both platforms provide links into multiple databases, such as Microsoft SQL Server™, Oracle, Informix, MySQL and DB2. This section discusses the ways that both .NET Framework and Java applications connect to databases, as well as some best practices for sharing databases.

Before you can learn how to share databases, you need to appreciate how each platform connects to a database. Each platform has a built-in data access API:

- ADO.NET in the .NET Framework.
- JDBC in Java.

For the majority of implementations, your choice of database and platform should not be a factor.

Note: Although the samples in this section refer to SQL Server 2000, the strategies shown apply to all databases.

Connecting with JDBC

JDBC is the API that enables J2EE applications to access tables, records, fields and stored procedures in any compatible database. You can use JDBC to connect to almost any tabular data, including spreadsheets and information in flat file format.

JDBC 3.0 represents the most recent release of the specification, which a variety of vendors now endorse, including IBM, Hewlett-Packard, BEA, Simba, and Oracle. Sun has recently filed JSR221, which covers the JDBC 4.0 API specification.

Note: Java 2 Platform, Standard Edition (J2SE) 1.4 includes complete support for JDBC 3.0, located in the **Java.sql** and **Javax.sql** packages. The classes and interfaces in these packages allow Java applications to access any database for which they have a JDBC database driver.

There are four types of JDBC database drivers:

- Type 1 (JDBC to ODBC bridge with ODBC driver)—Type 1 drivers provide JDBC access through ODBC drivers. Sun supplies a JDBC to ODBC bridge driver in the J2SE that you can use if no other driver is available. Type 1 drivers require native code installation on the client computer.

- Type 2 (Native API with Java technology driver)—Type 2 drivers convert JDBC calls into calls to the client API. As with Type 1 drivers, this implementation requires native code installation on the client computer.

- Type 3 (Pure Java driver for database middleware)—Type 3 drivers translate the JDBC calls into a middleware vendor's protocol. The middleware then translates this protocol into DBMS calls. You do not have to install any native code on the client computer, but you must specify security configuration settings for Internet operation.

- Type 4 (Pure Java direct to database driver)—Type 4 drivers translate JDBC calls into DBMS calls directly, and use native protocols to access the database.

Note: Type 4 "Pure Java" drivers are the preferred option because they typically offer the best performance.

JDBC uses the concept of ResultSets. A **ResultSet** is a grouping of all the rows that satisfy the conditions within a SQL statement. You can access the data in the **ResultSet** using the **get** method, which enables you to traverse columns in the current row. You can also move to the next row using **ResultSet.next**.

Applications can execute statements and then process any number of result sets. The statement that generates a **ResultSet** automatically closes it, either by closing the statement, executing it again, or retrieving the next result from multiple result sequences.

Note: ResultSets are similar to ADO.NET DataSets. However, ResultSets are closer to ADO RecordSets, the pre-.NET database access API objects.

For more information about **ResultSets**, see "JDBC Guide: Getting Started" on the Java Web site. For more information about using JDBC, see "JDBC Data Access API" on the Java Web site.

Connecting to SQL Server 2000 with JDBC

You can access SQL Server 2000 from Java applications using any one of a range of JDBC drivers, either free or commercial in nature. For example, Microsoft provides the Microsoft SQL Server 2000 Driver for JDBC Service Pack 1. This is a Type 4 JDBC driver that provides highly scalable and reliable connectivity for J2EE applications. This driver provides JDBC access to SQL Server 2000 for any Java-enabled applet, application, or application server.

For more information about the Microsoft SQL Server 2000 Driver for JDBC Service Pack 1, including download information, go to the Microsoft Download Center.

Note: When connecting to SQL Server 2000 using a JDBC driver, ensure the security settings on SQL Server use SQL Server and Windows authentication (mixed mode authentication). Also, ensure that you set a complex (mixed case letters and numbers) password for the **sa** account.

For more information about connecting to SQL Server 2000 with the Microsoft JDBC driver, see Microsoft Knowledge Base article Q313100, "HOW TO: Get Started with Microsoft JDBC."

Connecting with ADO.NET

Accessing data in relational databases has always been a feature with Microsoft platforms. Before the arrival of the .NET Framework, ActiveX Data Objects (ADO) API was the primary database access mechanism. The .NET Framework introduced ADO.NET as the new API for connecting to databases on Microsoft platforms.

ADO.NET represents the abstract design concepts that you need to build data access classes within the .NET Framework. ADO.NET lets you work with data irrespective of data source, data format, or physical location. It includes a new object model and promotes new concepts such as the **DataSet** and the **DataReader** classes.

ADO.NET improves on ADO by being less database-centric and more aligned with modern Web service based programming. It works well in a distributed environment and enables developers to link to data sources quickly and reliably.

There were several main design goals for ADO.NET:

- **Explicit and factored object model**—ADO.NET provides a simple to use object model in which developers have complete control over how to control data source connectivity, command execution, and data manipulation.

- **Disconnected data cache model**—N-tier programming and XML Web service architectures require that applications work in a disconnected, loosely coupled manner. ADO.NET provides a comprehensive caching data model for marshaling data between applications or services and then updating the original data source.

- **Common data representation with data combination**—ADO.NET gives you the ability to combine data from multiple and varied data sources.

- **XML support**—XML is a key component in building interoperable applications and more robust data processing models. ADO.NET uses the XML support in the .NET Framework by interacting with XML in either a relational manner or in native XML.

- **Use existing ADO knowledge**—Although the ADO.NET object model differs from the previous ADO model, the basic constructs remain the same. The ADO.NET object model consists of a provider, connection, and command objects, enabling current ADO developers to migrate easily to ADO.NET.

From a developer's perspective, ADO.NET represents the concrete implementation of classes inside the .NET Framework that you can use for data access. These classes exist within the **System.Data** namespace of the .NET Framework.

Note: The ADO.NET classes in **System.Data.dll** are integrated with the XML classes found in **System.Xml.dll**. Hence to compile code that uses the **System.Data** namespace, you should add a reference to both **System.Data.dll** and **System.Xml.dll** in your Visual Studio .NET projects.

ADO.NET introduces the concepts of datasets, as provided by the **DataSet** class. You can compare a dataset to a **ResultSet** object in JDBC, but datasets provide a disconnected view of the data. You can take datasets offline, modify them, and then update the database with the amended values.

ADO.NET also introduces the concept of data readers, as provided by the **SqlDataReader**, **OleDbDataReader**, and **OracleDataReader** classes. A data reader object retrieves a read-only, forward-only stream of data from a database. You can use the data reader object to increase application performance and reduce system overhead as only one row at a time is held in memory.

To determine whether to use a dataset or data reader when you design your application, consider the level of functionality that you need in the application.

Use a dataset in order to do the following:

- Navigate between multiple discrete tables of results.

- Manipulate data from multiple sources (for example, a mixture of data from more than one database, from an XML file, and from a spreadsheet).

- Exchange data between tiers or using an XML Web service. Unlike data readers, you can pass a dataset to a remote client.

- Reuse the same set of rows to achieve a performance gain through caching (such as when sorting, searching, or filtering the data).

- Perform a large amount of processing per row. Extended processing on each row returned using a data reader ties up the connection serving the data reader longer than necessary, affecting performance.

- Manipulate data using XML operations such as Extensible Style Language Transformations (XSLT transformations) or XPath queries.

Use a data reader in your application for the following reasons:

- You do not need to cache the data.

- You are processing a set of results too large to fit into memory.

- You need to access data quickly and once only, in a forward-only and read-only manner.

ADO.NET connects to a database through managed providers. These are database drivers that expose APIs using classes operating from managed code. You can obtain managed providers for SQL Server, Oracle 8i, MySQL and IBM's DB2, as well as several other databases.

Alternatively, managed providers can access OLEDB or ODBC-based drivers. OLEDB and ODBC are two older database-independent connection APIs that you can use to connect to any compliant data store. If you use the ADO.NET managed provider for either of these APIs, you can access virtually any database with one set of code; however, you add the overhead of another API layer.

The managed providers for each database (such as the managed provider for SQL Server 7.0 or SQL Server 2000) link directly to the database at the binary level, giving a substantial performance advantage. For this reason, you are recommended to use the managed provider for the database you are connecting to instead of the more generic OLEDB or ODBC-based drivers.

Using the managed provider for a particular database does imply that your application is then tied to that database and switching to another database would require rewriting the database access code. However, it is rare for an organization to change its database, and it is certainly not something that companies do just for fun. Hence the performance benefits are worth the minor inconvenience of dedicated database access code.

Note: There are techniques in this chapter that cover how to enable your application to use different databases without significant code rewriting.

Connecting to Microsoft SQL Server 2000 with ADO.NET

You can access SQL Server 2000 from .NET Framework applications through the SQL Managed Provider for ADO.NET. You can find most of the APIs you need to access the SQL Managed Provider for ADO.NET in the **System.Data.SqlClient** namespace. This is the namespace that you import at the beginning of your code.

The **Connection, Command, Data Reader**, and **Data Adapter** objects provide the core functionality of the ADO.NET data provider model. Each managed provider provides its own implementation of these core objects prefixed with the provider name. For example, the SQL Managed Provider for .NET Framework contains classes such as **SqlConnection** and **SqlCommand**. ADO.NET classes prefixed with **Sql** address the SQL Server managed provider and only work with SQL Server.

Using these SQL Server managed provider classes offers two major advantages over their OLE DB provider counterparts. Firstly, these classes use the native Tabular Data Stream (TDS) interface for maximum performance and the additional interface layers that the OLE DB classes require no longer exist, resulting in faster database access. Secondly, the SQL classes that these controls create have additional methods that take advantage of features specific to SQL Server. This provides you with greater flexibility in design and programming with SQL Server.

In a simple connection scenario, you can use objects in the following manner. First, you define a connection to the database using the **SqlConnection** class. This class builds a connection string including the computer name, database name, and authentication details, such as user name and password. You then use the **Open** method to open the connection to the database.

To fetch data from the database, you construct a **SqlCommand** object that contains the relevant **select** statement. The **ExecuteReader** method called on the **SqlCommand** object returns a **SqlDataReader** object containing the results from the **select** statement. Finally, you extract the fields from the reader, index them with the **GetValue** method and use them however you want within the application. For more information about implementing these commands, see the References section at the end of this chapter.

Sharing Data Between ADO.NET and JDBC

You have seen how both JDBC and ADO.NET provide database connectivity for .NET Framework and J2EE applications to a range of databases. You should now appreciate that both environments can point to a single data source to add, read, update, and delete records. It is now time to look at some best practices for implementing database connectivity.

Abstracting database access code from the rest of your application is best practice in both .NET Framework and J2EE application architectures. For ease of coding and consistency, you should implement a layer that abstracts the database code from the business logic, as Figure 5.2 shows.

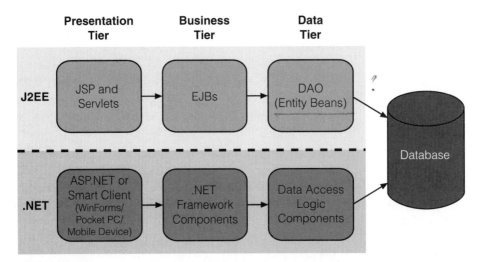

Figure 5.2
The Data Access Logic Components abstract the database code from the Business tier

This abstraction pattern has different names depending on the platform. In J2EE, this is the Data Access Object (DAO) pattern. The *Application Architecture for .NET: Designing Applications and Services* guide refers to this as Data Access Logic Components or simply Data Access Logic. The next section looks at the benefits of implementing a Data Access Logic layer in both .NET Framework and J2EE applications.

Note: This book refers to the Data Access Logic Components pattern for both .NET and Java applications.

Implementing Data Access Logic Components

Regardless of the data store you choose, your application should use Data Access Logic Components to access the database. These components abstract the semantics of the underlying data store and data access technology (such as ADO.NET or JDBC) and provide a simple programmatic interface for retrieving and performing operations on the stored data.

Data access logic components usually implement a stateless design that separates the business processing from the data access logic. Each data access logic component typically provides methods to perform create, read, update, and delete (CRUD) operations on a specific business entity in the application.

For example, in an e-commerce application, you can design a data access logic component for handling all data interactions with the data relating to customer orders. This data access logic component is not necessarily tied to one table in the database; it can access any of the tables that relate to order data. Typically, this data access logic component retrieves complex data types that represent a business entity, in this case, an **OrderData** object.

For more information about implementing data access logic, see the References section at the end of this chapter.

Taking this concept further, if you have multiple data access logic components, it is a good idea to implement a *database helper* class to handle common tasks such as database connections, execute commands, and cache parameters, and so on. The data access logic components provide the logic to access specific business data, while the database helper class centralizes data access API code to a specific database. This helps to reduce code duplication.

You have already seen that if you use a managed provider class to communicate with a database, you may need to write code that is specific to that database. When you implement a database helper class, you can keep all database specific code within that class. The database helper class enables you to keep your data access logic components database independent. Changing database types means simply replacing your database helper class with one that can communicate with the new database. Additionally, environments with more than one database type can use multiple database helper classes in order to access data from the different databases.

Microsoft provides the Data Access Application Block (DAAB) for the .NET Framework, which can be used as a database helper for accessing SQL Server. For more information about the DAAB, including download information, see "Data Access Application Block Overview" on MSDN.

Benefits of Implementing Data Access Logic Components

Implementing Data Access Logic Components gives the following interoperability benefits:

- Creates a common approach for accessing data from either environment, enabling developers to write business logic code with a consistent feel regardless of the underlying platform.
- Provides the ability to abstract access to different underlying databases.
- Enables the integration of further logic and processes for accessing databases, such as:
  - Caching for added performance.
  - Authentication and authorization for user connections.
  - Transaction support and locking.
  - Data paging for large results sets.

The common approach benefit opens the door for a further interoperability scenario where the Business tier on one platform can call the Data Access Logic tier of the other platform. This advances the concept of sharing a database between .NET Framework and Java applications by allowing you not only to share the database, but also the data access logic that communicates with the database. The XBikes sample application included in this guide provides the ability to implement this scenario through one of its configuration options.

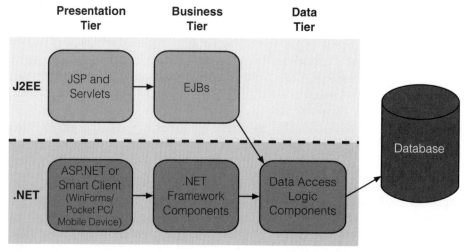

Figure 5.3

Sharing Data Access Logic Components between .NET Framework and Java applications

Implementing Asynchronous Interoperability

So far, you have looked at synchronous calls between .NET Framework and Java applications using .NET Remoting and Web services. Synchronous calls require a response from the provider component that returns the results to the consumer, with the requester waiting until it receives the response. With high-speed, permanent link WAN links, this is the preferred approach. Even in the higher latency environment of the Internet, synchronous calls can be more than adequate.

However, what do you do if there is no guarantee that the provider application is available? What if the link to that component is non-permanent, or other factors (such as loading levels and queuing) prevent synchronous operation? In this case, you can implement asynchronous communication.

With asynchronous communication, there is no guarantee that the provider application is available. Hence the consumer application adds its request into a messaging queue, and then it awaits the response when the provider can process it. Another example might be where the provider needs to expend significant processing resources in producing a result, possibly contacting other providers for information before being able to formulate a response.

Asynchronous processing is ideal to use in many situations—especially on the Web, where a user's request could take a long time to process, but you want to provide a response back to the user immediately. By handling the user's request asynchronously, your system can respond regardless of how long that request may actually take to execute.

Operations that fall into this category include placing an order at an online store with a credit card or making a request to a fulfillment center. Rather than keep the user waiting while the credit card company authorizes the payment or the fulfillment center puts the order together, the application lets the user know the order was placed successfully. A later e-mail notification could confirm that payment was made or the order assembled.

Asynchronous operations fall into two main types:

- **Non-blocking operations**—This is where the client handles the asynchronous call. The call itself is synchronous, but the client switches the call to another process or thread, allowing other operations to proceed uninterrupted until the response returns.
- **One-way operations**—This is a true asynchronous operation, in that the client makes the request which is handled by a separate server component. The client can then check up on the progress of the request by looking at status information before receiving the result of the transaction.

This next section looks at using Web services to make non-blocking asynchronous calls between .NET Framework and Java applications. The rest of the chapter then moves on to address the true one-way asynchronous operation support available in message queuing products.

Connecting with Web Services Using Asynchronous Calls

Although Web services are synchronous in nature, you can use them to implement non-blocking asynchronous connectivity. Non-blocking asynchronous calls are not truly asynchronous, but they allow a client application to continue to function by spawning a separate process that handles the asynchronous operation. This section looks at the techniques for implementing non-blocking asynchronous connectivity with Web services.

It is important to start out by differentiating the two following scenarios:

- Implementing an asynchronous call to a Web service.
- Implementing a Web service that is itself asynchronous.

In the first scenario, a client application calls a "slow" Web service asynchronously to allow the application to continue processing while the slow Web service call is in progress. The second scenario is where a Web service operates asynchronously on the Web server to increase its performance. However, this second option still results in a Web service that accepts synchronous connections. This guide discusses only the first scenario.

When you call a Web service from a .NET Framework client application, you can either call the method synchronously or asynchronously. In Chapter 4, "Interoperability Technologies: Point to Point," you saw how a Web service client uses methods in an auto-generated proxy class to make calls to a Web service. You create this proxy class for your client when you add a Web reference to your client project, or when you use the Web Services Description Language tool (Wsdl.exe), which automatically creates methods for calling the Web service method synchronously or asynchronously. This is true even if there is only a synchronous implementation of the XML Web service method.

For example, if the Web service exposes the method **GetProductsByCategory**, the proxy file would contain three methods named **GetProductsByCategory**, **BeginGetProductsByCategory**, and **EndGetProductsByCategory**. The first method calls the Web service synchronously as normal. The second two handle the asynchronous call. The **Begin** method initiates the call to the Web service, while the **End** method retrieves the results. Calling the **Begin** method in the proxy class from the client starts a second process that makes the synchronous call to the Web service, allowing the client to continue while the Web service call executes.

The obvious question is how does the client know when to call the **End** method? There are four main ways of doing this:

- Pass a callback function into the **Begin** method. The second process then calls the callback function when the message has finished processing. This is the preferred method as the callback functions do not block threads while awaiting the response.

- Use one of the **WaitHandle** methods of the **IAsyncResult.AsyncWaitHandle** object. When using the methods of the **WaitHandle** class, the client can also specify a timeout after which it abandons waiting for the results.

- Poll the value of **IAsyncResult.IsCompleted**. When this property returns true, the XML Web service response is available.

- Call the *End* method directly. This method does not return until the asynchronous operation is complete since it uses **IAsyncResult.AsyncWaitHandle**.

Using asynchronous communication improves system usage and avoids the situation where the client has to wait while the Web service delivers the results of an operation. Your decision to call a Web service method synchronously or asynchronously should be based upon performance. However, communication from the client application is still one-way, so this is not a true asynchronous implementation.

For more information about asynchronous calls to Web services, see the References section at the end of this chapter.

Using Callbacks in Client Applications

Implementing this "pseudo-asynchronous" operation is easy to achieve in .NET Framework Web service client applications. You can also achieve this style of operation in Java Web service clients, depending on the features that your Java Web Services Toolkit provides.

However, a call to a Web service using this asynchronous technique would not survive the client going offline and coming back online later in the week. If the transaction takes more than a few minutes (or even seconds), the user is unlikely to keep the connection open. Hence implement non-blocking asynchronous operation only if the following factors are true:

- The client and Web service have permanent connectivity.
- The call to the Web service does not take too long to complete.
- The client can work on other tasks during the Web service call.

If any of these factors are not true, you should consider moving beyond the non-blocking implementation with Web services toward true asynchronous operation using a messaging or queuing infrastructure.

Using Message Queues for Asynchronous Interoperability

You have seen how you can call Web services to simulate non-blocking asynchronous calls. Now, you will look at how to use message queuing to achieve true asynchronous communication, and then how to connect .NET Framework and Java applications.

Message queuing is a technique where processes or program instances can exchange or pass data through an interface to a system-managed queue of messages. Messages can have different lengths, types, and uses. You can have one process create a message queue with which multiple processes can interact, by reading or writing messages. For example, a client process can write messages to a message queue which a server process can later read or vice versa.

By placing a message representing a task (for example, an order for fulfillment) into a queue rather than processing the task synchronously, the application only has to post the message to the queue. Any number of different applications (potentially on different platforms) can post messages to a queue, and any number can be used to retrieve and process those same messages, providing scalability to your application.

Figure 5.4 shows an overall view of how message queuing works between two applications. Using a messaging API, an application creates a message with a data payload. The message queue system, through the queue manager, takes care of marshaling the data in the proper format to place the message in the queue. The queue manager also takes care of locating the destination queues (there may be more than one), whether they are on the local computer or on a remote computer on the network.

Note: In Figure 5.4, the sender and receiver applications may be on different platforms.

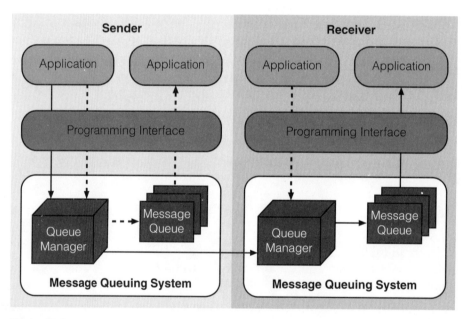

Figure 5.4

Example of a message queuing application

Several vendors produce message queue products, including:

- Microsoft Message Queuing (also known as MSMQ)
- IBM WebSphere MQ (formerly known as MQSeries)
- Sun ONE Message Queue
- BEA Message Q

These message queue products typically are responsible for managing the queues on a system. Applications typically send and receive messages from a queue using an API.

To discuss interoperability between .NET Framework and Java applications, this guide focuses on Microsoft Message Queuing and IBM's WebSphere MQ. The reason for discussing IBM's WebSphere MQ is because it is quite popular in enterprise environments, particularly those using Java. The next few sections look at using both Microsoft Message Queuing and WebSphere MQ to enable interoperability between .NET Framework and Java applications.

Using Microsoft Message Queuing

Microsoft Message Queuing (MSMQ) is a feature of the Windows operating system. MSMQ provides an inter-application messaging infrastructure, implementing the features for sending messages between disconnected applications. This is a crucial requirement for using Business tier components in an application.

MSMQ has been through several releases. MSMQ 1.0 was introduced as a part of the Windows NT 4.0 Options Pack and was also available for Windows 95 and Windows 98. MSMQ 2.0 is part of Windows 2000. The latest version, MSMQ 3.0 now ships with Windows XP Professional and Windows Server 2003. There is also a version of MSMQ for Windows CE.

Note: MSMQ in Windows NT 4.0 Workstation Windows 2000 Professional and Windows XP Professional can access only local private queues.

Because it is tightly integrated with Windows, MSMQ offers several benefits, such as the ability to utilize COM+ transactions, alignment with the Windows security model, and clustering. MSMQ 3.0 provides some additional features such as the ability to use HTTP as a transport, SOAP Reliable Messaging Protocol (SRMP) support, multicast options, triggers, and a number of management and deployment upgrades.

MSMQ fulfils a number of application requirements:

- **Message transport**—MSMQ handles packaging the message and transporting it across the network to the receiving application. It uses its own IP-based protocol as well as HTTP for transport (version 3.0 only), and COM/DCOM for object serialization when the body includes an object.

- **Resilient queues**—An MSMQ queue is an in-memory or persistent store of messages waiting for delivery. An application can view messages in the queue without removing them, filter them, and retrieve them from the queue.

- **Patient disconnection**—Unless you specify otherwise, a message sits and waits in a queue until an application comes looking for it. This means that MSMQ supports disconnected applications, where computers are not connected to the same physical network. After the computer reconnects, it can receive any waiting messages.

- **Transactional messages**—The optional transaction features of MSMQ guarantee that messages arrive once and only once, that multiple messages appear in a particular order, and if anything goes wrong, the entire set of messages rolls back to its initial state. MSMQ is a standard resource manager, so it can coordinate activity with other resource managers, such as Microsoft SQL Server, therefore allowing reading and writing of messages and data in the same transaction.

- **Error handling and auditing**—A lot can go wrong with any kind of disconnected application, and MSMQ has to provide robust support for error and audit conditions, such as undeliverable messages or auditing and journaling messages.

For more information about MSMQ features, see the Microsoft Message Queuing (MSMQ) Center Web site.

MSMQ is not part of the default installation of Windows Server 2003. To install MSMQ, add it using **Add/Remove Windows Components** under **Add or Remove Programs** in Control Panel. Go to the **Application Server** section and select the **Message Queuing** check box.

For detailed instructions about how to install MSMQ, see Chapter 9, "Implementing Asynchronous Interoperability." For more generic information, see "Installation Overview for Message Queuing" in Windows Help.

Administering MSMQ

You can administer MSMQ through the Computer Management console. You can use this tool to create, view, and manage queues. In this tool, you find MSMQ items under the Message Queuing object. There are four containers:

- **Outgoing Queues**—Holds outgoing messages, normally for routing purposes.
- **Private Queues**—Lets you create a private queue to which you can send messages.
- **Public Queues**—Enables you to create a queue that Active Directory publishes.
- **System Queues**—Contains system level queues, such as "dead letter" queues to store messages that MSMQ could not deliver.

For more information about administering and configuring MSMQ, see Windows Help.

Choosing Between Private and Public Queues

MSMQ offers the choice of creating public queues or private queues. The main differences between public and private queues are as follows:

- Public queues appear in Active Directory and private ones do not, so you can only access private queues by knowing the queue address.
- Private queues do not incur any overhead from the Active Directory.
- Public queues are only available in a domain environment. In a workgroup environment, you can use only private queues.
- Private queues can operate when the Active Directory directory service is unavailable.

Note: Unless your design is tightly bound to Active Directory authentication, use private queues.

Now that you understand the basics of MSMQ, this next section shows you how to use it to enable asynchronous interoperability between .NET Framework and Java applications. Chapter 3, "Interoperability Fundamentals," described how to get .NET Framework and Java applications to agree on a common format for exchanging data. Assuming you have created a common data format, then in theory if you can send and receive messages to and from MSMQ using .NET Framework as well as Java applications, MSMQ can act as an asynchronous link between the two platforms, as Figure 5.5 shows.

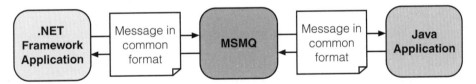

Figure 5.5

Message Queuing enabling asynchronous interoperability between .NET Framework and Java applications

Connecting to MSMQ from .NET Framework Applications

Programmatic access to MSMQ from a .NET Framework application is now a relatively easy process, although this was not always the case. Although MSMQ is conceptually quite simple, the original Win32® APIs involved significant low-level programming. The first improvement was the development of a COM interface. However, in the .NET Framework, Microsoft provides a namespace and a set of classes that support MSMQ. The **System.Messaging** namespace makes programming MSMQ consistent with programming the .NET Framework.

System.Messaging contains the set of classes that wrap the underlying MSMQ infrastructure. From these classes, there are three classes that you find yourself using most often when programming MSMQ:

- **MessageQueue**
- **Message**
- **MessageEnumerator**

The next sections describe each of these classes.

MessageQueue Class

The **MessageQueue** class is the primary class for interacting with message queues on local or remote computers. You can use it to perform tasks such as enumerating the queues on a particular computer, retrieving messages from a queue, sending messages to a queue, and creating and deleting queues. Almost everything you do with MSMQ in the .NET Framework starts with an instance of the **MessageQueue** class.

Message Class

The **Message** class lets you access and manipulate individual messages in a queue, as well as format and fine-tune a message that you add to a queue. In most cases, you use a **Message** object to receive a reference to a specific message as you loop through a collection of messages.

The **Body** property of the **Message** object stores the message data. Sending the message serializes the contents of the **Body** property, using the **Formatter** property you specify. This is similar to the serialization techniques discussed in Chapter 3, "Interoperability Fundamentals." MSMQ provides both a binary and an XML formatter. You can find the serialized contents in the **BodyStream** property. You can also set the **BodyStream** property directly, to perform tasks such as sending a file as the data content of a message. You can change the **Body** or **Formatter** properties at any time before sending the message, which serializes the data appropriately when you call the **Send** method of the **MessageQueue** object.

MessageEnumerator Class

The **MessageEnumerator** class is unique in that it provides very flexible access to the messages in a queue, as a dynamic collection of messages. It is the best means to process multiple messages because it gives you the flexibility to peek at or to receive messages as necessary. A **MessageEnumerator** object is a cursor with references to messages in the order the messages appear in the queue, ranked according to message priority. You can use a **MessageEnumerator** to step through the queue and examine or access the messages in the order in which they appear in the queue. However, the **MessageEnumerator** class provides a forward-only cursor, so you cannot step back through the queue with **MessageEnumerator**.

Note: An enumerator does not remove the messages from the queue when it queries the queue. It returns information about the message at the current cursor position, but it leaves the message in the queue.

For more information about the MSMQ-related classes in the **System.Messaging** namespace and how to program against MSMQ, see the ".NET Framework Class Library" on MSDN.

Working with MSMQ Queues

You have to be able to specify a message queue before you can use it. To do this, you need a way to describe a queue uniquely and consistently in your applications. The .NET Framework provides three different ways to access a specific queue:

- **Specify a queue by its path**—A path to a queue looks like **<servername> \private$\<queuename>, netserver\private$\Orders**, which specifies the computer name (or "." for the local server) and the full path to the queue.

- **Specify a queue by format name**—This option uses **Format Name**, which is a string that describes the queue through some connection details and the queue's path, for example, **DIRECT=OS:netserver\private$\Orders** or using a special GUID that uniquely identifies the message queue.

- **Specify a queue by label**—This method uses the queue's label ("**My Orders**"), a value that you can assign through code or through the Message Queuing administration interface.

Using either the label or the path methods adds overhead, because MSMQ must resolve those descriptions into the **Format Name** that it uses internally to describe individual queues.

Using a **Format Name** directly avoids the name resolution, making it a more efficient method; it is the only way you can refer to a queue if you want your client application to be able to function when a queue is offline. However, specifying a queue by its path is the only option available when creating a new queue, because the other two reference options rely on properties of the queue that can be set only once the queue exists.

Sending Queue Messages

Sending a message to a MSMQ queue is a relatively straight forward process.

► To send a message to a MSMQ queue

1. Open the queue you want to send a message to by creating an instance of a **MessageQueue** object and specifying the queue name as a parameter to the constructor.

2. Set the **Formatter** property of the **MessageQueue** object to use the type of formatter (binary or XML) you want to be used for serializing the contents of your message on the queue. If you do not specify the **Formatter** property, the XML formatter will be used.

3. Create a new **Message** object and set the value of its **Body** property to the object you want to send to the queue. For example, an **OrderData** object containing the details of an order.

4. Send the message to the queue by calling the **Send** method on the **MessageQueue** object with the **Message** object as a parameter.

For a detailed example of sending a message to a MSMQ queue from a .NET Framework client, see Chapter 9, "Implementing Asynchronous Interoperability."

Retrieving Queue Messages

The **MessageQueue** class supports the MSMQ ability either to peek at or to receive messages. Peeking means that you examine the first message in a particular queue without removing it from the queue. This is a handy way to look at the queue and implement logic for handling messages in a different order from the order they appear in the queue. However, **Peek** allows you to see only the first message in the queue. Because peeking does not remove that message from the queue, you cannot then peek at subsequent messages.

Note: If you want to see all the messages in a queue without removing them from the queue, you can use the **GetAllMessages** method or the **GetMessageEnumerator** method.

After the application peeks at a message in the queue, it can elect to receive the message, or it can directly receive it without peeking. Receiving a message means that the message leaves the queue, and the application can do whatever is appropriate with the message. When an application receives a message, that message leaves the queue permanently, unless some process returns it to the queue.

Retrieving a message from a MSMQ queue is also a straightforward process.

▶ To retrieve a message from a MSMQ queue

1. Open the queue you want to receive a message from by creating an instance of a **MessageQueue** object and specifying the queue name as a parameter to the constructor.

2. Set up the correct formatter using the **MessageQueue.Formatter** or **Message.Formatter** properties. The formatting on the sender side must match that on the receiver.

3. Call the **Receive** method of the **MessageQueue** object to return a **Message** object.

4. Cast the value of the **Body** property of the **Message** object into the type of object you are expecting to receive.

Note: An application can peek or receive messages either synchronously or asynchronously. The **MessageQueue** class provides **PeekCompleted** and **ReceiveCompleted** events you can use to receive events asynchronously. Typically, an application using these events specifies a timeout to limit the duration an application sits waiting for messages.

For a detailed example of retrieving a message from a MSMQ queue in a .NET Framework application, see Chapter 9, "Implementing Asynchronous Interoperability."

Connecting to MSMQ from J2EE

So far, this guide has described how a .NET Framework application can implement asynchronous connectivity by sending and receiving messages to and from MSMQ. But what can MSMQ do for J2EE services and Java clients?

In general, enabling Java applications to interoperate with MSMQ is not an easy thing to do. Microsoft does not currently provide an MSMQ client for Java. To access MSMQ from a Java application, you need to implement other strategies.

At present, there are three ways of doing this:

- Using a Java to COM Bridge.
- Using a JMS Provider for MSMQ.
- Creating a Web service interface.

The following sections describe each of these techniques.

Using a Java-to-COM Bridge

Although native Java clients cannot talk direct to MSMQ, existing COM clients can talk direct to MSMQ by using the COM API. COM clients include Microsoft Visual Basic and C/C++ applications based on the Win32 platform. Third-party vendors supply products that let you call the COM API from a Java client, in effect linking Java clients to MSMQ through COM as shown in Figure 5.6.

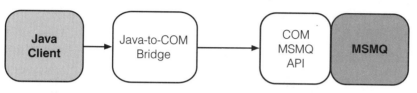

Figure 5.6

Accessing Message Queuing through a Java-to-COM bridge

The benefits of this approach are that the MSMQ COM libraries are quite extensive and provide a rich interface to MSMQ without requiring you to create any additional wrapper or interface. However, one disadvantage in this approach is that the Java client must be Windows-based to use the Java-to-COM bridge, and you must install the COM libraries for MSMQ. This requirement rules out using Java clients running on operating systems other than Windows.

The second issue is that network connectivity needs to use DCOM over a custom TCP socket. DCOM does not work well in Internet-based distributed environments.

Note: Intrinsyc provides a Java-to-COM bridge called J-Integra that does not require you to use a Windows-based Java client or to install the COM libraries for MSMQ. For more information, see the References section at the end of this chapter.

Using a JMS Provider for MSMQ

JMS is the Java Messaging Service API and is part of the J2EE specification. It provides an abstraction layer for several message queuing products, and all J2EE vendors implement JMS support. To access a queue using JMS, you need a JMS provider for that type of queue. Although this would be a good solution for accessing MSMQ from Java, there are currently no JMS providers for MSMQ.

Creating a Web Service Interface

A more involved approach to connecting Java to MSMQ is to use a Web service interface. In this approach, you create a .NET Framework Web service that exposes the functionality of MSMQ. A Java client can then access MSMQ by making calls to the Web service. Figure 5.7 shows this approach.

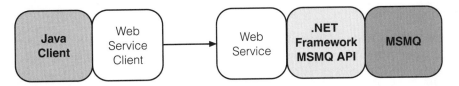

Figure 5.7

Accessing MSMQ using a Web service interface

For an example of a Web service interface that exposes MSMQ to Java clients, see the section named "Creating a Web Service Interface for MSMQ" in *Microsoft .NET and J2EE Interoperability Toolkit* by Simon Guest.

The Web service interface provides an interesting approach for linking J2EE to MSMQ. Again, with interest building in Web services, there is a lot of momentum in developing Web service interfaces for a range of components.

However, implementing a Web service interface for MSMQ does not provide all the answers and in some areas could be viewed as a backward step. Certain functionality that MSMQ provides would suffer from this approach, in particular:

- Reliable messaging.
- Transactional support.
- True callback.

There are new and emerging Web services specifications that offer solutions in the first two cases, as this next section illustrates.

Reliable Messaging

The problem with reliable messaging and Web services is that Web services use HTTP as the underlying transport protocol. Although HTTP contains features that enable connection retries, you cannot regard it as a reliable protocol. For example, HTTP does not report back to IIS on successful or unsuccessful message delivery. Hence if you link to MSMQ using Web services, you sacrifice the delivery guarantee that MSMQ provides.

The Web services reliable messaging protocol (WS-ReliableMessaging) is a new specification for providing reliable messaging over Web services. WS-ReliableMessaging consists of a protocol that can identify, track, and manage message delivery between two computers. The protocol itself uses SOAP headers and bindings to provide reliability. For more information about WS-Reliable Messaging, see "Web Services Reliable Messaging Protocol (WS-ReliableMessaging)" on MSDN.

Transactional Support

The Web services Basic Profile 1.0 specification does not implement support for transactions. Transaction support involves guarantees that a set of operations or transaction, either completes successfully or rolls back to the state before the operations started.

The standard example is one of transferring money from one bank account to another. This process involves reducing the balance on one account and incrementing the balance on the other. If one operation completes and the second operation does not, you can end up with money disappearing out of one account and not appearing in the other. By making these two operations a transaction, you ensure that either both complete or both roll back to the starting position, thus undoing all changes.

Implementing transaction support within a Web service is difficult, but not impossible. The transaction process in the preceding example requires a number of steps:

1. Create the transaction.

2. Send message requesting money from account #1.

3. Send message adding money to account #2.

4. Commit or abort the transaction.

A Web service is capable of handling only one action at a time. Also, Web service calls are stateless, so there is no affinity between the client and the service. For example, the Web service could send a message to a queue that requests money from the first account, but after it completes that task, it is finished. If the client calls back again, there is no inherent way for the server to know that it is the same client.

One approach to implementing transactional support in Web services is to store session state information in the Web application. In the preceding example, the Web service can hold the client requests for each of the four tasks in session state, and then process them only after it receives the commit request. Figure 5.8 shows an example of this scenario.

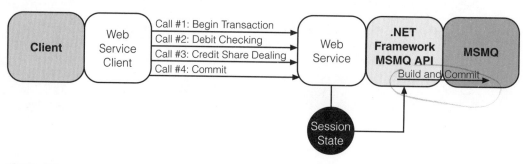

Figure 5.8

Handling a transaction using a Web service

Implementing session state in a Web service is not without penalties. Storing session state uses a lot of memory resources. This resource usage can cause limitations on scalability. It can also make you susceptible to denial of service attacks or even simple overload when the Web server runs out of memory due to the creation of multiple state objects.

Web Services Transaction (WS-Transaction) is a new specification that applies transactional support to Web services. It covers both atomic transactions and business activities. Atomic transactions are discrete, self-contained, short-lived transactions, whereas business activities cover transactions that take significant time to execute, and that you cannot simply roll back to the previous state. For more information about WS-Transaction, see "Web Services Transaction (WS-Transaction)" on MSDN.

True Callback

True callback support in MSMQ enables a messaging server to notify a client of the arrival of a message in a queue or of other events. To do this, you provide the queue with a callback location when connecting to the queue or sending a message. The queue registers the callback location and then sends notifications according to the selected criteria. Alternative approaches use UDP multicasting to notify multiple clients immediately. MSMQ version 3.0 implements the Pragmatic General Multicast (PGM) reliable multicast protocol.

This differs from pseudo-callback support, where the client has to poll the queue to see what is in it. **AsyncCallBack** is an example of this pseudo-callback function. The **System.Messaging** namespace supports **AsyncCallBack** through the **BeginReceive** and **EndReceive** methods within the **MessageQueue** class.

Note: AsyncCallBack is not a true callback function because although the operation spawns a second, non-blocking thread, the mechanism is still of a request-response nature.

Today's Web services can offer only pseudo-callback support, again because the current implementations depend on HTTP as the transport protocol. HTTP supports only request-response type interactions; this makes notification very difficult. If Web services become truly protocol independent (as in the Web services definition), it may then be possible to implement a true callback function using Web services.

Using IBM WebSphere MQ

WebSphere MQ (formerly MQ Series) is IBM's equivalent of MSMQ and has evolved from IBM's mainframe days. WebSphere MQ provides assured, once-only delivery of messages. If the receiving application or the communication channel to the receiving application is unavailable, WebSphere MQ automatically stores the message and forwards it at a later time. You can also configure WebSphere MQ to provide acknowledgement messages.

One of the main differences between MSMQ and WebSphere MQ is that WebSphere MQ runs on multiple operating systems, including Linux, UNIX, AIX, HP-UX, Sun Solaris, and Windows. It also supports messaging to more than 35 different platforms. You enable applications to use message queuing using a programming interface known as the MQI (Message Queue Interface). This is a cross platform API, so application calls on one platform easily port to another. WebSphere MQ provides both a Java and .NET Framework implementation of the MQI functionality, together with J2EE JMS Support.

In WebSphere MQ, queue managers manage the queues. Queue managers provide the messaging services for applications and process the Message Queue Interface (MQI) calls from applications. The queue manager handles the placing of a message in a queue or the routing of a message to another queue manager.

Note: Before you can do anything with WebSphere MQ, both the queue manager and queue must have been created and be accessible to the computer running the application.

For an application to send or receive a message, it must first connect to the queue manager. The queue manager provides a *connection handle*; the application uses the connection handle for MQI calls during that session.

After the queue manager creates this connection handle, the next task is to open a queue. You can open a queue for getting (reading) or putting (writing) a message. The queue manager is responsible for opening the queue, and returns an *object handle* if successful. Your application uses the object handle and the connection handle whenever it gets or puts messages on the queue.

When sending a message, you must open the queue for putting. Sending a message involves packaging the data you want to send into a data buffer and providing other information such as destination and message type. To receive a message, the queue must be open for getting.

Note: The maximum message size that WebSphere MQ supports is 4 MB, although not all operating systems support this range. For example, Windows and DOS applications have a 32 KB message size.

Administering WebSphere MQ

WebSphere MQ for Windows provides a Microsoft Management Console (MMC) snap-in for managing queue managers and queue definitions. When you install WebSphere MQ, this creates the default queue manager, which you can then configure. You can add different queue managers, and even change the default using the MMC tools.

Part of the function of the queue manager is to provide access to the queues. You can use the MMC snap-in to create four types of queues:

- **Local Queue**—A queue that belongs to the local queue manager.
- **Alias Queue**—A queue definition that uses another queue for its implementation, letting clients connect to the alias name but transferring the queue requests to another local queue.
- **Model Queue**—Allows you to define a model or template that an application can use to create queues dynamically.
- **Remote Queue Definition**—Lets you to provide a hook into queues configured on different computers.

Note: You can only send messages to remote queues, not receive them.

For more information about administering WebSphere MQ, see the IBM WebSphere MQ Web page.

Accessing WebSphere MQ from a Remote Computer

WebSphere MQ has a client component that you can install on a separate computer. The client enables applications to communicate with queue managers residing on a different computer, which could even run on a different platform.

Understanding the Role of JMS

In Chapter 2, "Understanding Enterprise Platforms," you saw that Java Messaging Service (JMS) is an API that provides application abstraction when accessing message queues. You also saw that JMS is not a product but a service definition. The JMS specification and API is part of J2EE, but it is up to third-party vendors to implement the standard. For more information about the JMS standard, see "Java Message Service API" on the Java Web site.

Several message queue vendors with a Java background have implemented JMS providers for their products. This provider acts as a binder between the message product and the JMS API. Ideally, this should enable portability by allowing you to switch operating system vendors without affecting the operation of the JMS component.

With JMS, you can implement two types of messaging support or messaging domains:

- Queue-based or point to point.
- Publish/Subscribe.

Queue-based messaging is similar to that in MSMQ. Both the sender and receiver agree on a pre-defined queue, using the JMS type **javax.jms.Queue** to handle asynchronous messages. A client can send a message to **MyPrivateQueue**, and the receiver receives the message back from the same queue. The receiver then acknowledges successful processing of the message.

Note: With point-to-point messaging, each message has only one consumer.

JMS also supports the Publish/Subscribe model by categorizing queues into topics using the **javax.jms.Topic** class. Publishing applications publish new messages to the topic (or queue) and any subscribers then receive the published message. You can create one-to-many, many-to-one, and many-to-many relationships between subscribers and topics.

The JMS specification enables you to control how durable topic messages are and therefore how long they remain in the topic queue after publication. Figure 5.9 shows an example of the Publish/Subscribe model. A feed provides a continuous flow of information, which the queue manager pushes out to subscribers. Applications, such as a stock trading program, can consume this information and traders then use it as a basis for buying and selling stock.

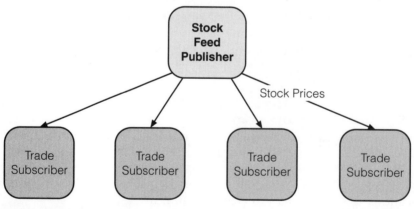

Figure 5.9
Publish/Subscribe domain in the JMS specification

> **Note:** A major difference between point-to-point and Publish/Subscribe is in timing. Point-to-point messaging works even if the client is offline. With Publish/Subscribe, clients need to be active to consume messages. *Durable subscriptions* provide a workaround to this, receiving messages while subscribers are offline.

Topic management can be an interesting challenge because clients can create and modify topics dynamically, meaning that fixed queues cannot be guaranteed. However, message vendors generally implement mechanisms for the management of topics. For example, the SupportPac MA0C for WebSphere MQ uses predefined system queues and channels.

JMS supports five message types:

- **javax.jms.TextMessage**—For simple string messages.
- **javax.jms.BytesMessage**—For sending raw bytes as messages.
- **javax.jms.ObjectMessage**—Sends a serializable Java object as a message.
- **javax.jms.MapMessage**—Sends a message that supports name/value pairs similar to a hash table.
- **javax.jms.StreamMessage**—Supports the same types as **MapMessage**, but where the contents of the message must be in order.

> **Note:** These message types all implement the **javax.jms.Message** interface.

Connecting to WebSphere MQ from J2EE Applications

There are three ways to connect to WebSphere MQ from a J2EE application:

- Using the WebSphere MQ Classes for Java.
- Using the WebSphere MQ Classes for JMS to Achieve Point-to-Point Messaging.
- Using the WebSphere MQ Classes for JMS to Achieve Publish/Subscribe Messaging.

The following sections discuss each technique.

Using the WebSphere MQ Classes for Java

The proprietary WebSphere MQ classes for Java allow you to connect to WebSphere MQ server, either directly or through the WebSphere MQ client. These classes allow Java applications, applets, and servlets to communicate with WebSphere MQ. The WebSphere MQ classes for Java are part of a package named **com.ibm.mq**. You must import this package to use classes in your Java code.

Sending and receiving messages using the WebSphere MQ classes for Java is a trivial task. You create a connection to a queue manager, open the queue, create a message, and then put it in the queue. The following code demonstrates this with a simple "Hello World" message.

```
// Create a connection to the QueueManager
MQQueueManager queueManager = new MQQueueManager("QM_MYQM");

// Open the desired queue
MQQueue queue = queueManager.accessQueue("myQ", MQC.MQOO_OUTPUT,
                                         "QM_MYQM", "myQ", "");
// Create a new message
MQMessage myMessage = new MQMessage();

// Specify the message format
myMessage.format = MQC.MQFMT_STRING;

// Populate the message data buffer with the "Hello World" string
myMessage.writeString("Hello World");

// Create the default message options
MQPutMessageOptions pmo = new MQPutMessageOptions();

// Put the message into the queue
queue.put(myMessage,pmo);
```

In addition to placing primitive data types or strings, you can also write Java objects out to the queue. This uses the standard Java serialization mechanism to write the contents of your object into the message buffer.

Note: While this is great for Java-to-Java applications, other platforms, including .NET Framework, do not understand the format of the serialized message.

If you want to use the WebSphere MQ classes for Java for interoperability, you have several challenges ahead. First, you must be aware the MQ classes for Java are not part of the J2EE specification, and therefore only WebSphere MQ implements these classes. If you are using a different message queuing product, you cannot use the **com.ibm.mq** package.

If you are happy using WebSphere MQ, your next problem is how to handle complex data. The differences between the serializers in the .NET Framework and Java means that you cannot put objects in a queue from one platform and take them out from the other. Hence interoperability at the object level is not possible.

However, you can serialize your data as an XML string, as discussed in the section about Web services in Chapter 4, "Interoperability Technologies: Point to Point." Java, the .NET Framework, and WebSphere MQ can all handle strings, so you can package up a customer object as an XML formatted string and then place it in the queue.

Using the WebSphere MQ Classes for JMS for Point-to-Point Messaging

The WebSphere MQ classes for JMS implement Sun's Java Message Service (JMS) interfaces, allowing Java programs to access WebSphere MQ. The WebSphere MQ classes for JMS support both the point-to-point and Publish/Subscribe models of JMS.

This section describes the point-to-point JMS messaging model. The next section describes the Publish/Subscribe JMS messaging model.

There are several key differences if you use the JMS classes to address WebSphere MQ. The most important is that you do not create a connection directly, but create a connection factory. These factory objects then exist within the JNDI namespace, protecting the application from vendor specific details. To obtain the connection factory, you need to retrieve the object from the JNDI namespace.

Note: If you do not have a JNDI namespace available, it is possible to create the factory at runtime.

After you have the connection factory, use the factory to create a connection that you then start. The following code shows how to obtain the connection factory and create the connection.

```
InitialContext ic = new InitialContext();
QueueConnectionFactory factory =
        (QueueConnectionFactory) ic.lookup(connectionName);
QueueConnection connection = factory.createQueueConnection();
connection.start();
```

After you create the connection, the next task is to create a session. The session provides the context for creating and consuming messages as well as the methods to create the **MessageProducer** object (used to send messages) and the **MessageConsumer** object (used to receive messages). You can create a simple, non-transactional, automatic acknowledgement session using the following code.

```
QueueSession session =
        connection.createQueueSession(false, Session.AUTO_ACKNOWLEDGE);
```

After the application obtains a session, it can create a queue and send a message using a **MessageProducer**. The definition for the queue can be stored in a JNDI namespace or created at run time. It is best practice to use JNDI to define the queues. An application can obtain a queue using the following code.

```
Queue queue = (Queue) ic.lookup(queueName);
```

Using the queue as a parameter, you can create a **MessageProducer** using the **QueueSession**. In the point-to-point messaging model, the **MessageProducer** will be a **QueueSender** as the following code shows.

```
QueueSender sender = session.createSender(queue);
```

Finally, you need to create a message of the correct type. Methods on the **QueueSession** object allow you to create any of the five types of JMS messages. You can then populate this message with the data you want to send as the following code shows.

```
ObjectMessage message = session.createObjectMessage(myObject);
sender.send(message);
```

You can use the **QueueReceiver** to receive a message using the **MessageConsumer**. You can create this from the session in the same manner as the **QueueSender**. You can then make a blocking or non-blocking call to receive a message from the queue. The following code shows how to receive a message from the queue. The code blocks until either a message arrives or the timeout expires.

```
QueueReceiver receiver = session.createReceiver(queue);
Message message = receiver.receive(1000);
```

The message type received is of one of the five types of supported JMS messages. To extract the correct message payload, you must cast the returned message into the correct message type.

Note: It is also possible to receive messages asynchronously.

JMS messages on WebSphere MQ have a different structure to that of standard WebSphere MQ messages, and the JMS messages need mapping to the WebSphere MQ format. However, this mapping is not important if you send a message through JMS and the receiving application is non-JMS, because you can then configure the queue's target client as MQ.

Using WebSphere MQ Classes for JMS for Publish/Subscribe Messaging

The preceding section described how to use the WebSphere MQ classes for JMS to achieve publish/subscribe messaging. This section describes how to achieve Publish/Subscribe messaging.

When you work with Publish/Subscribe messaging, you must decide early on which broker you want to use and configure it to run the WebSphere MQ classes for JMS. The broker has a record of all the subscribers registered for a topic. When an application publishes a message to a topic, the broker forwards the message to the subscribers.

Note: You add Publish/Subscribe support to WebSphere MQ through a SupportPac. For information about how to do this, see the References section at the end of this chapter.

WebSphere MQ offers three types of brokers:

- MQSeries Publish/Subscribe
- WebSphere MQ Integrator Broker
- WebSphere MQ Event Broker

Broker setup depends not only upon which broker you choose but on how you want to use it. Each broker has its own documentation for configuration and setup.

After the broker is sorted out, you must create JMS objects similar to those used in point-to-point messaging. Specifically, you need to obtain or create the following objects:

- **TopicConnectionFactory**
- **TopicConnection**
- **TopicSession**
- **Topic**
- Either a **TopicPublisher** or **TopicSubscriber**

The steps are similar to those for the point-to-point technique, as the following code sample shows.

```
// Create a connection
InitialContext context = new InitialContext();
TopicConnectionFactory factory = (TopicConnectionFactory) context.lookup(tcfName);
TopicConnection connection = factory.createTopicConnection();
connection.start();

// Create a session
TopicSession session =
      connection.createTopicSession(false, Session.AUTO_ACKNOWLEDGE);

// Create a topic
Topic topic = (Topic) context.lookup(topicName);

// Create a publisher...
TopicPublisher publisher = session.createPublisher(topic);
// ...or create a subscriber
TopicSubscriber subscriber = session.createSubscriber(topic);
```

Finally, you either publish messages or receive messages in the same way as in the earlier section on point-to-point messaging.

Connecting to WebSphere MQ from .NET Framework Applications

There are two ways to connect to WebSphere MQ from .NET Framework applications:

- Using the WebSphere MQ Classes for Microsoft .NET
- Using JMS and Third-Party Bridging Products

The following sections discuss each technique and describe the advantages and disadvantages of each.

Using the WebSphere MQ Classes for Microsoft .NET

The WebSphere MQ classes for Microsoft .NET provide access to WebSphere MQ in much the same way as the WebSphere MQ classes for Java. However, although they both use the same object model, the .NET Framework version does not support connection pools or sending messages to multiple queues or topics. Figure 5.10 shows how a .NET Framework client can connect to WebSphere MQ using the WebSphere MQ classes for .NET.

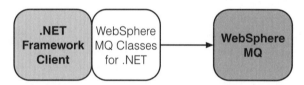

Figure 5.10

A .NET Framework client using the WebSphere MQ Classes for .NET to connect to WebSphere MQ

You can obtain the .NET Framework classes from IBM as part of MQ v5.3 CSD05, which stands for Corrective Service Distribution #5 (equivalent of a service pack). This fixpack installs the **Amqmdnet.dll** library in the **WebSphere/bin** directory. The DLL provides a set of classes that you can use with any .NET Framework application.

Note: CSD05 is supported by IBM. You can obtain CSD05 from the IBM Web site.

Although **Amqmdnet.dll** exposes managed classes, you should be aware that these classes make **PInvoke** calls to other MQ client libraries. Hence if your application makes calls to classes in **Amqmdnet.dll**, you need to install the WebSphere MQ client on the computer on which the application runs if you have not done so already.

Note: PInvoke enables managed code to call methods and functions on a Win32 DLL file. This avoids using COM for interoperability, but the .NET Framework cannot provide managed code functionality such as garbage collection for these calls.

Amqmdnet.dll exposes classes that are remarkably similar to those in the Java environment, helping developers to port code between the two systems. Data transfer between the Java and .NET Framework clients uses a raw format without any packaging or serialization.

You can send and receive messages from the queue using the same object and method calls as the Java classes, as demonstrated in the following code sample.

```
// Create a connection to the QueueManger
MQQueueManager queueManager = new MQQueueManager("QM_pagdal");

// Open the desired queue
MQQueue queue = queueManager.AccessQueue("XBikesQ",MQC.MQOO_OUTPUT,
                             "QM_pagdal", "XBikesQ", "");
// Create a new message
MQMessage myMessage = new MQMessage();

// Specify the message format
myMessage.Format = MQC.MQFMT_STRING;

// Populate the message data buffer with the "Hello World" string
myMessage.WriteString("Hello World");

// Create the default message options
MQPutMessageOptions pmo = new MQPutMessageOptions();

// Put the message into the queue
queue.Put(myMessage,pmo);
```

Note: Apart from the capitalization of the methods (lowercase in Java, uppercase in .NET), this code sample is identical to the Java version. This is a design goal of the MQI API.

Using JMS and Third-Party Bridging Products

You can use third-party bridging products such as Ja.NET or JNBridgePro to access the WebSphere MQ JMS functionality from .NET Framework applications. You can do this exactly like accessing JMS functionality from a Java client, with your .NET client making calls directly to the JMS API. To do this, create .NET proxies of all the Java classes that you require to send a message using JMS and invoke them from .NET. The proxies manage the communication between the .NET client and WebSphere MQ. Accessing JMS functionality through bridging has the advantage of allowing you to use familiar JMS APIs to implement messaging from .NET. At the same time, it makes the JMS API look like a regular .NET Framework API.

Figure 5.11 shows how a runtime bridge can allow a .NET Framework client to connect to WebSphere MQ using JMS.

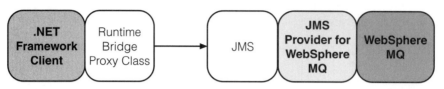

Figure 5.11

Using a runtime bridge to access WebSphere MQ JMS functionality from .NET Framework clients

Chapter 9, "Implementing Asynchronous Interoperability," shows a detailed example of how to access JMS functionality in WebSphere MQ from a .NET client using both JNBridge and JaNET.

Accessing JMS Messages from .NET Framework Clients

You have seen how .NET Framework clients can consume messages from WebSphere MQ with the WebSphere MQ classes for Microsoft .NET or using JMS through a third-party bridge product. However, there are some issues of which you need to be aware when consuming messages in a .NET Framework client that are placed on a WebSphere MQ queue using JMS.

The main issue with accessing JMS messages from WebSphere MQ is that JMS messages have extra headers that non-JMS applications do not understand. For example, the WebSphere MQ classes for .NET cannot un-package a JMS formatted message. However, if you use a third-party bridging product to connect to WebSphere MQ through JMS, this is not an issue as the bridging product handles and translates the JMS message headers.

To enable a .NET Framework client to consume JMS messages from WebSphere MQ using the WebSphere MQ classes for .NET, ensure that the Java application sending the messages sets the target client in JMS to MQ. This allows the Java application to send JMS messages without the troublesome headers. While the WebSphere MQ classes for .NET cannot un-package a JMS formatted message, they have no trouble un-packaging an MQ message.

Note: .NET Framework clients cannot reconstruct objects serialized from Java so any messages must be sent as basic data types.

A major interoperability issue with the JMS Publish/Subscribe model is that it is impossible to link in to the model with a .NET Framework client using the WebSphere MQ classes for .NET. The only way to access the Publish/Subscribe model from .NET is to use a bridging product that wraps the JMS calls. This is because clients create topics in a dynamic fashion.

WebSphere MQ does not implement a one-to-one relationship between queues and topics, because this restricts the number of allowed topics. The WebSphere MQ Classes for .NET do not support accessing topics. Also, because WebSphere MQ handles topic queues as system objects, .NET Framework clients cannot access the queues. Even the **MQQueueManager** class does not enable you to associate a queue with a topic. Hence only JMS clients can access JMS topics or act as publishers or subscribers. This makes interoperability using direct communication from .NET Framework clients using the WebSphere MQ classes for .NET very difficult to achieve.

Note: You can achieve this interoperability using a bridging product, such as JNBridgePro or Ja.NET.

In the next section, you go on to see how you can use the bridging functionality within Host Integration Server to link .NET and Java applications.

Using Host Integration Server 2000

This chapter has described how both MSMQ and IBM WebSphere MQ can enable asynchronous interoperability between .NET Framework and Java clients and you can connect Java clients to MSMQ or .NET Framework clients to WebSphere MQ. However, there are several drawbacks to each technique such as the loss of reliable operations or transactional support.

An alternative way to implement asynchronous connectivity between .NET Framework and Java applications is by linking MSMQ and WebSphere MQ through the use of a bridge. In this approach, the .NET Framework application connects to MSMQ and the Java application connects to WebSphere MQ. You then use a bridge to connect the two queues. Figure 5.12 shows a high-level view of this approach using the MSMQ-MQSeries Bridge that is part of Microsoft Host Integration Server (HIS) 2000.

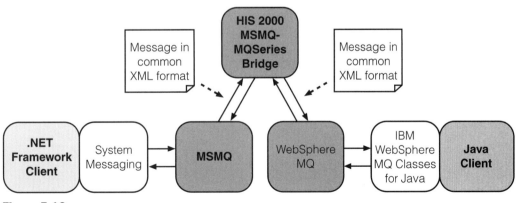

Figure 5.12
Using the MSMQ-MQSeries Bridge in HIS 2000 to enable asynchronous interoperability

HIS evolved from Microsoft SNA Server and enables organizations to connect Windows and LAN-based networking to host-based mainframe equipment. Most importantly from the interoperability perspective, HIS provides an MSMQ-MQSeries Bridge. By using the native message queue implementations, the bridge guarantees reliability and transactional message queue qualities.

For more information about HIS, see the Host Information Server Web site.

Bridging MSMQ and WebSphere MQ with HIS 2000

The MSMQ-MQSeries Bridge gives HIS the capacity to exchange messages in either direction between MSMQ and WebSphere MQ components. HIS can take messages from MSMQ queues and deliver them to WebSphere queues and back again.

Note: The MSMQ-MQSeries Bridge works with IBM WebSphere MQ, even though the bridge product name refers to MQSeries.

The MSMQ-MQSeries Bridge system contains two main components:

- **MSMQ-MQSeries Bridge**—Converts and transmits messages between the MSMQ and MQSeries environments.
- **MSMQ-MQSeries Bridge Manager**—Lets you configure, monitor, and control the messaging traffic through the MSMQ-MQSeries Bridge.

The MSMQ-MQSeries Bridge maps the fields or properties of a message to the corresponding fields or properties of the destination message queuing system. For example, if you send a message from WebSphere MQ to MSMQ, MSMQ-MQSeries Bridge analyzes the fields of the WebSphere MQ message and maps each value to its MSMQ counterpart.

In cases where one system needs an additional field that does not exist in the other, MSMQ-MQSeries Bridge provides the field during the conversion process. For example, suppose that a MSMQ message includes the **PROPID_M_TIME_TO_BE_RECEIVED** property with a specific value. The MSMQ-MQSeries Bridge maps this property to the **MQMD.Expiry** WebSphere MQ property and multiplies the value by 10 to change the units from seconds to tenths of seconds.

Note: The MSMQ-MQSeries Bridge does not restrict the content of a message. The message body can contain its own internal structure, which only the sending and receiving applications recognize. The MSMQ-MQSeries Bridge does not interpret this structure in any way.

For detailed information about how the MSMQ-MQSeries Bridge maps and converts properties from Message Queuing to WebSphere MQ and from WebSphere MQ to Message Queuing, see the "Microsoft Host Integration Server 2000 Developer's Guide" on MSDN.

Formatting Messages

The MSMQ-MQSeries Bridge in HIS 2000 enables you to exchange messages between MSMQ and WebSphere MQ. However, as Chapter 3, "Interoperability Fundamentals," discusses at length, mere message exchange does not guarantee interoperability.

You now know that the MSMQ-MQSeries Bridge does not manipulate the contents of a message as it is passes between the two queuing systems. Hence it is up to you to ensure that messages are in a common format that both the .NET Framework and Java applications understand.

To ensure that messages exchanged through the MSMQ-MQSeries Bridge are in a common format, you need to understand how .NET Framework and Java applications send and receive messages to their respective queues, starting on the .NET Framework side.

When a .NET Framework client sends an object to a MSMQ queue, either a binary or XML formatter serializes the contents of the object. Likewise, when a .NET Framework client receives a message, it expects the message to be serialized in either binary or XML format.

Java handles sending and receiving messages to or from a queue differently from the .NET Framework. A Java client can send messages to a WebSphere MQ queue using either the native WebSphere MQ API or JMS. If the client uses the WebSphere MQ API, the object travels as a simple byte stream rather than in serialized form.

Note: JMS also sends the object as a byte stream, but wrapped with additional JMS header information.

Sending Messages from .NET Framework to Java Applications

You can choose whether a .NET Framework client uses a binary or XML serializer when sending messages to MSMQ. However, Chapter 3, "Interoperability Fundamentals," described how the binary serializers in the .NET Framework and Java are incompatible. Therefore, when sending a complex data type object to MSMQ for transferring to WebSphere MQ and a Java client, the .NET Framework client should only use the XML formatter.

The message that the Java client receives from WebSphere MQ consists of a string object containing the serialized XML representation of the original .NET Framework object. Using the techniques described in Chapter 3, "Interoperability Fundamentals," the Java client must then interpret this string as XML, and de-serialize it into a matching object in Java. This process assumes that the data type object that the .NET Framework client side passes derives from the same common XML Schema as the one in Java. It is up to you to de-serialize the received object in the Java client correctly, as described in Chapter 3, "Interoperability Fundamentals."

Sending Messages from Java to .NET Framework Applications

As discussed earlier, messages sent to a WebSphere MQ queue using JMS include additional header information. Unfortunately, the .NET Framework does not understand this information. Therefore, if you want to send messages to a .NET Framework application, your Java client should use the native WebSphere MQ API or, if using JMS, set the target client to MQ.

In addition, because the WebSphere MQ API does not serialize messages that Java clients place into the queue, the Java client needs to serialize the object into XML format before sending it. You can accomplish this using the techniques in Chapter 3, "Interoperability Fundamentals." This ensures that the .NET Framework client can de-serialize the XML formatted message it receives back into an object.

Implementing the MSMQ-MQSeries Bridge

There are several requirements for implementing the MSMQ-MQSeries Bridge. This section provides an overview of these requirements, and the architecture required to set up the bridge.

Note: For detailed instructions about setting up and configuring the bridge, consult the HIS 2000 product documentation.

The MSMQ-MQSeries Bridge requires an instance of Microsoft Active Directory to be in place to function properly. This dependency springs from how the MSMQ-MQSeries Bridge works.

From MSMQ to WebSphere MQ, the MSMQ-MQSeries Bridge picks up messages from public queues published in Active Directory. These queues exist in a defined foreign site. The bridge then delivers the messages to a nominated queue on WebSphere MQ.

The reverse path involves the bridge picking up messages from the nominated WebSphere MQ queue and delivering them to a public MSMQ queue. Because you can only define foreign sites and public queues in Active Directory, operation of the bridge requires that you have Active Directory installed and configured.

You install the MSMQ-MQSeries Bridge on a computer running Windows 2000 or Windows Server 2003 that acts as a connection point between the networks. You must install a MSMQ routing server on the same computer as MSMQ-MQSeries Bridge, and this computer must be able to connect by a TCP/IP or LU 6.2 link to an MQSeries Queue Manager.

You must install WebSphere MQ on a Windows server to use the bridge to connect to MSMQ. This could be seen as a complicating factor if your existing WebSphere MQ implementation is on another operating system. One of the reasons for this requirement is to ensure that authentication works by enabling the computer hosting WebSphere MQ to participate in the same Active Directory forest. However, you can work around this issue by setting up a computer running Windows and WebSphere MQ, installing the bridge component, and configuring that computer to link automatically to the queues in your existing non-Windows environment.

In a test environment, you could run the MSMQ-MQSeries Bridge on the same computer as WebSphere MQ. However, this is not recommended in production. The computer running the bridge must either be a member server in an Active Directory domain (production environments) or a domain controller (test environments only).

Summary

This chapter first described how you can achieve interoperability by sharing a database between two platforms. It covered the current best practice for accessing data stores, including protecting code against changes. The second part of the chapter covers message-based interoperability mechanisms that provide support for transactions and for long-running operations. It described how you can use message queuing products from either Microsoft or J2EE vendors to make connections to Data tier components hosted either on the .NET Framework or on J2EE. With this knowledge, you can now look at the application architecture of the XBikes Web site and see how the developers applied the techniques in Chapters 4 and 5.

References

For more information about ResultSets
See the "JDBC Guide: Getting Started"
http://java.sun.com/j2se/1.4.2/docs/guide/jdbc/getstart/resultset.html

For more information about using JDBC
See "JDBC Data Access API"
http://java.sun.com/products/jdbc/

For more information about the Microsoft SQL Server 2000 Driver for JDBC Service Pack 1, including download information
http://www.microsoft.com/downloads/details.aspx?FamilyID=4f8f2f01-1ed7-4c4d-8f7b
-3d47969e66ae&DisplayLang=en

For more information about connecting to SQL Server 2000 with the Microsoft
JDBC driver
Microsoft Knowledge Base article Q313100, "HOW TO: Get Started with
Microsoft JDBC"
http://support.microsoft.com/default.aspx?scid=kb;en-us;313100

For more information about MSMQ features
http://www.microsoft.com/windows2000/technologies/communications/msmq/default.asp

For more information about the MSMQ-related classes in the System.Messaging
namespace and how to program against MSMQ
See the ".NET Framework Class Library"
*http://msdn.microsoft.com/library/default.asp?url=/library/en-us/cpref/html
/frlrfSystemMessaging.asp?frame=true*

For an example of a Web service interface that exposes MSMQ to Java clients
See the section about Creating a Web Service Interface for MSMQ in *Microsoft .NET
and J2EE Interoperability Toolkit,* by Simon Guest, Microsoft Press, ISBN 0-7356-1922-0.

For more information about J-Integra
http://j-integra.intrinsyc.com/

For details about implementing J-Integra
See "Introducing J-Integra 1.5.5"
http://www.intrinsyc.com/support/j-integra/doc/

- and -

"Java Servlet to MSMQ Example"
http://www.intrinsyc.com/support/j-integra/doc/servlet_com/ServletToMsmqExample.html

For more information about WS-Reliable Messaging
See "Web Services Reliable Messaging Protocol (WS-ReliableMessaging)"
*http://msdn.microsoft.com/library/default.asp?url=/library/en-us/dnglobspec/html
/ws-reliablemessaging.asp*

For more information about WS-Transaction
See "Web Services Transaction (WS-Transaction)"
*http://msdn.microsoft.com/library/default.asp?url=/library/en-us/dnglobspec/html
/ws-transaction.asp*

For more information about administering WebSphere MQ
http://www-3.ibm.com/software/ts/mqseries/messaging

For more information about the JMS standard
See "Java Message Service API"
http://java.sun.com/products/jms/index.html

You can obtain CSD05 at
http://www-3.ibm.com/software/integration/mqfamily/support/summary/wnt.html

For more information about HIS
http://www.microsoft.com/hiserver/

For detailed information about how the MSMQ-MQSeries Bridge maps and converts properties from Message Queuing to WebSphere MQ and from WebSphere MQ to Message Queuing
See the "Microsoft Host Integration Server 2000 Developer's Guide"
http://msdn.microsoft.com/library/default.asp?url=/library/en-us/his/htm
/his_dg_devguide_intro_libd.asp

For an example of how to use the managed provider for SQL Server to connect to a SQL Server database
See "Connecting to SQL Server Using ADO.NET"
http://msdn.microsoft.com/library/default.asp?url=/library/en-us/cpguide/html
/cpconnectingtosqlserverusingadonet.asp

For an example of how to retrieve data from a database using a data reader object
See "Retrieving Data Using the DataReader"
http://msdn.microsoft.com/library/default.asp?url=/library/en-us/cpguide/html
/cpcontheadonetdatareader.asp?frame=true

For more information about designing Data Access Logic Components in the .NET Framework
See Chapter 2, "Designing the Components of an Application or Service,"
of *Application Architecture for .NET: Designing Applications and Services*
http://msdn.microsoft.com/library/default.asp?url=/library/en-us/dnbda/html/distapp.asp

For more information about implementing Data Access Logic Components in .NET Framework
See the *.NET Data Access Architecture Guide*
http://msdn.microsoft.com/library/default.asp?url=/library/en-us/dnbda/html/daag.asp

For information about implementing the DAO pattern in J2EE
See *Core J2EE Patterns Best Practices and Design Strategies* by Deepak Alur, Dan Malks, and John Crupi (ISBN 0-13-064884-1).

For an example of calling a Web service asynchronously in the .NET Framework
See "Communicating with XML Web Services Asynchronously"
http://msdn.microsoft.com/library/default.asp?url=/library/en-us/cpguide/html
/cpconinvokingwebservicesasynchronously.asp

To install MQSeries–Publish/Subscribe support
Download the SupportPac MA0C from the Business Integration Web page on the IBM Web site
http://www.ibm.com/software/ts/mqseries/txppacs

6

Implementing Interoperability Design Elements

Introduction

The first five chapters of this book reviewed interoperability techniques in general without considering how to implement them in a distributed application within an enterprise environment. This chapter describes architectural patterns and programming techniques that you can apply to enable interoperability between .NET Framework and Java in a multi-tiered application.

This chapter refers extensively to the XBikes sample application. XBikes is a demonstration of best practices for implementing interoperability in a typical multi-tiered application.

This chapter starts with a high-level architectural overview of the XBikes sample application, then it reviews the typical three-tier architecture used in many enterprise applications, and then it introduces the new layers and components recommended for implementing interoperability. The chapter highlights the recommended interoperability components and compares them to those that the developers implemented in XBikes.

Understanding the XBikes Sample Application

Chapter 1 introduced the XBikes sample application as an e-commerce enabled Web site through which you can simulate buying bicycles and related accessories. XBikes is a three-tier distributed application that creates the Downhill Bikes online bicycle store.

There are two versions of the XBikes application, one built on the .NET Framework and one built on J2EE, both of which are functionally equivalent. Two teams of developers created these versions to demonstrate the following interoperability scenarios:

- You have an existing J2EE application and you want to add .NET Framework elements.

- You have an existing .NET Framework application and you want to add J2EE elements.

The Downhill Bikes online store is loosely based on a sample application also called Downhill Bikes, part of the original version of Visual Studio .NET and the .NET Framework 1.0. The first implementation of Downhill Bikes was a .NET Framework application designed to show off the features of the then new Web application framework, ASP.NET.

Note: Although XBikes implements the user interface from Downhill Bikes, it is important to note that both the .NET Framework and Java versions of XBikes were designed and built from scratch to demonstrate interoperability techniques.

The reworked sample application took the name XBikes or "CrossBikes" to reflect its new purpose in life, which is to demonstrate cross-platform interoperability.

The Java developers implemented the J2EE version of XBikes using best practice recommendations from Sun and IBM. Likewise, the .NET Framework developers implemented the .NET Framework version using the equivalent Microsoft patterns. Taking the two functionally equivalent versions, the developers then re-engineered both the .NET Framework and Java applications to implement multiple interoperability techniques, so that application elements in one environment can call corresponding elements on the alternate technology.

Note: XBikes illustrates multiple interoperability principles, so some design elements in XBikes show several methods of linking J2EE and .NET Framework, whereas in a practical design, you would select only one of these techniques.

The XBikes application design implements the pattern of use cases. Each possible user action, such as logging in or placing an order, is a use case. This equivalence appears in the names and breakdown of the various components within the application. The following are the six use cases or possible user actions in XBikes:

- **AuthenticateCustomer**—Logs a customer into the application.

- **GetCategories**—Returns and displays a list of categories from the product catalog.

- **GetProductsByCategory**—Returns and displays a list of products from the catalog that belong to a specific category.

- **GetCustomerOrders**—Returns and displays a list of all orders a customer has placed.
- **GetSearchResults**—Returns and displays search results from a user initiated product search.
- **PlaceOrder**—Places an order for selected products in the catalog.

Note: While both versions of XBikes provide the functionality of the six use cases, they do not handle some things that are essential to a production environment, such as security. XBikes is only a sample use case implementation to demonstrate interoperability and does not illustrate recommended practice for implementing security in a production application.

The next few sections review architectural best practices for multi-tiered applications in both .NET Framework and Java. These sections contain implementation references to the overall architecture of the two XBikes applications. Chapters 7 to 9 cover the details of how the developers implemented these interoperability components.

The companion CD to this book contains both the .NET Framework and J2EE versions of the XBikes sample application. For information about how to install and configure XBikes, see Appendices A and B.

Reviewing .NET Framework and J2EE Application Architecture

A central assumption in this guide is that your existing applications are designed according to best practice recommendations for application design on each application's host environment, whether it is .NET Framework or J2EE. Unfortunately, this is not always the case, because many application design specifications have developed over time or even evolved from previous architectures. Additionally, application designs rarely include interoperability as a factor. However, you can still apply the interoperability strategies described in this chapter to an existing application even if the application does not follow architectural best practice, although this makes implementing interoperability more of a challenge.

Before describing implementing interoperability, it is important to review recommended application architecture for multi-tier applications in both .NET Framework and J2EE. For recommended practices for distributed and multi-tiered .NET Framework application architecture, see *Application Architecture for .NET: Designing Applications and Services* on MSDN (*http://msdn.microsoft.com/library /default.asp?url=/library/en-us/dnbda/html/distapp.asp*). Figure 6.1 is from this guide and represents the recommended best practice for .NET Framework application design.

Note: Sun also provides best practices for J2EE application architecture, but this design applies equally well to J2EE applications.

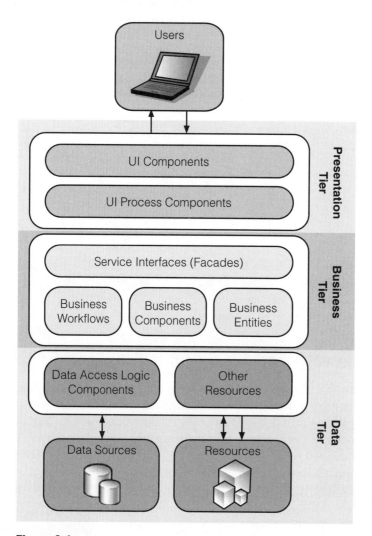

Figure 6.1

.NET Framework application architecture best practice design

As Figure 6.1 shows, it is recommended best practice to divide multi-tiered applications into three logical layers:

- Presentation tier
- Business tier
- Data (or Resource) tier

The following sections discuss the functions of the components within each tier and correlate them with the components implemented in both the .NET Framework and J2EE versions of XBikes.

For more details about each of the elements within the recommended application architecture, including best practices for implementing them, see *Application Architecture for .NET: Designing Applications and Services* on MSDN.

Implementing Presentation Tier Elements

The Presentation tier contains the necessary elements to enable user interaction with the application. The components of this tier can make up different types of applications, including the following:

● **Web applications**—ASP.NET or JSPs and servlets.

● **Desktop applications**—Windows Forms or Java's Swing or Abstract Windowing Toolkit (AWT).

● **Smart Clients**—Such as Pocket PCs and mobile phones.

This chapter considers the Presentation tier as a Web application, although this may not always be the case. However, this choice does not affect the interoperability architecture strategies that you implement.

The Presentation tier can consist of two types of components:

● User interface (UI) components

● User interface process components

In its simplest form, the Presentation tier can contain UI components, such as an ASP.NET Web Form or a JSP Web page. These components are only responsible for rendering the UI and handling direct interaction with the user. For more complex user interactions, you can design UI process components to orchestrate the user interface elements and control the user interaction. UI process components are useful when the user interaction follows a predictable flow of steps, such as when a user starts a wizard to complete a task.

The Java version of XBikes implements its Presentation tier as a combination of JSPs and Struts. Struts is part of the Apache Jakarta Project and provides a flexible control layer based on standard Java technologies. It also gives you a framework to underpin the Presentation tier. While the JSPs and servlets act as UI components, Struts provides the functionality of UI process components.

The .NET Framework version of XBikes Presentation tier uses ASP.NET, implementing a number of ASP.NET Web Forms that allow the user to interact with the application. This interaction then causes the initiation of one or more of the six use cases. There are no UI process components in the .NET Framework Presentation tier.

Implementing Business Tier Elements

The Business tier contains the necessary elements to implement the business logic and processing that the Presentation tier requests and consumes. Business tier components can then exchange data with the Data tier or any external services. Within the Business tier are programmatic elements that execute the business logic.

A Business tier can consist of the following elements:

- Business components
- Business workflows
- Business entities
- Service interfaces

Business Components

In a simple Business tier implementation, business components encapsulate and implement the functionality of a particular task or use case. In J2EE, these are also referred to as use case components or commands.

You could implement these components as classes or methods in a .NET Framework component library, or as COM+ ServicedComponents in a .NET Framework application. In a J2EE application, these could be plain ordinary Java objects or Enterprise JavaBeans (EJB) session beans. A Presentation tier client can then call these Business tier objects synchronously or asynchronously.

Using separate business components to implement individual use cases enables you to separate the functions within the Business tier logic, allowing the updating of individual use cases without affecting the remainder of the application. This provides useful change protection and reduces the risk associated with making changes to production applications. Implementing business components for each use case also makes it easier for large software teams to collaborate when developing applications.

The Business tier of XBikes implements business components for each of the six use cases that the application supports. To keep consistent with the functionality they implement, both the .NET Framework and J2EE versions of XBikes refer to these components as use case commands. These commands take the corresponding use case names with the word "Command" as a suffix, as in the following examples:

- **AuthenticateCustomerCommand**
- **GetCategoriesCommand**
- **GetProductsByCategoryCommand**
- **GetCustomerOrdersCommand**
- **GetSearchResultsCommand**
- **PlaceOrderCommand**

Both versions of XBikes implement the use case business components through the Command design pattern, common in J2EE architectures. The developers of XBikes decided to use the Command design pattern in the .NET Framework version of XBikes to keep the interfaces for each use case consistent.

For more information about the Command design pattern, see *Design Patterns: Elements of Reusable Object-Oriented Software*, by Erich Gamma, Richard Helm, Ralph Johnson, and John Vlissides (ISBN 0-201-63361-2).

The J2EE version of XBikes implements the use case commands as plain ordinary Java objects. The .NET Framework version of XBikes has separate .NET Framework classes for each use case. Each use case command implements a common **IUseCaseCommand** interface the developers defined as part of the Command pattern.

Business Workflows

Business workflows are usually only a requirement if you have long-running transactions or procedures that involve multiple steps that need to be orchestrated. Typically, business workflows involve the use of an orchestration product such as Microsoft BizTalk Server. Other orchestration or workflow product vendors have equivalent products.

Note: XBikes does not implement business workflows; it is only a demonstration application and does not require the additional functionality.

Business Entities

In multi-tier applications, data passes back and forth across the Application tiers. Business entities are objects that represent data within the application. Entities contain "snapshot" data, acting as an effective local cache of information. Other Business tier or Presentation tier elements can connect to business entities.

The data that business entities represent is typically not tied to a particular database table. A business entity usually incorporates a schema that is a de-normalization of the underlying database schemas. They can also represent data aggregated from many sources.

Chapter 3, "Interoperability Fundamentals," described complex data types made up from simple data types and used to store information about a particular business object. An example was where you design a custom complex data type to represent data about a customer, named **CustomerData**. The object can store data such as the name, address, and zip code of a customer. This **CustomerData** object would be considered a business entity component when implemented within the architecture of a multi-tiered application.

There are many data formats that you can use for defining a business entity in both .NET Framework and J2EE. Common formats include the following:

- An XML document.
- **DataSet** (.NET Framework only).
- Typed **DataSet** (.NET Framework only).
- Entity beans (J2EE only).
- A custom object with properties that map to data fields, and methods that perform data modifications through data access logic components, known as the Value Object pattern in J2EE applications.

Note: Custom business entity components are not a mandatory part of all applications. Many solutions (especially ASP.NET applications and .NET Framework business components) do not use custom representations of business entities; instead they use datasets or XML documents because they provide all the required information and the development model is more task and document oriented rather than object-oriented.

Business Entities in XBikes

Both versions of the XBikes application define the following business entities to represent the data that the six use cases require:

- **CustomerData**—Contains data representing a customer.
- **CategoriesData**—Contains data representing product categories.
- **ProductsData**—Contains data representing store products.
- **OrderData**—Contains data representing an order and its order details.

Deciding on a data format to represent the business entities in XBikes was one of the first tasks that the XBikes developers faced. As explained in Chapter 3, agreeing on a common data format for exchanging data across platforms is one of the fundamental requirements for implementing interoperability. There were several choices considered for the data formats on both the .NET Framework and J2EE versions of the application.

The ideal situation is where you develop both the .NET Framework and J2EE applications from scratch. Chapter 3 described how you could generate a custom data type object on each platform from a common XML Schema. The two environments could then exchange the serialized XML version of these objects. However, this situation rarely occurs.

The interoperability scenarios that Chapter 1 presents show a more realistic approach to interoperability projects, such as the following:

- Integrating .NET Framework components at the Presentation tier.
- Integrating .NET Framework components at the Business tier.

The first scenario integrates a new .NET Framework ASP.NET application on the Presentation tier that communicates with the existing J2EE Business tier. The second involves having an existing J2EE-based JSP and servlet Presentation tier communicate with a new .NET Framework Business tier. Both scenarios share the common feature in that a new .NET Framework application operates alongside an existing J2EE application.

Within these scenarios, there are factors that can make it difficult to agree on a common format for exchanging data between the platforms:

- Lack of ability to modify or change the data types used in the existing application.
- Application developers not able to work together or to establish a process for agreeing on a common data format.
- Non-ideal data type mapping with common XML Schemas.

An example of the last case might be in .NET Framework, where using a dataset or typed dataset is recommended over a custom data type. This is because datasets provide richer functionality at the Presentation tier level where you can use data binding to populate a data grid with the contents of the dataset with very little code.

Based on these factors, the XBikes developers decided to use the data format best suited for the given platform in each version of XBikes. Hence each version of XBikes uses data types specific to the platform on which it is built. To exchange data between the .NET Framework and Java versions, some extra components (interoperability adapters and service interfaces) were necessary to convert the data types into a common format. This chapter discusses these components in a later section.

The J2EE version of XBikes uses custom Java classes to implement the four business entities. The developers implemented these custom Java classes using the Value Object design pattern. This design pattern is common in J2EE applications when implementing business entity components.

For more information about the Value Object pattern, see *Core J2EE Patterns Best Practices and Design Strategies* by Deepak Alur, Dan Malks, and John Crupi, (ISBN 0-13-064884-1).

The .NET Framework version of XBikes uses typed datasets to implement the four business entities. Typed datasets are a feature of ADO.NET. A typed ADO.NET dataset is a class with an associated XML Schema, rather than an untyped dataset that is a class and has no associated schema. The typed dataset class derives from a dataset class, which inherits all of the methods, events, and properties of a dataset. This allows your application to use some of the rich features provided by a dataset, such as data binding.

Additionally, a typed dataset provides strongly typed methods, events, and properties meaning you can access tables and columns by name, instead of iterating through collections. A typed dataset also incorporates table and column names into the statement completion feature of Visual Studio. This lets you create code that is easier to write and read. Additionally, with a typed dataset, you can catch type mismatch errors when compiling the code rather than at run time. Creating or modifying a typed dataset is a very easy process using the XML Schema designer in Visual Studio .NET 2003.

For these reasons, you are recommended to use typed datasets to implement business entity components in a .NET Framework application. For more information about implementing typed datasets in .NET Framework, see "Creating XML Schemas and Datasets" on MSDN.

While datasets and typed datasets are recommended for use within a .NET Framework application, it is generally not recommended that you use them to exchange data with Java applications. The main reason for this recommendation is because there is no equivalent data type in J2EE to which you can map a dataset. Also, while you can serialize datasets into XML format, this XML format is specific to the .NET Framework, so a J2EE client cannot understand how to properly de-serialize them.

In XBikes, the developers used Java collections on J2EE and typed datasets on .NET Framework. This decision requires the use of interoperability layers to enable the two platforms to exchange data.

Note: However, you can use the typed dataset's **GetXML** method to generate an XML document based on the schema associated with the typed dataset and containing data from the typed dataset. The typed dataset's **ReadXML** method takes an XML document formatted according to the XML Schema associated with the typed dataset and populates the typed dataset with the contents of that document. Chapter 7 and 8 show how the developers used these methods to enable cross-platform data transfer in XBikes.

Service Interfaces

A service interface is a software element that handles mapping and transformation services to allow communication with a service, while also enforcing a process and a policy for communication. For example, you could have a service interface that exposes your business functionality as a Web service.

The .NET Application Architecture best practice design covered earlier in this chapter includes service interfaces as one of the elements in the Business tier. Service interfaces are useful if you plan to expose your business functionality as a service. They provide a client entry point that abstracts the implementation of your Business tier. They can also be extremely useful for implementing interoperability.

Note: Most application architectures implement a service interface as a façade.

Service interfaces can also act as a gatekeeper to your business components, handling more complex tasks such as authentication, validation, or caching. However, service interfaces should not implement business logic. Using a service interface in this manner enables you to concentrate any policy related code, such as auditing or validations, into one place. A simple service interface that implements the Façade design pattern can act as a pass through class. This class then implements member methods that call each of the underlying business components directly, aggregating them into a single interface.

In the Web service example, you would expose your business functionality through a Web service service interface (WS service interface). The WS service interface then handles the implementation details of the Web service itself. However, your interoperability scenario may require you to expose your business functionality through different interoperability mechanisms, such as message queuing or .NET Remoting.

Your application may also need to expose its business functionality through different communication channels, which you should implement as a simple service interface or façade. This service interface then aggregates your underlying business components into a single interface. It also consolidates policy-related code so that you can reuse this code across multiple service interfaces that handle different interoperability mechanisms. A later section covers how you can use multiple service interfaces in interoperability scenarios.

Using the Façade Design Pattern

Using the Façade design pattern to encapsulate Business tier functionality is a popular and recommended practice for J2EE applications. You can apply this pattern to both .NET Framework and J2EE applications to abstract multiple business components within a Business tier. The Façade design pattern provides a single client interface to access the Business tier functionality.

Note: You may see references to façades that encapsulate business functionality as service façades.

You should implement a façade for a core set of business functionality that you want to expose as a single interface. A simple application may have one façade that encapsulates all of your core business functionality. Larger applications may contain multiple façades that expose different sets of business functionality.

For more information about the Façade design pattern, see *Design Patterns: Elements of Reusable Object-Oriented Software*.

Business Façades in XBikes

Both the .NET Framework and J2EE versions of XBikes implement a business façade, named the business service façade, to encapsulate the functionality of the Business tier into a single interface. The business service façade provides an interface for the Presentation tier components at its front end redirecting calls from the JSP/Struts application in J2EE or the ASP.NET application in .NET Framework to the relevant use case command in the Business tier logic.

For example, in the J2EE version of XBikes, when the user logs on to the XBikes Web site, the JSP Presentation tier components make a call to the business service façade, which redirects the call to the **AuthenticateCustomer** use case command. The **AuthenticateCustomer** use case command then makes a call to the Data tier to check for the existence of the user's log on name and to verify the password. The same application flow occurs when a user logs into the XBikes Web site of the .NET Framework version.

In the J2EE version of XBikes, the developers implemented the business service façade as an EJB session bean. Using an EJB to implement the business service façade provides additional enterprise functionality such as session state, caching, and object pooling. Calls to the business service façade session bean create calls to the underlying use case commands that are implemented as plain ordinary Java objects.

For details about how to implement a façade in J2EE, see the Session Façade design pattern in *Core J2EE Patterns: Best Practices and Design Strategies*.

In the .NET Framework version of XBikes, the developers implemented the business service façade as a COM+ ServicedComponent. This approach provides the benefits of the enterprise features of Windows Server Component Services such as just-in-time activation, object pooling, role-based security, and transactional support. The business service façade ServicedComponent makes calls into the underlying use case command classes which then run as part of the façade's COM+ application process.

Note: In XBikes, the developers implemented the business service façade as a ServicedComponent to demonstrate how to create a service façade in an enterprise-class application. However, XBikes uses COM+ for demonstration purposes only and does not use the additional features.

Implementing Data Access Logic Tier Components

Almost all applications need to access or store data in some sort of data store or database. The Data Access Logic tier contains the elements necessary to access data from data sources and returns it to the Business tier. In Chapter 5, "Interoperability Technologies: Data Tier," the section "Sharing Data between ADO.NET and JDBC" looked at implementing a Data Access Logic layer within your application in order to abstract the functionality accessing the Database from the Business tier. Abstracting your database access code from the Business tier is a recommended best practice for both .NET Framework and J2EE applications.

The Data Access Logic tier can contain the following elements:

- Data Access Logic Components
- Data Access Logic Service Façade
- Databases

The next sections describe each of these elements.

Data Access Logic Components

Data Access Logic Components provide simple access to database functionality such as queries and data operations, and they return both simple and complex data structures. They hide invocation and format idiosyncrasies of the data store from the business components and user interfaces that consume them. Implementing your Data Access Logic in Data Access Logic Components allows you to encapsulate all the Data Access Logic for the entire application in a single, central location, making the application easier to maintain or extend.

Chapter 5 also described how the implementation of a Data Access Logic tier is different between .NET Framework and J2EE applications. J2EE applications use the Data Access Object (DAO) design pattern in conjunction with Java entity beans to implement components that encapsulate create, read, update and delete (CRUD) database operations for a particular business entity. In .NET Framework applications, Data Access Logic Components handle the CRUD operations for a particular business entity, possibly with the addition of database helper classes such as the Microsoft Data Access Application Block (DAAB) to handle direct communications with the database.

Note: For simplicity, this book uses the term Data Access Logic Components from the .NET Framework architecture to refer to the J2EE entity bean components that implement the DAO design pattern.

While you implement Data Access Logic Components differently on each platform, the principles of this abstraction layer are similar for both platforms. In general, you should implement Data Access Logic Components to handle database operations for each business entity.

The Java version of XBikes implements five data access logic components using entity beans. Each of these entity beans contains the logic to call the individual areas within the SQL Server database. These five entity beans are the following:

- **CategoriesDataAdapterBean**
- **CustomerDataAdapterBean**
- **OrderDataAdapterBean**
- **OrderDetailsDataAdapterBean**
- **ProductsDataAdapterBean**

An XML deployment descriptor provides the mapping between the entity beans and the SQL database tables. These deployment descriptors refer to a JNDI name for the database (**XBikesDB**).

The XBikes design uses Container Managed Persistence (CMP), so the Data Access Logic container handles all the SQL processing. This is in contrast to bean managed persistence (BMP), where the developer must write the SQL code. The container configuration contains the information to connect to SQL Server. The container passes this connection information, manages connection pooling and sends the native SQL call to the database to retrieve the necessary data.

The .NET Framework version of XBikes implements four data access logic components. These four components correspond to the four business entities defined in the XBikes application, as follows:

- **Customer**
- **Categories**
- **Products**
- **Orders**

The Data Access Logic components in .NET Framework implement the interfaces necessary to perform CRUD operations on the business entities' data. Chapter 5 covers how you can use the Microsoft-provided DAAB for .NET Framework to encapsulate all of the common code for accessing a database. The .NET Framework version of XBikes uses the DAAB to provide this encapsulation. Each of the Data Access Logic Components makes calls into the DAAB to access the database.

Data Access Logic Service Façade

The Data Access Logic service façade handles calls from the use case commands in the Business tier and sends them to the Data Access Logic Components or entity beans in the Data Access Logic tier. For example, in the .NET Framework version, the Data Access Logic service façade passes calls from the **GetCustomerOrders** use case command to the **OrderData** Data Access Logic Component.

Implementing a façade for the Data Access Logic provides the equivalent functionality of implementing a façade in the Business tier. You can implement a Data Access Logic service façade to encapsulate the underlying Data Access Logic Components in the Data Access Logic tier into a single interface that business components in the Business tier can consume.

You should implement a Data Access Logic service façade for your Data Access Logic tier if you intend to expose your Data Access Logic tier as a service. In most applications, the business components within the Business tier call the Data Access Logic components directly. However, it is not as common to expose your Data tier functionality as a service as it is with the Business tier.

Both versions of the XBikes application implemented a Data Access Logic service façade to support the different interoperability scenarios. The J2EE version of XBikes implements the Data Access Logic service façade as an EJB session bean. The .NET Framework version of XBikes implements the Data Access Logic service façade as a regular .NET Framework component.

Databases

At the root of any application's Data Access Logic tier is a database, normally relational in nature. The XBikes design uses SQL Server 2000 to implement the database for both the Java and .NET Framework versions. This sharing is possible because both the .NET Framework and J2EE version store their application data using the same database schema. Chapter 5 covered how you can share a database between applications built on different platforms.

Implementing Message Queuing Services

Chapter 5 also looks at using message queuing services to implement interoperability. Normally, you use message queuing to implement asynchronous connectivity between components running in a single environment. Asynchronous connectivity is desirable when you have long running transactions, or portions of your application (particularly at the client end) that are not always online or available.

A good example of this scenario is when a user places an order at an online store. When the user places an order, there are a number of items that need processing and these items can take some time. Because orders directly affect the profitability of the Web site and can be long running, you need to be able to run the order process asynchronously, so that the user can continue with other operations while the order process checks stock levels, authorizes payment details, and (importantly) takes other orders.

In order to support these scenarios, you can implement asynchronous connectivity through message queuing. When a user places an order, it goes into a queue until the order processing application can receive it. In the meantime, the application that placed the order on the queue can continue operating without interruption.

Both versions of the XBikes applications implement asynchronous message queuing to support placing an order on the Web site. Although they differ in actual implementation, the basic concepts are similar. The **PlaceOrder** use case command in both the .NET Framework and J2EE Business tiers calls a message queue component which places **OrderData** message objects onto a queue.

Note: While the XBikes applications implement message queuing to demonstrate asynchronous connectivity, they do not actually do any processing with the order and orders are simply placed onto a queue. Both applications have sample console applications that read order messages from a queue and insert the order into the database through the Data Access Logic tier.

The J2EE version of XBikes uses IBM WebSphere MQ for message queuing services. This design allows the developers to address the WebSphere MQ component either using the Java Message Service (JMS) API or through IBM's WebSphere MQ API.

Note: XBikes uses the JMS API.

The .NET Framework version of XBikes uses MSMQ for message queuing services. MSMQ provides the equivalent asynchronous support for the .NET Framework design.

XBikes Application Architecture for .NET Framework and J2EE

This section provides a summary of the architecture of the two XBikes applications without considering the interoperability components. The composition of the three tiers of the XBikes application is as follows:

- Presentation tier (JSP/Struts or ASP.NET)
- Business tier, consisting of:
  - Business service façade
  - Business components that implement logic for the six use cases

- Data tier, consisting of:
  - Data Access Logic service façade
  - Data Access Logic Components (five in the J2EE version, and four in the .NET Framework version)
  - The DAAB (.NET Framework version only)
  - SQL Server 2000 database
  - IBM WebSphere MQ Queue (J2EE) or MSMQ (.NET Framework)

Figure 6.2 shows the architecture of the .NET Framework version of XBikes.

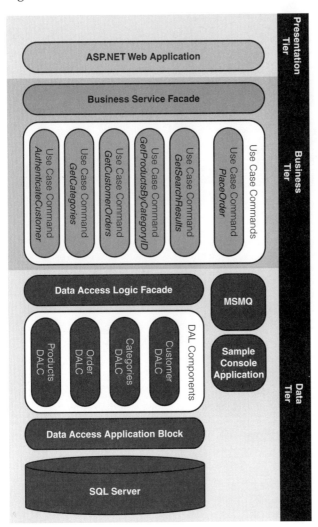

Figure 6.2

Application architecture for .NET Framework version of XBikes

Compare this to Figure 6.3, which shows the architecture of the J2EE version.

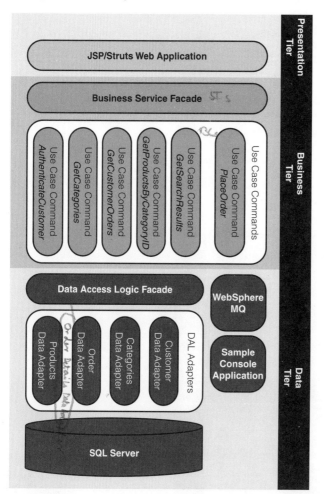

Figure 6.3

Application architecture for J2EE version of XBikes

Figures 6.2 and 6.3 show how similar the application architectures are.

Linking to the Reference Design

You can now link the architectural elements from the reference design to build up a table of component equivalence. Table 6.1 shows how the elements in the .NET Framework architectural best practice correspond with the components in both the .NET Framework and J2EE version of XBikes.

Table 6.1: Comparison of.NET Framework Application Architecture and XBikes Implementations

.NET Framework Application Architecture	XBikes .NET Framework Implementation	XBikes J2EE Implementation	Comments
UI components/UI process components	ASP.NET client	JSP/Struts	No equivalent of UI process components
service interfaces	Business service façade (implemented as a serviced component)	Business service façade (implemented as an EJB session bean)	None
Business workflows	Not applicable	Not applicable	Business workflows not implemented due to application simplicity
Business components	Use case commands implemented as .NET Framework components	Use case commands implemented as session beans	None
Business entities	.NET Framework typed datasets	Custom Java objects (using Value Object design pattern)	None
Data Access Logic Components	Data Access Logic service façade Data Access Logic Components DAAB	DAO pattern Entity beans with CMP	None
Data sources	SQL Server	SQL Server	None

Note: There is not direct equivalence at all levels between the two architectures. However, there is broad functional and conceptual equivalence.

The next section looks at how to implement interoperability between Java and .NET Framework enterprise-class applications, with reference to the implementation of the two versions of XBikes.

Implementing Interoperability

Chapter 1 described three main scenarios for interoperability between .NET Framework and J2EE applications:

- Integrating .NET Framework components at the Presentation tier.
- Integrating .NET Framework components at the Business tier.
- Implementing asynchronous interoperability.

The interoperability architecture and implementation strategies in this guide apply to all three scenarios. However, certain exceptions and restrictions apply, such as when you cannot modify an existing application, regardless of whether the application runs on .NET Framework or J2EE. The XBikes sample application takes a middle path—it does not represent the ideal scenario, with both .NET Framework and J2EE applications under development at the same time by the same programming teams. However, it does not take the rigid approach where you cannot modify the existing application at all.

Chapters 4 and 5 showed that you have several interoperability mechanisms to choose from:

- Web services.
- .NET Remoting with runtime bridges.
- Asynchronous interoperability through a message queuing system.

Each of these mechanisms applies best in different scenarios. Web services are best when you want to design your applications to use open standards and for compatibility with future applications. Runtime bridges such as Ja.NET and JNBridgePro are best for when you need high performance. Asynchronous interoperability usually involves only Business to Data tier interaction. However, the interoperability requirements for your application are likely to change, although hopefully not as quickly as the Web services specifications.

Your application design should reflect the reality that the interoperability mechanism it uses will probably change over time. Therefore, it is recommended that you implement additional interoperability layers and components to abstract the various connection points between your .NET Framework and Java applications.

These interoperability layers and components correspond to how you implement a service oriented architecture. The next section details these interoperability layers, makes recommendations for implementing them, and refers to how the developers implemented these in the XBikes sample application.

Describing Interoperability Connection Points

A connection point represents at a basic level, a client/server relationship where a client component consumes the services of provider. The diagrams in Chapter 1 show a matrix of possible connection points. Figure 6.4 demonstrates a basic connection point.

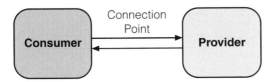

Figure 6.4
Simple connection point example

In two multi-tiered applications, there can be multiple connection points. Figure 6.5 shows a high level diagram of the possible interoperability points between two applications, one on J2EE, the other on .NET.

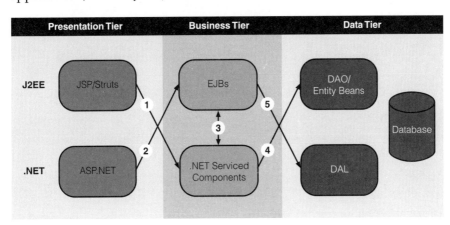

Figure 6.5
Interoperability points in multi-tiered applications

When designing your application for interoperability, consider each provider's connection point as a service. For example, in Figure 6.5, path 2 represents an ASP.NET Presentation tier client connecting to a J2EE Business tier EJB. In this example, the ASP.NET client considers the J2EE Business tier EJB to be a service. In service-oriented architectures, applications can communicate with a service through different channels or communication mechanisms. It is recommended that you create an abstraction layer between a client consumer and service provider that isolates the provider and consumer, thus masking the details of how they communicate from each other.

The XBikes sample application design supports the interoperability paths 1, 2, 4, and 5 in Figure 6.5. However, it does not cover the connection point that path 3 represents. This interoperability scenario depicts point-to-point connectivity between a Business tier application in .NET Framework and a Business tier application in J2EE. If you consider each provider end of each connection point as a service, the Business tier component on the alternate platform appears to the calling Business tier component as just another service. Hence the path 3 implementation is similar to that of any of the other paths.

The next section discusses the components that make up the interoperability layer which abstracts the details of the interoperability mechanisms for each connection point.

Interoperability Layers and Components

When implementing interoperability, you should incorporate the ability to cope with changes into your application architecture. The following are examples of the changes your application must cope:

- The interoperability requirements may change, requiring a different interoperability mechanism.
- Your application's interoperability requirements may require different interoperability mechanisms for distinct parts of your application at the same time.
- The interoperability mechanism itself may change as new technology appears.

To implement change-tolerant interoperability between a .NET Framework and J2EE application, it is recommended that you implement the following programmatic elements:

- Service interfaces
- Interoperability adapters
- Interoperability adapter factories

Figure 6.6 shows how these components fit in to a point-to-point interoperability scenario.

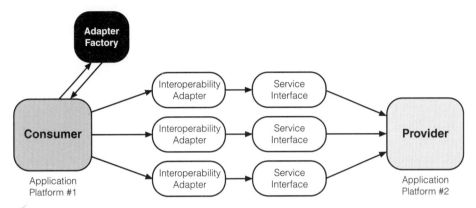

Figure 6.6

Programmatic elements for point to point interoperability

The following sections examine these interoperability elements in detail.

Service Interfaces

This guide has already described that a service interface enables an application to expose functionality to a consumer. It has also described how you can implement a simple service interface that follows the Façade design pattern to consolidate all policy-related code into one location. In addition, this service interface can aggregate the methods from multiple business components into one interface. This section explores how you can use service interfaces to enable interoperability between application components on J2EE and .NET Framework.

A service interface handles the details of the communication mechanism between a client and service, including mapping and transformation of data types between the client application and the service itself. This approach allows you to decouple the mechanism needed to communicate with the service from the service's business logic. It is this functionality that makes implementing service interfaces ideal for interoperability scenarios.

When designing your application for interoperability, implement service interfaces to handle the details of the interoperability mechanism you choose. Using service interfaces in your application provides greater flexibility when modifying the application later.

For example, you may have implemented a business service façade that exposes your Business tier functionality as a single interface. You can then create additional service interfaces to expose your business service façade through a Web service or through a runtime bridge such as Ja.NET or JNBridge. In this example, the service interface handles the details of the Web service or runtime bridge implementations.

> **Note:** It is important to appreciate that the data types used on one platform are unlikely to be the same as the data types on the alternate platform. The service interface transforms data from the common data type that the interoperability mechanism exchanges to the native data type of the service provider.

Consider the example where your Java Business tier interface works with custom Java collection data types and your .NET Framework Presentation tier works with typed datasets. Using the techniques discussed in Chapter 3, you can develop a common data format for data exchange between the two environments. In this scenario, the Java Business tier service interface accepts and returns data in the common data format. The Java service interface then transforms the data from the collection objects in the Java Business tier to the common data format the service interface exposes. On the .NET Framework side, a similar process occurs, except that the .NET Framework Business tier exchanges typed datasets with the service interface. Chapter 7, "Integrating .NET in the Presentation Tier," shows how the XBikes developers implemented these service interfaces.

For more information about the service interfaces pattern, see "Enterprise Solution Patterns: Service Interface" on MSDN.

Interoperability Adapters

Interoperability adapters provide the corresponding piece of the puzzle on the client side of the interoperability scenario. An interoperability adapter enables a client to communicate with a service provider through a specific service interface.

Interoperability adapters hide the implementation details of the interoperability mechanism from the connected client application. Interoperability adapters are responsible for transforming the data between the format that a client application uses and a common data format for interoperability.

Taking the example in the "Service Interfaces" section, the .NET Framework client uses a **CustomerData** typed dataset. The interoperability adapter then handles the data mapping from the .NET Framework typed dataset to the common data format for exchange with the Java application through one of the service interfaces.

You can compare an interoperability adapter to three established concepts:

- The service gateway pattern.
- The service agent pattern.
- A business delegate in J2EE.

The closest match is to the service gateway pattern, but for terminology reasons, this book refers to interoperability adapters. The comparison to the service agent pattern is less strict, because interoperability adapters provide only a subset of the functionality in a service agent. Like an interoperability adapter, a J2EE business delegate provides an abstraction of the implementation of the business services, reducing coupling between the Presentation and Business tiers.

You should create interoperability adapters based on the design of the service interface and the level of fine control that you require. Taking a service that implements the logic for one or more use cases, you may choose either to build an interoperability adapter for each use case or a single interoperability adapter for the service interface.

Implementing an interoperability adapter for each use case provides you with the flexibility to use a different interoperability mechanism for each use case. For example, you could set up your ASP.NET application so that one use case implements a Web service interoperability adapter to communicate with the J2EE Business tier, while another use case (requiring higher performance) connects through a runtime bridge.

Implementing an interoperability adapter for each use case also enables a migration scenario where you may have some uses cases running on one platform and others on another. For example, you may have an ASP.NET Presentation tier that calls an interoperability adapter for one use case that a J2EE Business tier implements, and at the same time have a different interoperability adapter for another use case that calls directly into the .NET Framework Business tier.

Interoperability Adapter Factory

An interoperability adapter factory enables dynamic selection of the correct interoperability adapter at run time. Although not a requirement for interoperability, the adapter factory provides the flexibility to change interoperability adapters easily. By implementing an adapter factory, you can configure adapter selection through a configuration file rather than by making changes to the code. An interoperability adapter factory also provides the flexibility in your design to incorporate as yet undeveloped interoperability mechanisms.

The interoperability adapter factory implements the Factory design pattern. The Factory design pattern is a well known pattern that allows a client to create an object based on predetermined settings.

You are recommended to implement one or more interoperability adapter factories to enable flexibility in which interoperability mechanisms you can use. For example, you may have multiple interoperability adapters that call into the same service, but through different interoperability mechanisms. A client calls the interoperability adapter factory to determine which interoperability adapter to use to call the service. The interoperability adapter factory looks in the configuration settings to see which interoperability adapter to use, and then it creates and returns an instance of the proper adapter to the client.

The interoperability adapter factory should return objects with only one type of interface. If you implement multiple interoperability adapters to communicate with the same service, but through different service interfaces, each interoperability adapter should implement the same interface.

You should implement an interoperability adapter factory for each service with which you want you communicate. For example, your Business tier application might communicate with both a Data Access Logic tier and a message queuing service. The Data Access Logic tier and message queuing service do not implement the same interfaces, so you need a separate factory to return the appropriate interoperability adapter for each one.

For more information about the Factory design pattern, see *Design Patterns: Elements of Reusable Object-Oriented Software*.

Adding Interoperability Components to a Multi-Tiered application

It is recommended to apply the following best practices when implementing interoperability layers between each of the interoperability connection points linking multi-tiered applications:

- Implement service interfaces that expose each tier's façade through the interoperability mechanisms you require.
- Create interoperability adapters either for each service interface or for each use case, depending on the level of fine control you require.
- Implement an interoperability adapter factory to enable dynamic selection of interoperability adapters for each service (or resource) with which your application needs to communicate.
- Provide multiple abstraction layers to ensure maximum flexibility for future developments.

Figure 6.7 shows how these interoperability elements link into the elements of a multi-tiered application from the best practices diagram in *Application Architecture for .NET: Designing Applications and Services.*

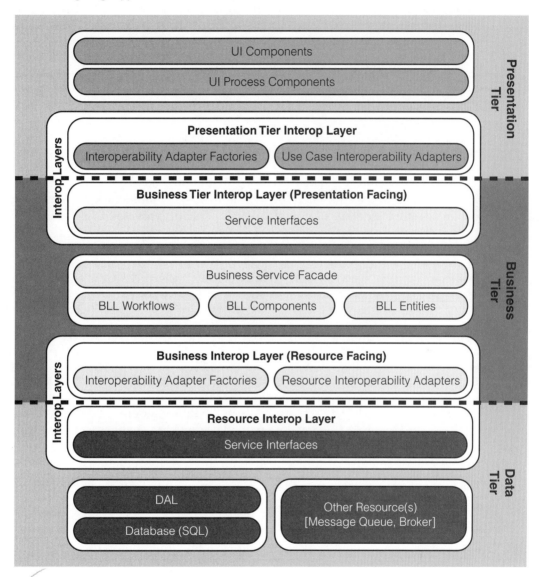

Figure 6.7
Linking interoperability elements into a multi-tiered application

Now that the interoperability elements have been described, it is time to see how the developers implemented these in the XBikes sample application.

Implementing Interoperability in XBikes

The development team faced several interesting and unusual challenges when they integrated the interoperability elements to the XBikes application:

- The application should demonstrate multiple interoperability techniques.
- The application should not be over-complicated.
- The application should be simple to configure.
- The application should not incur excessive performance penalties from the interoperability methods.

Achieving these aims involved adding interoperability components to the design of both the .NET Framework and J2EE versions of XBikes. This next section covers these changes at the architectural level, looking first at how the developers customized the J2EE version, and the equivalent process in the .NET Framework version. Chapters 7 to 9 then show the details of how the developers implemented these components.

Note: The XBikes application implements multiple service interfaces and interoperability adapters between each connection point to demonstrate how to use each interoperability mechanism. However, in a production environment, you would probably implement only one or two between each connection point, depending on your interoperability requirements.

Adding J2EE Presentation to Business Tier Interoperability

This section looks at the interoperability components that the developers designed into the Presentation and Business tiers of the J2EE version of XBikes to enable interoperability with the corresponding tiers in the .NET Framework version. The client-facing JSP/Struts components in the Presentation tier did not change significantly. However, the developers made significant changes to the way in which calls from the Presentation tier pass to the Business tier. These changes involved adding interoperability components to both the J2EE Presentation and Business tiers.

The following are components that add interoperability features to the J2EE version:

- Service interfaces in the Business tier.
- Use case interoperability adapters in the Presentation tier.
- Use case interoperability adapter factory in the Presentation tier.
- An XML configuration file for the use case interoperability adapter factory.

Figure 6.8 shows how the developers implemented these components.

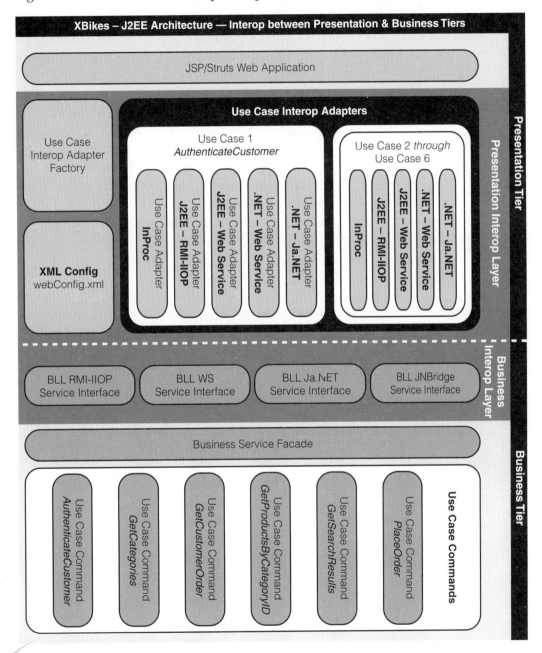

Figure 6.8

XBikes on J2EE Presentation and business tiers with interoperability elements added

The next section describes the interoperability components the developers added.

J2EE Service Interfaces

To expose the J2EE Business tier to both the J2EE and .NET Framework Presentation tiers, the developers added multiple service interfaces. Each service interface exposes the J2EE Business tier through different interoperability mechanisms. There are four services interfaces in the J2EE Business tier:

- **Remote Method Invocation over Internet Inter-ORB Protocol (RMI-IIOP)** — Exposes the J2EE Business tier through RMI-IIOP for remote consumption by the J2EE Presentation tier.

- **Web service** — Exposes the J2EE Business tier through a Web service for consumption by either the .NET Framework or J2EE Presentation tiers.

- **Ja.NET** — Exposes the J2EE Business tier through a Ja.NET runtime bridge for consumption by the .NET Presentation tier.

- **JNBridgePro** — Exposes the J2EE Business tier through a JNBridge runtime bridge for consumption by the .NET Presentation tier.

Although the RMI-IIOP service interface is specific to J2EE, the WS service interface can field requests from either environment.

Note: RMI-IIOP uses Remote Method Invocation, the Java equivalent of .NET Remoting.

J2EE Use Case Interoperability Adapters

To communicate with either the J2EE or .NET Framework Business tiers, the developers added interoperability adapters to the J2EE Presentation tier. For flexibility, the XBikes developers implemented a series of interoperability adapters for each use case, making it easy to select which interoperability technology to use, depending on whether the next tier is on the same or the alternate platform. The XBikes design refers to these interoperability adapters as use case interoperability adapters.

Take the example of the **AuthenticateCustomer** use case. For this use case, the J2EE developers implemented five use case interoperability adapters:

- **Inproc** — Addresses J2EE Business tier's business service façade directly through an in-process call in a single computer environment.

- **RMI-IIOP** — Addresses J2EE Business tier RMI-IIOP service interface.

- **J2EE Web service** — Addresses J2EE Business tier WS service interface.

- **.NET Framework Web service** — Addresses .NET Framework Business tier WS service interface.

- **Ja.NET** — Addresses .NET Framework Business tier Ja.NET service interface.

Here you can see that there are three ways of linking from the J2EE Presentation tier to the J2EE Business tier, and two ways of linking from the J2EE Presentation tier to the .NET Framework Business tier.

Because the design implements five interoperability adapters for each of the six use cases, there are a total of thirty use case interoperability adapters in the XBikes J2EE Presentation tier.

J2EE Use Case Interoperability Adapter Factory

To increase the flexibility in selecting interoperability adapters, the developers added an interoperability factory to the J2EE Presentation tier. Rather than call the use case interoperability adapters directly, the J2EE Presentation tier components first call an interoperability adapter factory, which the design calls the use case interoperability factory. The factory then checks with an XML configuration file to discover which use case interoperability adapter to select for each use case. The J2EE Presentation tier components then invoke that use case interoperability adapter to connect to the .NET Framework or J2EE Business tiers.

Note: This configuration technique allows you to specify different use case interoperability adapters for individual use cases, giving you maximum flexibility. If you do not foresee the need to change the adapters, you can omit the factory and simply load the correct adapter within your Presentation tier logic.

For example, when a user tries to log on to the XBikes Web site, this action requires the **AuthenticateCustomer** use case. Rather than select and call the use case interoperability adapter directly, the Web page calls the use case interoperability adapter factory. The use case interoperability adapter factory checks with the configuration file, which contains configuration information mapping use cases to use case interoperability adapters. The factory then returns and loads the correct use case interoperability adapter for the requested use case.

J2EE XML Configuration File

The use case interoperability adapter factory in the J2EE application retrieves configuration information from **WebConfig.xml.** This file contains a text-based listing of settings that link the use cases to the use case interoperability adapters. Hence the **AuthenticateCustomer** use case might be set to use the .NET Framework Web service use case interoperability adapter, whereas the **GetCategories** use case could be set to use the RMI-IIOP use case interoperability adapter. This ensures no interdependence between use cases.

For more information about the settings available to the use case interoperability adapter factory in the J2EE Presentation tier, see Appendix A.

Adding J2EE Business to Data Tier Interoperability

The developers added interoperability components on the J2EE Business and Data tiers to enable interoperability. The J2EE XBikes application has two resources in the Data tier—the SQL Server database and a WebSphere MQ message queuing system. Instead of calling resources in the Data tier directly, the J2EE Business tier components make calls through the various interoperability components.

Interoperability components added to enable interoperability on the J2EE Business and Data tiers include the following:

- Service interfaces in the Data tier.
- Resource interoperability adapters in the Business tier.
- Resource interoperability adapter factories in the Business tier.
- An XML configuration file for the resource interoperability adapter factories.

Figure 6.9 shows how these elements appear.

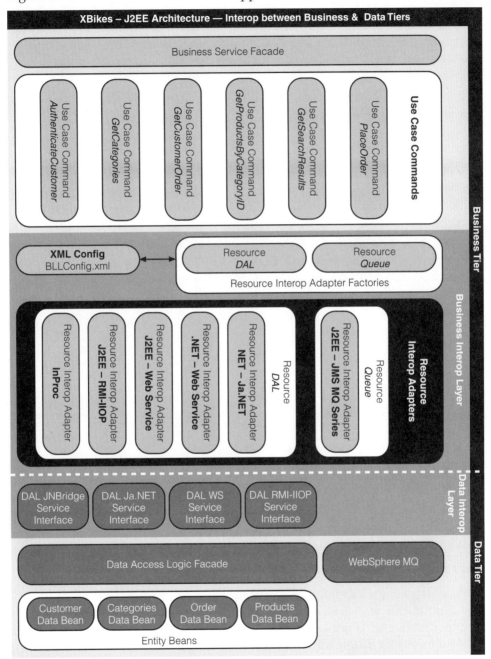

Figure 6.9

XBikes on J2EE Business and Data tiers with interoperability elements added

The next section describes the interoperability components the developers added.

J2EE Service Interfaces

The developers added multiple service interfaces to expose the resources in the J2EE Data tier to both the J2EE and .NET Framework Business tiers. Each service interface exposes a resource in the J2EE Data tier through a different interoperability mechanism.

There are four service interfaces to expose the database resource, or Data Access Logic tier, in the J2EE Data tier:

- **Remote Method Invocation over Internet Inter-Orb Protocol (RMI-IIOP)** — Exposes the J2EE Data Access Logic resource by way of RMI-IIOP for remote consumption by the J2EE Business tier.
- **Web service** — Exposes the J2EE Data Access Logic resource through a Web service for consumption by either the .NET Framework or J2EE Business tiers.
- **Ja.NET** — Exposes the J2EE Data Access Logic resource through a Ja.NET runtime bridge for consumption by the .NET Framework Business tier.
- **JNBridgePro** — Exposes the J2EE Data Access Logic resource through a JNBridge runtime bridge for consumption by the .NET Framework Business tier.

Like with the Presentation to Business tier interface, the RMI-IIOP service interface is J2EE-specific; whereas the WS service interface can field requests from either environment.

There are three service interfaces that expose the WebSphere MQ message queuing resource:

- **RMI-IIOP-JMS** — Exposes the WebSphere MQ resource for remote consumption by the J2EE Business tier.
- **Ja.NET-JMS** — Exposes the WebSphere MQ resource through a Ja.NET runtime bridge that uses JMS to connect to the .NET Framework Business tier.
- **JNBridge-JMS** — Exposes the WebSphere MQ resource through JNBridge that uses JMS to connect to the .NET Framework Business tier.

The developers also implemented a sample console application that reads messages from the WebSphere MQ message queue and sends them to the Data Access Logic service façade.

J2EE Resource Interoperability Adapters

The developers also added interoperability adapters to the J2EE Business tier to communicate with either the J2EE or .NET Framework Data tiers. They also implemented a set of interoperability adapters for each resource in the Data tier to demonstrate multiple interoperability techniques. The design refers to these as resource interoperability adapters. Unlike the use case interoperability adapters in the J2EE Presentation tier where there is a set of interoperability adapters for each use case, there is only one set of resource interoperability adapters for each resource's service interface.

To communicate with the Data Access Logic resource in both the .NET Framework and J2EE Data tiers, the developers implemented the following resource interoperability adapters:

- **InProc**—Addresses the Data Access Logic service façade in the J2EE Data tier directly through an in-process call in a single computer environment.
- **RMI-IIOP**—Addresses the Data Access Logic resource RMI-IIOP service interface in the J2EE Data tier.
- **J2EE Web service**—Addresses the Data Access Logic resource WS service interface in the J2EE Data tier.
- **.NET Framework Web service**—Addresses the Data Access Logic resource WS service interface in the .NET Framework Data tier.
- **Ja.NET**—Addresses the Data Access Logic resource Ja.NET service interface in the .NET Framework Data tier.

This gives you three ways of linking from the J2EE Business tier to the Data Access Logic resource in the J2EE Data tier, and two ways of linking from the J2EE Business tier to the Data Access Logic resource in the .NET Framework Data tier.

To communicate with the WebSphere MQ message queuing resource in the J2EE Data tier, the developers implemented only one resource interoperability adapter. This uses the JMS API to place messages in the WebSphere queue. The **PlaceOrder** use case command in the Business tier is the only process that calls this resource interoperability adapter.

J2EE Resource Interoperability Factories

The developers added interoperability adapter factories to the J2EE Business tier to provide flexibility when selecting the interoperability mechanism for connecting to Data Access Logic and queue resources in the J2EE Data tier. Instead of calling the resource interoperability adapters directly, the J2EE Business tier components first call the interoperability adapter factory, which the design calls the resource interoperability factory. The factory checks with an XML configuration file to discover which interoperability adapter to select to connect to the resource. The J2EE Business tier components then use that resource interoperability adapter to connect to the corresponding resource in the .NET Framework or J2EE Data tiers.

The XBikes design implements two resource interoperability adapter factories:

- Data Access Logic
- Queue

The resource interoperability adapter factories work the same way as the use case interoperability adapter factory in the Presentation tier. The only difference is that they return interoperability adapters for the Data Access Logic and message queue resources in the Data tier.

Like with the Presentation tier, this configuration technique allows you to specify different resource interoperability adapters for two resources, giving you maximum flexibility. If you do not foresee the need to change the adapters, you can omit the factory and simply load the correct adapter within your Business tier logic. However, it is recommended that you implement interoperability adapter factories to keep your application responsive to future changes.

J2EE XML Configuration File

The resource interoperability adapter factory in the J2EE application retrieves configuration information from an XML configuration file named Bllconfig.xml. This XML file contains settings linking the resources to the resource interoperability adapters. For example, you might configure the Data Access Logic resource interoperability factory to use the .NET Framework Web service resource interoperability adapter for all calls to the Data Access Logic.

For more information about the settings available to the resource interoperability adapter factories in the J2EE Business tier, see Appendix A.

Adding .NET Framework Presentation to Business Tier Interoperability

The interoperability components the developers implemented in the .NET Framework Presentation and Business tiers are very similar to those in the corresponding tiers of the J2EE version of XBikes. The components that add interoperability features to the .NET Framework version include the following:

- Service interfaces in the Business tier.
- Use case interoperability adapters in the Presentation tier.
- Use case interoperability adapter factory in the Presentation tier.
- An XML configuration file for the use case interoperability adapter factory.

Figure 6.10 shows how the linking of the Presentation and Business tiers with the .NET Framework interoperability components added.

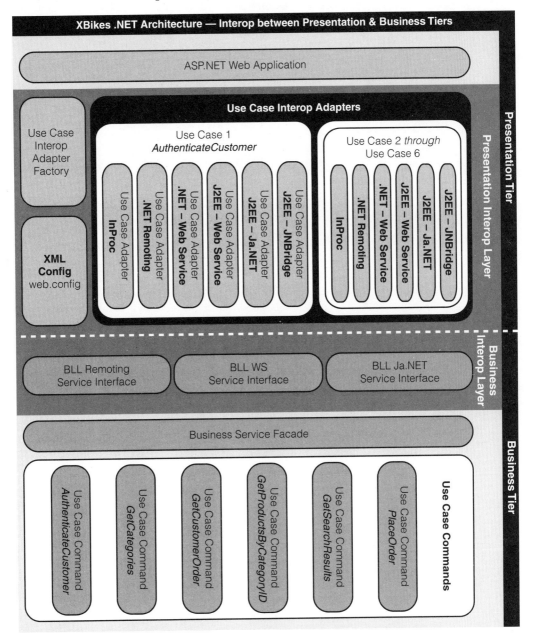

Figure 6.10

XBikes on .NET Framework Presentation and Business tiers with interoperability elements added

The next section describes the interoperability components the developers added.

.NET Framework Service Interfaces

To expose the .NET Framework Business tier to both the .NET Framework and J2EE Presentation tiers, multiple service interfaces were added. In the J2EE Business tier, each service interfaces exposes the .NET Framework Business tier by way of different interoperability mechanism. There are three services interfaces in the .NET Framework Business tier. The service interfaces are the following:

- **.NET Remoting**—Exposes the .NET Framework Business tier by way of .NET Remoting so that it can be consumed by the .NET Framework Presentation tier remotely.

- **Web service**—Exposes the .NET Framework Business tier by way of a Web service so that it can be consumed by either the .NET Framework or J2EE Presentation tiers.

- **Ja.NET**—Exposes the .NET Framework Business tier by way of Ja.Net for consumption by the J2EE Presentation tier.

Although the .NET Remoting service interface is .NET Framework-specific, the WS service interface can field requests from either environment.

Note: The .NET Remoting service interface uses typed datasets to exchange data between .NET Framework components. There is a known performance issue when sending **DataSet** objects across .NET Remoting calls. This is due to the way **DataSet** objects are serialized in the .NET Framework version 1.0 and 1.1. In a production application, consider implementing surrogate classes that implement their own serialization process for higher performance.

.NET Framework Use Case Interoperability Adapters

As in the J2EE version, to communicate with either the J2EE or .NET Framework Business tiers, interoperability adapters were added to the .NET Framework Presentation tier. In the J2EE Presentation tier, a series of interoperability adapters were implemented for each use case. This enables you to choose different interoperability mechanisms to connect for each use case. These interoperability adapters are referred to as use case interoperability adapters.

The .NET Framework application requires different use case interoperability adapters than the J2EE application to reflect the mechanisms for communicating between the .NET Framework and J2EE Presentation and Business tiers. The .NET Framework developers implemented the following six interoperability adapters for each use case:

- **InProc or native mode adapter**—Addresses .NET business façade directly.
- **.NET Remoting adapter**—Addresses .NET Remoting service interface.
- **.NET Web services adapter**—Addresses .NET WS service interface.
- **J2EE Web services adapter**—Addresses J2EE WS service interface.
- **J2EE Ja.NET adapter**—Addresses J2EE Ja.NET service interface.
- **J2EE JNBridge adapter**—Addresses J2EE JNBridge service interface.

There are three ways of linking from the .NET Framework Presentation tier to the .NET Framework Business tier and three ways of linking from the .NET Framework Presentation tier to the J2EE Business tier for each use case. Because six interoperability adapters are implemented for each of the six use cases, there are a total of 36 use case interoperability adapters in the XBikes .NET Framework Presentation tier.

Note: The InProc use case interoperability adapter can only be used in a single computer environment when calls can be made natively to the Business tier on the same computer without the need for going across the network.

.NET Framework Use Case Interoperability Adapter Factory

An interoperability adapter factory was added to the .NET Framework Presentation tier so you can use a variety of interoperability mechanisms. Instead of calling the use case interoperability adapters directly, the .NET Framework Presentation tier components first call an interoperability adapter factory, referred to as use case interoperability factory, which then checks with an XML configuration file to discover which use case interoperability adapter to use for each use case. The .NET Framework Presentation tier components then use that use case interoperability adapter to connect to the .NET Framework or J2EE Business tiers.

The use case interoperability adapter factory in the .NET Framework Presentation tier is similar to the one in the J2EE Presentation tier.

.NET Framework XML Configuration File

The use case interoperability adapter factory in the .NET Framework version of the XBikes application retrieves configuration information from the XML-based Web.config configuration file of the ASP.NET Presentation tier application. Like the J2EE version, this file contains a text-based listing of settings linking the use cases to the use case interoperability adapters.

For more information about the settings available to the use case interoperability adapter factory in the .NET Framework Presentation tier, see Appendix B.

Adding .NET Framework Business to Data Tier Interoperability

The developers added components to the .NET Framework Business and Data tiers to enable interoperability. Like the J2EE version, the .NET Framework XBikes application has two resources in the Data tier. These are the SQL Server database and a message queuing system. Instead of calling resources in the Data tier directly, the .NET Framework Business tier components make calls through the various interoperability components.

The following are interoperability components added to enable interoperability on the .NET Framework Business and Data tiers:

- Service interfaces in the Data tier.
- Resource interoperability adapters in the Business tier.
- Resource interoperability adapter factories in the Business tier.
- An XML configuration file for the resource interoperability adapter factories.

Figure 6.11 shows how the developers implemented these components.

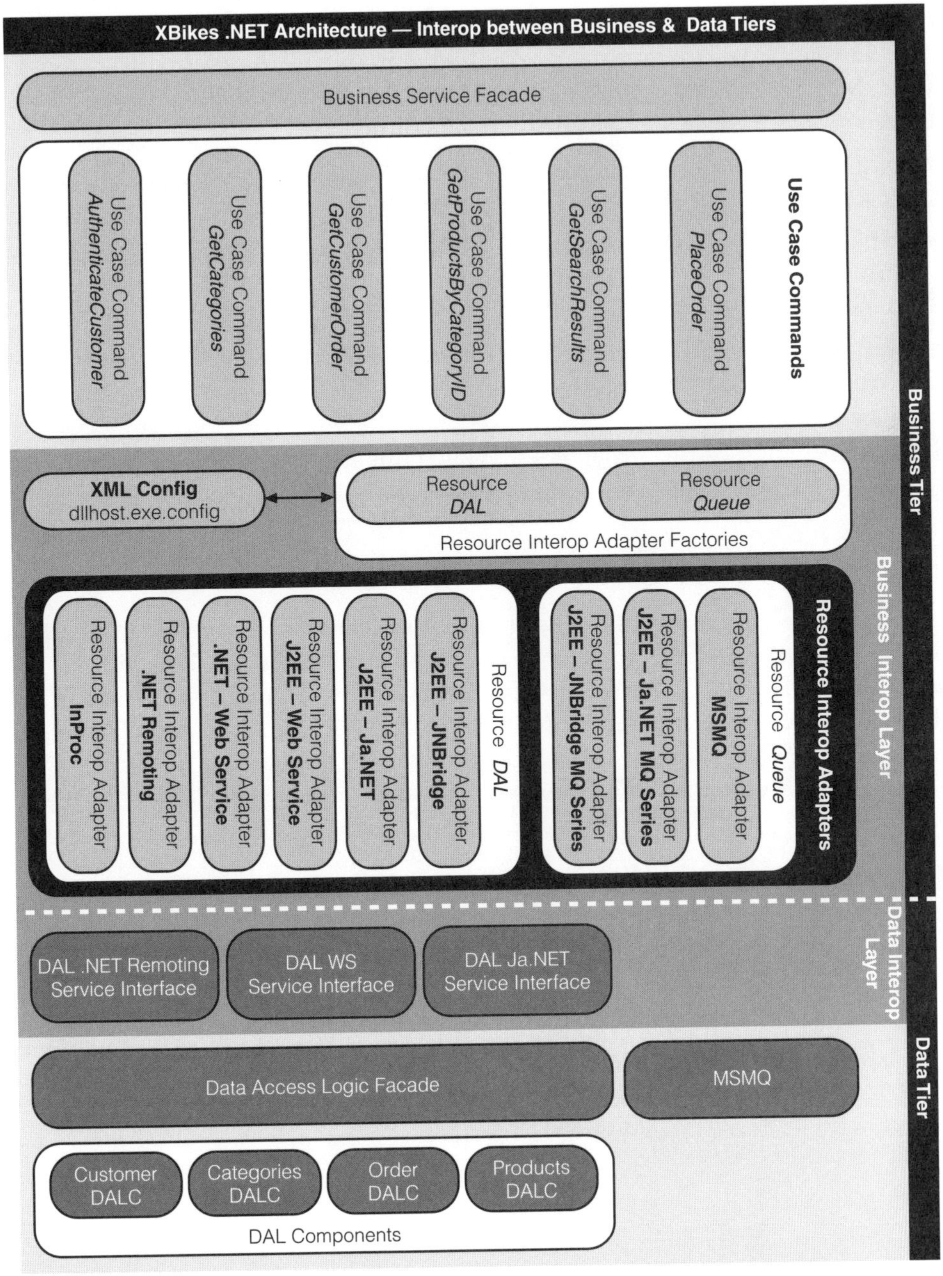

XBikes .NET Architecture — Interop between Business & Data Tiers

- Business Service Facade
- Use Case Command *AuthenticateCustomer*
- Use Case Command *GetCategories*
- Use Case Command *GetCustomerOrder*
- Use Case Command *GetProductsByCategoryID*
- Use Case Command *GetSearchResults*
- Use Case Command *PlaceOrder*
- **Use Case Commands**
- **Business Tier**
- XML Config dllhost.exe.config
- Resource *DAL*
- Resource *Queue*
- Resource Interop Adapter Factories
- **Business Interop Layer**
- Resource Interop Adapter **InProc**
- Resource Interop Adapter **.NET Remoting**
- Resource Interop Adapter **.NET – Web Service**
- Resource Interop Adapter **J2EE – Web Service**
- Resource Interop Adapter **J2EE – Ja.NET**
- Resource Interop Adapter **J2EE – JNBridge**
- Resource *DAL*
- Resource Interop Adapter **J2EE – JNBridge MQ Series**
- Resource Interop Adapter **J2EE – Ja.NET MQ Series**
- Resource Interop Adapter **MSMQ**
- Resource *Queue*
- **Resource Interop Adapters**
- **Data Interop Layer**
- DAL .NET Remoting Service Interface
- DAL WS Service Interface
- DAL Ja.NET Service Interface
- **Data Tier**
- Data Access Logic Facade
- MSMQ
- Customer DALC
- Categories DALC
- Order DALC
- Products DALC
- DAL Components

Figure 6.11

XBikes on .NET Framework Business and Data tiers with interoperability elements added

Architecturally, this diagram is very similar to the J2EE version in Figure 6.9.

.NET Framework Service Interfaces

The developers added multiple service interfaces to expose the resources in the .NET Framework Data tier to both the J2EE and .NET Framework Business tiers. Each service interfaces presents a resource in the .NET Framework Data tier through a different interoperability mechanism.

There are three service interfaces that expose the database resource or Data Access Logic tier in the .NET Framework Data tier:

- **.NET Remoting**—Exposes the .NET Framework Data Access Logic resource through .NET Remoting for remote consumption by the .NET Framework Business tier.

- **Web service**—Exposes the .NET Framework Data Access Logic resource through a Web service for consumption by either the .NET Framework or J2EE Business tiers.

- **Ja.NET**—Exposes the .NET Framework Data Access Logic resource though a Ja.NET runtime bridge for consumption by the J2EE Business tier.

Although the .NET Remoting service interface is .NET Framework-specific, the WS service interface can field requests from either environment.

Like the J2EE version of XBikes, a sample console application reads **OrderData** messages off of a MSMQ queue then calls the Data Access Logic service façade and adds the order to the database. You can consider this sample console application (**DALMSMQServiceInterface**) a fourth service interface for the Data Access Logic. Unlike the J2EE version, the .NET Framework version requires no service interfaces to expose MSMQ to the .NET Framework Business tier, because the MSMQ resource interoperability adapter can communicate with MSMQ directly.

.NET Framework Resource Interoperability Adapters

The developers added multiple interoperability adapters were added to the .NET Framework Business tier to communicate with either the J2EE or .NET Framework Data tiers. To demonstrate multiple interoperability techniques, the design implements a set of interoperability adapters or resource interoperability adapters for each resource in the Data tier. Unlike the use case interoperability adapters in the .NET Framework Presentation tier, there is only one set of resource interoperability adapters for each resource's service interface.

To communicate with the Data Access Logic resource in both the .NET Framework and J2EE Data tiers, the developers implemented the following resource interoperability adapters:

- **InProc or native mode adapter**—Addresses the .NET Framework Data Access Logic service façade directly through an in-process call in a single computer environment.
- **.NET Remoting adapter**—Addresses the Data Access Logic resource in the .NET Framework Data tier through a .NET Remoting service interface.
- **.NET Web services adapter**—Addresses the Data Access Logic resource in the .NET Framework Data tier through a WS service interface.
- **J2EE Web services adapter**—Addresses the Data Access Logic resource in the J2EE Data tier through a WS service interface.
- **J2EE Ja.NET adapter**—Addresses the Data Access Logic resource in the J2EE Data tier through the Ja.NET service interface.
- **J2EE JNBridge adapter**—Addresses the Data Access Logic resource in the J2EE Data tier through the JNBridge service interface.

These adapters give you three ways of linking from the .NET Framework Business tier to the Data Access Logic resource in the .NET Framework Data tier and three ways of linking from the .NET Framework Business tier to the Data Access Logic resource in the J2EE Data tier.

Note: You can only use the InProc use case interoperability adapter in a single computer environment as InProc does not support connections to a remote computer.

To communicate with the message queuing resources in the .NET Framework and J2EE Data tiers, the developers implemented the following three resource interoperability adapters:

- **MSMQ**—Uses the **System.Messaging** namespace addresses to address the MSMQ queue resource in the .NET Framework Data tier.
- **WebSphere MQ-Ja.NET-JMS**—Uses Ja.NET and JMS to address the WebSphere MQ queue in the J2EE Data tier.
- **WebSphere MQ-JNBridge-JMS**—Uses JNBridge and JMS to address the WebSphere MQ queue in the J2EE Data tier.

Again, the **PlaceOrder** use case command in the Business tier is the only use case that accesses these resource interoperability adapters.

.NET Framework Resource Interoperability Factories

The developers added interoperability adapter factories to the .NET Framework Business tier to increase flexibility in selecting which interoperability mechanism connects with the Data Access Logic and queue resources in the .NET Framework Data tier. The design implements these interoperability adapter factories in the same fashion as the corresponding ones in the J2EE Business tier and refers to them as resource interoperability adapter factories.

The developers implemented two resource interoperability adapter factories in XBikes, one for the Data Access Logic and one for the queue.

.NET Framework XML Configuration File

The resource interoperability adapter factory in the .NET Framework application retrieves configuration information from an XML configuration file named Dllhost.exe.config. This file in the \System32 folder and contains a text-based listing of settings linking the resources to the resource interoperability adapters. For example, you could configure the Data Access Logic resource interoperability factory to use the J2EE Web service resource interoperability adapter for all calls to the Data Access Logic.

Note: This configuration is for illustrative purposes only. A production application should not read configuration settings from the \System32 folder. For application security best practices, refer to *http://www.microsoft.com/practices*.

For more information about the settings available to the resource interoperability adapter factories in the .NET Framework Business tier, see Appendix B.

Summary

This chapter reviewed the elements that you need to add to an application to enable interoperability. It also covered best practice recommendations for interoperability. It then looked at how the developers implemented these elements in the application architecture for the XBikes sample application. It described how this enabled the developers to link the two platforms using multiple techniques and, importantly, to change the linking method. The remaining chapters describe how the developers added these interoperability elements.

References

For more information about the Command, Façade, and Factory design patterns *Design Patterns: Elements of Reusable Object-Oriented Software*, by Erich Gamma, Richard Helm, Ralph Johnson, and John Vlissides (ISBN 0-201-63361-2).

For more information about the Value Object pattern, see *Core J2EE Patterns Best Practices and Design Strategies* by Deepak Alur, Dan Malks, and John Crupi (ISBN 0-13-064884-1).

For more information about implementing typed datasets in .NET Framework See "Creating XML Schemas and Datasets" *http://msdn.microsoft.com/library/default.asp?url=/library/en-us/vbcon/html /vboriCreatingSchemasDataSets.asp*

For more information about the service interfaces pattern See "Enterprise Solution Patterns: Service Interface" *http://msdn.microsoft.com/practices/type/patterns/enterprise/DesServiceInterface/*

7

Integrating .NET in the Presentation Tier

Introduction

You should now understand the architecture of the XBikes application and the interoperability techniques that XBikes uses. In this chapter, you look in detail at the code that allowed the XBikes developers to implement interoperability by integrating an ASP.NET Presentation tier application with a J2EE Business tier.

When deciding to add an ASP.NET Presentation tier to a J2EE application, there are three areas you need to address, regardless of the technology you decide to use:

- Which data format to use for interoperability.
- How to design and build the service interfaces in the J2EE application.
- How to design and build the interoperability adapters in the .NET Framework application.

There are several factors to consider when deciding on which interoperability technology is best for your project. Performance, standards compliance and cost are just some of the factors that affect your choice and each choice has advantages and disadvantages.

Web services offers an industry standard solution, supported by many vendors on a variety of platforms including .NET and Java. However, while being fairly easy to implement, Web services do not offer the performance of some third party binary interoperability technologies.

JNBridgePro from JNBridge and Ja.NET from Intrinsyc both offer high performance, high control binary solutions, although they do not completely conform to open industry standards.

Note: Choose Web services as the interoperability technology unless performance is an overriding requirement. This is because Web services follow open standards and are the best way to ensure interoperability with future applications and industry developments.

For a detailed discussion about choosing an interoperability technology, see Chapters 3 to 5.

Determining Data Exchange Formats and Types

In Chapter 3, "Interoperability Fundamentals," you saw how Java and .NET complex data types are unlikely to correlate between the two platforms. You also saw how it is possible to create a common format for exchanging data between the platforms through the use of custom serializable classes generated from a common XML Schema.

In Chapter 4, "Interoperability Technologies: Point to Point," you saw how Ja.Net and JNBridgePro can create proxies for Java data classes that a .NET Framework application can then use. While these are two valid solutions for getting data from Java to .NET, using custom data classes or proxy Java classes may not be desirable within the .NET Presentation tier. It is likely that you will want to use native .NET data types, such as a typed **DataSet**, to take advantage of the rich features provided by ASP.NET such as data binding.

To get around this issue, you either need to package the data up on the Java side into the format you want for .NET, or send the Java data and repackage it on the .NET side. To do this, your service interfaces and interoperability adapters may need to manipulate the data. In the XBikes application, the mapping techniques differ, depending on the interoperability technology.

For a detailed discussion about data exchange factors, see Chapter 3.

Designing and Building the Service Interface

The XBikes sample application follows the J2EE best practices described in Chapter 6, "Implementing Interoperability Design Elements," so access to the Business tier is through the session bean **BusinessServiceFacade**. To expose this functionality to the .NET Framework application, the developers created a service interface that exposes **BusinessServiceFacade**. Depending upon the interoperability technology in use, this service interface class *either* calls the existing service façade directly *or* manipulates the data before calling the service façade. Again, on the return path the service interface either returns the data to the service interface caller directly or manipulates it before returning it. Figure 7.1 shows this arrangement.

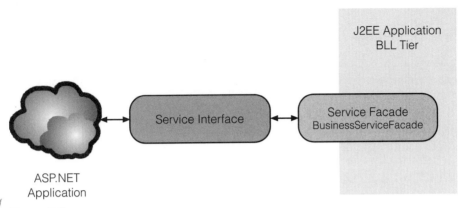

Figure 7.1
Implementing a service interface and service façade to link the J2EE Business tier to the .NET Presentation tier

For a detailed discussion of service interfaces, see Chapter 6.

Designing and Building the Interoperability Adapters

In the XBikes application, the developers created an Interoperability adapter for each use case. This choice allows selection of the interoperability technology at the use case level.

Note: Implementing interoperability adapters at the use case level was mainly for demonstration purposes. Your application may not require that level of granularity.

Figure 7.2 shows the interoperability adapters linking the ASP.NET application to the service interface.

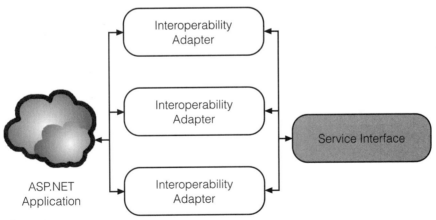

Figure 7.2
Interoperability adapters connecting the ASP.NET application to the service interface

For more information about implementing interoperability adapters, see Chapter 6.

Using Web Services for Interoperability

Web services are the recommended interoperability technique, unless performance or other considerations require a binary solution. This section looks at how you can use Web services to implement interoperability. It covers the data format choices, how to build the service interface for the Web service in Java using GLUE, from The Mind Electric (recently acquired by webMethods, Inc.) and how to build the .NET interoperability adapters.

Deciding on a Data Format

With a Web service interface, the temptation is to use the service interface to return complex types, allowing the adapters to create proxies of these complex types and consume them. However, because of the issues of handling XSD-based complex types in Web services, not all Web services stacks are compatible. Experience shows that what works for one Web service stack may break another. To solve this problem, you should look at exchanging only primitive data types, such as strings, integers and so on. All Web service stacks support these data types, and these provide the greatest levels of flexibility and client access.

If you use primitive data types and need to return something more complex, like an order, you have to package the data as a string. The best solution for this is to populate a string with an XML representation of the data. This XML encoding should follow an agreed schema.

Note: There is little performance difference between passing Java data types directly and serializing them and passing them as strings, because the Web service has to serialize the Java data into XML anyway.

In the XBikes application, the J2EE and .NET developer teams decided upon a common data format for the Web services. They created an XSD Schema from this design, which both teams then used to create the appropriate classes and mapping files.

Building the Service Interface in J2EE

You now need to create a service interface that exposes the J2EE Business tier façade through Web services. This becomes the J2EE Web service service interface. This publication refers to these as WS service interfaces.

Building the Java Web service is a fairly straight forward process. First, create Java data classes based upon the XSD schemas for the messages. Then you need to create Java helper classes that parse the data classes based upon the XSD schema and convert the data to and from XML formatted strings. The Java data classes can then be serialized in to XML formatted strings and back again using the helper classes.

You then build a Java class that exposes the correct methods for the Web service. This class accepts and returns primitive data types, performs any data conversion between what the Web service uses and what the Business tier service façade(s) expect, and calls the correct method on the service façade. Once you create this Java class, you can expose this as a Web service using whatever techniques your Web service stack provides.

To build your Java Web service, complete the following tasks:

1. Create the XSD-based data types and XML mapping for serialization.
2. Create a Java Helper Class
3. Create and expose the Java class as a Web service.

Creating the Data Types and XML Mapping

The first part in creating the WS service interface is to create any data manipulation code you need. Since you should have an XSD Schema to work with, you can use one of the many Java XML products to generate a Java class from this schema.

Many Java XML products contain mapping files, which map a field in the class to an element or attribute in the XML Schema. Sometimes your existing classes map to the correct Schema without needing an intermediary. If this is the case, create mapping files for your existing classes, as this removes the step of taking the data from the existing Java classes into the Schema-based Java classes.

The XBikes developers used GLUE as the Java Web services stack. GLUE also contains Electric XML in the same package. Electric XML includes tools for building Java classes from an XSD. Electric XML also produces a mapping file which GLUE uses when reading or writing the XML data to or from Java classes.

The developers used these tools to build the Java classes from the XSD files. Conveniently, the generated classes were almost the same as the existing Java data classes. In these cases, the developers modified the created mapping files and then serialized the existing classes.

The following steps illustrate how to create the Java class from the **CustomerData** XSD files, which the developers implemented in the **AuthenticateCustomer** use case using the GLUE tools:

1. The XBikes developers designed the **CustomerData** XSD file using the XSD Designer in Visual Studio .NET 2003. For more information about XSD Designer and XSD files, see Chapter 3.

Note: These steps assume the computer has a licensed copy of GLUE installed and a valid Java path configured.

2. The developers created the Java classes based on the CustomerData.xsd file. GLUE provides a **schema2java** tool, which the developers used to create the Java class in the correct package for the project by running the following command.

```
schema2Java CustomerData.xsd -g -p xbikes.common.dataconverters.customers
```

This command generated two classes, **Customers_TYPE.Java** and **CustomerData_TYPE.Java**. The tool also generated a **CustomerData.map** which the serializer uses to map the fields to the correct XML elements.

Creating the Java Helper Class

After you have these XSD-based classes, you should move the data from the original Java data classes into the XSD-based classes. After you populate the XSD classes, you need to serialize them to an XML formatted string. It makes sense to put this serialization code into a method in a *helper class*, and this is what the XBikes developers did.

The following steps illustrate how the developers created the Java *helper* class for the **CustomerData** XSD based classes:

1. The Developers created a helper class containing two methods to read and write the data to and from a string. The methods accepted a single parameter for the type of data you want to convert, and returned a single value of the converted type. The following method signatures show this.

```
public static String orderToString(Order o);
public static Order StringToOrder(String o);
```

2. The developers then added the files created in steps 1 and 2 to the Java project, placing them in the common package for easy access. As you can see from the **schema2Java** command line in step 1, the package destination was **xbikes.common.dataconverters.customers**.

3. As GLUE is the chosen environment, the team added Glue.jar to the build path.

4. Next the developers generated the helper class to perform the conversion to and from the Java classes into the strings. They added a new class called **CustomerConverter** to the **xbikes.common.dataconverters** package.

5. The developers added two methods to the **CustomerConverter** class, one to convert the Java data into a string, and the other to convert a string into the Java data. These methods use the GLUE serializer to read and write the XML. Because the existing Java **CustomerData** class is not compatible with the schema, this requires population of the **CustomerData_TYPE** and **Customers_TYPE** classes as part of the conversion. This code listing shows the completed **CustomerConverter** class.

```java
public final class CustomerConverter
{
    private static final String WRITER = "CustomerData";
    private static final String NAMESPACE =
        "http://tempuri.org/CustomerData.xsd";

    public static CustomerData stringToCustomerData(String xml)
        throws XBikesInteropException
    {
        try
        {
            // Need to convert the string into xml
            Document d = new Document(xml);
            IReader reader = new LiteralReader(d);
            CustomerData_TYPE myCustomer =
                (CustomerData_TYPE) reader.readObject(CustomerData_TYPE.class);
            Customers_TYPE customer = myCustomer.getCustomers();
            CustomerData cd = new CustomerData();
            cd.setAddress(customer.getEmailAddress());
            cd.setCustomerID(customer.getCustomerID());
            cd.setName(customer.getFullName());
            cd.setPassword(customer.getPassword());
            cd.setZip(customer.getZipCode());
            return cd;
        }
        catch (Exception e)
        {
            System.out.println(e.getMessage());
            throw new XBikesInteropException(e.getMessage());
        }
    }
    public static String customerDataToString(CustomerData cd)
        throws XBikesInteropException
    {
        try
        {
            // Move the data from the internal Java classes into those
            // generated by the schema tool
            Customers_TYPE customer = new Customers_TYPE();
            customer.setCustomerID(cd.getCustomerID());
            customer.setEmailAddress(cd.getAddress());
            customer.setFullName(cd.getName());
            customer.setPassword(cd.getPassword());
            customer.setZipCode(cd.getZip());
            CustomerData_TYPE customerData = new CustomerData_TYPE();
            customerData.setCustomers(customer);
            // Write the object to a string, via the LiteralWriter / Document
            // and StringBuffer
            IWriter writer = new LiteralWriter(WRITER);
            writer.writeObject(customerData);
            writer.writeNamespace("", NAMESPACE);
            Document d = writer.getDocument();
```

(continued)

(continued)

```
            String sCustomerData = "";
            StringWriter sw = new StringWriter();
            d.write(sw);
            sCustomerData = sw.getBuffer().toString();
            return sCustomerData;
        }
        catch (Exception e)
        {
            System.out.println(e.getMessage());
            throw new XBikesInteropException(e.getMessage());
        }
    }
```

Creating and Exposing a Java Class as a Web Service

Your final task is to build and expose the Java Web service. The exact mechanics of this depend on which Web service stack you have decided to use. The XBikes developers used GLUE, so there may be steps that you do not need to carry out in your chosen stack.

The Mind Electric, like many other Java Web service vendors, implements Web services in GLUE through a servlet. Therefore you need a Web application to host this component. The Web service needs to contain all the methods that you want to expose from the **BusinessServiceFacade**, but rather than return the Java data types, you should return strings. The Web service therefore should convert any Java data types into strings containing XML, that has been formatted according to the XSD files. In the following example, you already have the code for this in a helper, so you simply need to make a method call. The flow of logic in any of the Web service methods is as follows:

1. Application calls the Web service method.
2. Web service passes any data that requires converting to the helper class.
3. The Web service creates the home interface for the **BusinessServiceFacade** session bean.
4. The Web service calls the appropriate method on the **BusinessServiceFacade**, passing the converted data.
5. If the **BusinessServiceFacade** returns data, use the helper class to convert this to a string.
6. Return the string representation of the data back to the calling application.

Figure 7.3 shows this in action.

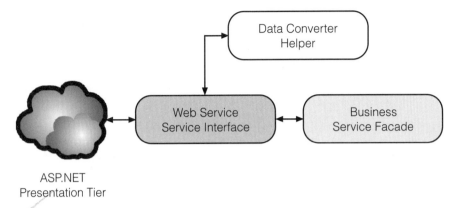

Figure 7.3
Using the Data Helper class in a Web service

You now have all the pieces you need to build the Web service. Because GLUE
implements the Web service stack as a servlet, you need to create a Web project in
the XBikes solution to host this servlet.

Note: GLUE also provides its own container to run GLUE Web services if you are not using an
application server.

The XBikes developers carried out the following steps to implement the Web service:

1. The developers created a new Web Project called **XBikesBLLServiceInterface**
   within IBM WebSphere Studio. They then added this project to the existing
   Enterprise Application Project called **SingleTierXBikes**.

2. The Web service needs to call objects within both the **XBikesCommon** and
   XBikesBiz projects, so the developers added these as module dependencies.

3. GLUE provides a template application that you can use. This template contains all
   the files required to run a GLUE Web service on an application server. You should
   find these files in the C:\Tme\Glue\App-Template folder. The developers copied
   these files into the project to get the basic GLUE files and the required folder
   structure. They also added the Glue.jar file to the build path.

4. The developers then built the class that the application exposes as the Web service.
   This class has the same methods as **BusinessServiceFacade**, but uses strings as the
   data type, rather than the existing Java classes.

5. The team created a new interface and class based upon the methods in **BusinessServiceFacade,** replacing the data types with strings. They added these classes to the **xbikes.bll.serviceinterface.j2ee.ws** package. The following code sample shows the methods added to **IBLLWSServiceInterface**.

```
public String authenticateCustomer(String email, String password)
       throws XBikesInteropException;
public String getCategories() throws XBikesInteropException;
public String getProductsByCategory(int categoryID)
       throws XBikesInteropException;
public String getSearchResults(String keyword)
       throws XBikesInteropException;
public String placeOrder(String order) throws XBikesInteropException;
public String getCustomerOrders(int customerID)
       throws XBikesInteropException;
```

6. The following code shows the implementation of the **AuthenticateCustomer** method in the **XBikesBLLServiceInterface** class.

```
package xbikes.bll.serviceinterface.j2ee.ws;
import javax.naming.InitialContext;
import javax.naming.NamingException;
import javax.rmi.PortableRemoteObject;

import xbikes.bll.facade.BusinessServiceFacade;
import xbikes.bll.facade.BusinessServiceFacadeHome;
import xbikes.common.data.CustomerData;
import xbikes.common.dataconverters.CustomerConverter;
import xbikes.common.exceptions.XBikesInteropException;

public class BLLWSServiceInterface implements IBLLWSServiceInterface
{
    private static final String BUSINESS_FACADE_JNDI =
        "ejb/xbikes/bll/facade/BusinessServiceFacadeHome";
    /**
    * @see
    xbikes.bll.serviceinterface.j2ee.ws.IBLLWSServiceInterface#authenticate
    Customer(String, String)
     */
    public String authenticateCustomer(String email, String password)
        throws XBikesInteropException
    {
        try
        {
            BusinessServiceFacade facade = getFacadeHome().create();
            CustomerData cd = facade.authenticateCustomer(email, password);
            String sCustomerData = CustomerConverter.customerDataToString(cd);
            // We now have a string that contains the xml.
            // We shall return that!
            return sCustomerData;
        }
```

(continued)

(continued)

```
        catch (Exception e)
        {
            throw new XBikesInteropException(e.getMessage());
        }
    }
}
```

Note: In this class the developers created a helper method to allow easy access to the **BusinessServiceFacade** session bean.

---

7. As you have now created the class that provides the functionality for the Web service, you simply need to tell GLUE about it. In XBikes, the developers went to the **XBikesBLLServiceInterface\Web Content\WEB-INF\services** folder, then copied and renamed the sample configuration file Sample.xml to make the new BLLWSServiceInterface.xml file.

8. The developers modified this file, changing the **constructor** tag with **xbikes.bll.serviceinterface.j2ee.we.BLLWSServiceInterface**. They altered the **description** tag to **Bikes Unsecure Web Service,** the publish tag to **yes** and the **style** to **document**. They also amended the **interface** tag, replacing **electric.util.sample.ISample** with **xbikes.bll.serviceinterface.j2ee.ws.IBLLWSServiceInterface** and the **targetNamespace** to **http://www.xbikes.com/**.

9. They then copied the maps created earlier into the **Web Content\WEB-INF\Maps** folder.

10. To test the Web service, the developers compiled and started the server. They opened a browser and pointed it to **http://localhost:9080 /XBikesBLLServiceInterface/Console** before using the GLUE console to invoke the **authenticateCustomer** method.

Creating the Interoperability Adapters in .NET

You have now created the Web service service interface in Java, so you can proceed to build the .NET interoperability adapters. The procedures to do this are as follows:

- Build the .NET data classes based on the XSD schema.
- Build a Web service proxy using the tools in Visual Studio .NET.
- Create an adapter for either the entire service interface, or one for each use case.

Note: In XBikes, the developers created an adapter for each use case.

The interoperability adapter calls the proxy, which then calls the Web service. The adapter also has to convert any .NET data to and from the correct string/XML format based on the XSD schema.

The logic flow for an adapter is as follows:

1. The application calls the adapter method.
2. The adapter converts any complex data to an XML string representation.
3. The adapter creates an instance of the Web service proxy.
4. The application calls the appropriate method in the Web service proxy.
5. If the proxy returns data, convert it into the correct .NET format if necessary.
6. Return the data back to the calling application.

Figure 7.4 shows this in operation.

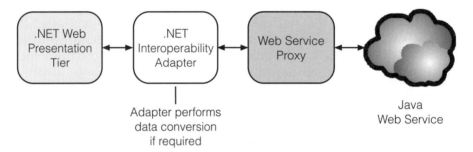

Figure 7.4
Web service proxy operation with .NET Framework applications

Creating the XSD based Data Classes

To enable .NET Framework applications to consume data from the Java Web service, you need to have a .NET class that you can populate with the returned XML string. Again you can use a tool that converts the schema into a class, which is the **XSD.EXE** tool.

XSD.EXE accepts the **/dataset** switch to generate a *sub-classed dataset*. If you are building the .NET Framework application from scratch, it may be worth considering using the datasets that XSD generates in your .NET Framework application. This removes the need to convert from the XSD-based classes into a differently formatted or structured .NET class.

The XBikes developers used the XSD tool with the **/dataset** switch to generate the .NET dataset classes. They then used these datasets throughout the entire .NET Framework application to remove the need to convert between data that the Java Web service returns and proprietary .NET classes.

Note: An alternative technique would be to use a graphical tool such as XML Schema Designer in Visual Studio .NET 2003.

To create the **CustomerData** data type in .NET the developers opened a Visual Studio .NET 2003 command prompt and executed the following command.

```
xsd CustomerData.xsd /dataset /namespace:xbikes.common.schemas
```

They then copied the generated file into the **XBikes-Common** project.

Creating the .NET Web Service Proxies

The next task is to build the proxy classes for the Web service. You can use Visual Studio .NET or the **wsdl.exe** command line tool depending on your preference. If you use Visual Studio .NET, add a Web reference to the project that contains your interoperability adapters. When you create the Web reference, enter the URL to the Java WSDL file. If you prefer the **wsdl.exe** command line tool, you should specify switches to create the proxy class in the correct namespace.

Note: When you add a Web reference to your project in Visual Studio .NET, it will have a default name which is the same as the server name portion of the URL where the Web service's WSDL is located. The proxy class generated by the Web reference belongs to a namespace which is the default namespace for the project suffixed with the name of the Web reference. It is good practice to give the Web reference, and thus the proxy namespace, a name other than the default name.

Because XBikes consumes a simple Web service, the developers used the **Add Web Reference** functionality of Visual Studio .NET to create the proxy. They added this proxy to the **XBikes-UseCaseInteropAdapters** project. The URL to the Java WSDL was **http://localhost:9080/XBikesBLLServiceInterface/services /BLLWSServiceInterface.wsdl**. The developer team renamed the Web Reference from its default value of **localhost** to **J2EE.BLLWSSI**. This new name reflects that this Web reference is for the J2EE business logic layer WS service interface. The proxy class generated by this Web reference then belongs to the **XBikes.UseCaseInteropAdapters.J2EE.BLLWSSI** namespace.

Creating the .NET Interoperability Adapters

Now that you have the data classes and Web service proxy, you can build the interoperability adapters. As discussed earlier in this chapter, you may choose to have a single adapter per Web service, or create an adapter for each use case, depending upon the level of fine control you require. The XBikes developers created an adapter for each use case to give maximum flexibility.

The XBikes use cases follow the command pattern, providing an execute and initialise method, and implement an interface called **IUseCaseCommand**. The adapters take names from the command they adapt, so **AuthenticateCustomerInteropAdapter** links to the **AuthenticateCustomerCommand**.

Creating the interoperability adapter for the **AuthenticateCustomer** use case was straight forward. In the **XBikes-UseCaseInteropAdapters** project the developers added a new class called **AuthenticateCustomerInteropAdapter** to the **J2EE\WS** folder. Next they changed the class to implement the **IUseCaseCommand** interface. This required them to implement both **execute** and **initialise** methods and to add code to the class constructor. The following code listing illustrates the **Constructor** and **Initialise** methods.

```
public AuthenticateCustomerInteropAdapter()
{
    try
    {
        // Instantiate the BLL service interface proxy.
        // Creates a J2EE-side BLL service interface
        _facade = new BLLWSServiceInterface();
    }
    catch (Exception e)
    {
        throw new XBikesInteropException("[AuthenticateCustomer]:
                                          J2EE WS Interop Adapter error: ", e);
    }
}
private string _email;
private string _password;

public void Initialise(object[] parameters)
{
    _email = (string) parameters[0];
    _password = (string) parameters[1];
}
```

The **execute** method needs to create an instance of the Web services proxy generated earlier. The returned string data then needs packaging up into a dataset before being returned. The next code listing shows the **execute** method.

```
public DataSet Execute()
{
    try
    {
        //Retrieve customer data as an XML Document in a string format.
        StringReader sr = new
            StringReader(_facade.authenticateCustomer(_email,_password));
        CustomerData ds = new CustomerData();
        //Load result string back into CustomerData typed DataSet.
        ds.ReadXml(sr);
        return ds;
    }
    //soap error
    catch (System.Web.Services.Protocols.SoapException soapExp)
    {
        string soapFaultMsg = soapExp.Message;
```

(continued)

(continued)

```
        //Parse SoapException message to get exception type.
        string ExceptionType =
            ExceptionHelper.GetSoapExceptionType(soapFaultMsg);
        //Throw the appropriate exception type based on the
        //exception type found in the SoapException.
        switch (ExceptionType)
        {
            case "Interop":
                throw(new XBikesInteropException(soapFaultMsg));
            case "Application" :
                throw(new XBikesApplicationException(soapFaultMsg));
            default:
                throw(new XBikesApplicationException(soapFaultMsg));
        }//switch
    }
    //general error
    catch (Exception e)
    {
        //Wrap in Interop Exception
        XBikesInteropException intExp = new
            XBikesInteropException("AuthenticateCustomer WS Interop
        Adapter error.",e);
        //Throw up the stack to client for logging.
        throw (intExp);
    }
}
```

When implementing this procedure, the string data that the Web service returns should be in the correct format according to the common XML Schema for **CustomerData**. Since the **CustomerData** typed **DataSet** is based on the common schema, you can load the XML string that the Web service returns into the **DataSet** using the **ReadXML()** method.

Note: The code example assumes the XML string returned matches the correct schema format, as the application generates an exception if this is not the case. You may wish to run the returned XML string through a validation process against the XSD schema file in order to confirm this before attempting to use the **ReadXML()** method to load the string into the typed **DataSet**.

In this section you saw how to create interoperability adapters and service interfaces in Java and .NET that use Web services to interoperate. In the next sections you look at how to implement interoperability adapters and service interfaces using JNBridgePro and Ja.NET to provide higher performance interoperability solutions.

Using JNBridgePro for Interoperability

This section shows how you can use JNBridgePro to perform bridging between a .NET Web tier and a J2EE Business tier. You look at the data format choices, how to build the service interface, and how to build the interoperability adapters.

Deciding on a Data Format

JNBridgePro has the ability to generate proxy classes in .NET for the Java data classes. You can then use these generated data classes throughout your .NET application. However, for reasons mentioned earlier in the chapter, it may make more sense to put this data into a dataset, which you can then easily use in the .NET Presentation tier.

Note: You are highly likely to carry out some form of data conversion when building the interoperability adapters in .NET.

Building the Service Interface for JNBridgePro

JNBridgePro can expose existing Java classes to .NET, so you could choose to expose an existing service façade to .NET. However, you should protect your code from changes by using a layered approach. To do this, create another Java class which is your service interface. Because you can return native Java data types to .NET with JNBridgePro, this service interface simply calls the appropriate methods on the service façade and returns any resultant data types.

Applications that use JNBridgePro for interoperability need JNBridge runtime components on both the .NET and J2EE sides. The Java-side runtime component acts as a .NET Framework remoting server, marshalling and unmarshaling parameters, returning values, dispatching methods, and managing the lifecycles of Java objects that .NET references.

Following the pattern of creating a service interface class, the developers built a Java class that implemented exactly the same methods as the existing **BusinessServiceFacade** session bean. This section shows the overall process of how the developers created the **AuthenticateCustomer** use case:

1. The developers created a new **Web Project** called **JNBridgeBLL** and added it to the existing **SingleTierXBikes** EAR. They then included the **XBikesCommon** and **XBikesBiz** projects as module references.

2. They then installed the JNBridgePro Java-side runtime component, **JNBCORE.JAR** to the **WEB-INF\lib** folder and added the **jnbcore_tcp.properties** file to the **WEB-INF** folder, copying these files from the JNBridge install folder.

3. Next they added the **JNBServlet** to the **Web Deployment Descriptor** and specified **Load on startup** and set the **Load Order** to **–1**, which loads the class when the application server starts.

4. The developers created the **BLLServiceInterface** class in the **xbikes.bll.serviceinterface.j2ee.jnbridge** package. This class simply passes any method call across to the existing service façade. The next code example shows the **BLLServiceInteface** class.

Source Code Listing

```
package xbikes.bll.serviceinterface.j2ee.jnbridge;

import javax.naming.*;
import javax.rmi.*;
import java.rmi.*;
import xbikes.bll.facade.*;
import xbikes.common.data.*;


public class BLLServiceInterface {

    BusinessServiceFacade facade=null;
    private final String BUSINESS_FACADE_JNDI =
        "BusinessServiceFacade";
    private final String BUSINESS_FACADE_CLASS =
        "xbikes.bll.facade.BusinessServiceFacadeHome";

    /**
     * Constructor for BLLServiceInterface.
     */
    public BLLServiceInterface() {
        try
        {
            InitialContext ic = new InitialContext();
            Java.lang.Object objRef = ic.lookup(BUSINESS_FACADE_JNDI);
            BusinessServiceFacadeHome home =
                (BusinessServiceFacadeHome) PortableRemoteObject.narrow(objRef,
                    Java.lang.Class.forName(BUSINESS_FACADE_CLASS));
            facade = home.create();
        }
        catch (Exception excp)
        {
            System.out.println(excp.getMessage());
        }
    }

    public CustomerData authenticateCustomer(String email, String password)
    throws Exception
    {
        return facade.authenticateCustomer(email, password);
    }
```

(continued)

(continued)

```java
public CategoriesListData getCategories()
throws Exception
{
    return facade.getCategories();
}

public OrderListData getCustomerOrders(int customerID)
throws Exception
{
    return facade.getCustomerOrders(customerID);
}

public ProductsListData getProductsByCategory(int categoryID)
throws Exception
{
    return facade.getProductsByCategory(categoryID);
}

public ProductsListData getSearchResults(String keyword)
throws Exception
{
    return facade.getSearchResults(keyword);
}

public void placeOrder(OrderData theOrder)
throws Exception
{
    facade.placeOrder(theOrder);
}
}
```

The **BLLServiceInterface** is mostly a pass-through to the existing **BusinessServiceFacade** EJB. The additional functionality that the wrapper class provides is the constructor, which encapsulates the code necessary to find and access the EJB.

While you can use JNBridgePro to generate proxies that access the **BusinessServiceFacade** and the supporting JNDI classes directly, it is more efficient if you perform these operations entirely on the Java side and encapsulate the operations within a wrapper. In other situations, where you cannot change the J2EE code, you might have to access JNDI and EJB classes directly. The section on Using the MSMQ-MQSeries Bridge in Chapter 9, "Implementing Asynchronous Interoperability," shows how to create an adapter that accesses the MQSeries APIs and demonstrates how you could create such an adapter if it were impossible to change the J2EE code.

Building the Interoperability Adapters using JNBridgePro

After you construct the service interface that you want the .NET application to consume, you need to generate a proxy assembly for .NET. This assembly contains .NET proxies for the service interface, as well as any data classes that the service interface uses. Therefore if the service interface returns Java data of the type **CustomerData**, the .NET assembly that JNBridgePro generates would contain a proxy for this class.

Note: In your code, consider prefixing the name of the proxy class with the name of the platform from where the proxy class originated, for example, if the .NET class was **CustomerData**, the Java proxy class would be **javaCustomerData**.

You can use the GUI tools that JNBridgePro provides to generate these proxy classes. You simply select the classes for which you wish to generate proxies and JNBridgePro creates them.

You can then add this assembly to your .NET project as a reference, along with the required JNBridgePro configuration files, and applications can consume it like any other .NET class, such as the interoperability adapter. Again, you should decide upon the level of fine control that you need with the interoperability adapters, either implementing one for each use case, or one for the whole service interface.

Note: The XBikes developers implemented an interoperability adapter for each use case.

Creating the Java Proxy Classes

The first stage for creating the interoperability adapters in XBikes was to generate the proxies for the Java service interface. The GUI-based proxy generation tool that is part of JNBridgePro was used to do this.

The first time this tool is executed, you have to setup the Java environment. This is done by specifying where the Java.exe program file is located. After that was done, the developers moved on to generating the adapters:

1. The developers loaded and configured the JNBProxy tool with the correct Java configuration, then added all the project folders and the Project Utility Jars that the service interface required to the class path created earlier. This included the following J2EE project folders and the Project Utility Jars:

   - C:\xbikes\J2EE-IBM\XBikesBiz\ejbModule, the root directory for the business façade classes.
   - C:\xbikes\J2EE-IBM\XBikesCommon, the root directory for the common data transfer objects.

- C:\xbikes\J2EE-IBM\JNBridgeBLL\Web Content\WEB-INF\classes, the root directory for the façade wrapper classes.
- C:\Program Files\IBM\WebSphere Studio\runtimes\base_v5\lib\j2ee.jar, the library containing various J2EE and EJB-related classes and exceptions.
- C:\Program Files\IBM\WebSphere Studio\runtimes\base_v5\mqjms\Java \lib\jndi.jar, the library containing various JNDI-related classes and exceptions.

Note: The folder and file paths may differ depending on your installation.

---

2. The development team had to select which classes they wanted to access from .NET, eventually adding the following classes, plus all the supporting classes:
   - **xbikes.bll.serviceinterface.j2ee.jnbridge.BLLServiceInterface**
   - **xbikes.common.data.CategoriesData**
   - **xbikes.common.data.CategoriesListData**
   - **xbikes.common.data.CustomerData**
   - **xbikes.common.data.OrderData**
   - **xbikes.common.data.OrderDetailsData**
   - **xbikes.common.data.OrderListData**
   - **xbikes.common.data.ProductsData**
   - **xbikes.common.data.ProductsListData**
3. **JNBProxy** then loaded the required Java classes. This only exposed the classes listed above, and the developers added these to the exposed proxies pane.
4. The goal was to create an assembly that would load into the GAC, so the developers configured **JNBProxy** to build a strong name, supplying the version number of **1.0.0.0**, and a strong name key file.
5. Finally, the developers instructed **JNBProxy** to build the assembly with the name **Jnbridgebllproxies.dll**.

JNBridgePro also ships with a configuration file that contains the settings for how the .NET Framework client can communicate with the Java application, such as the URL or location of the Java application. This file is named **jnbproxy_tcp.config**. Now that they had generated the proxies, the next task was to integrate this into the ASP.NET Presentation tier.

Note: This example focuses on the **AuthenticateCustomer** use case; however the rest follow the same pattern.

Implementing the Interoperability Adapters

The developers opened the .NET XBikes solution and added a new project named **XBikes-UseCaseInteropAdapters-JNBridge**. In this project the developers added a new class called **AuthenticateCustomerInteropAdapter** to the **J2EE\JNBridge** folder.

Note: The JNBridge and JaNET use case interoperability adapters reside in separate Visual Studio projects from the other XBikes .NET use case interoperability adapters. This avoids conflicts when using JaNET and JNBridge elements within the same project. In a production environment, it is unlikely that you would need both JaNET and JNBridge.

Because the interoperability adapter uses JNBridge, the developers copied both the created proxy assembly, Jnbridgebllproxies.dll and the JNBridge .NET support assembly Jnbshare.dll to the .NET computer and added them as project references. They also copied the configuration file Jnbproxy_tcp.config to the WWWroot folder on this computer and renamed it Jnbproxy.config.

The **AuthenticateCustomerInteropAdapter** handles the bridging between the .NET Web tier and the J2EE Business tier when authenticating the customer's identity. It implements the **IUseCaseCommand** interface, which means it implements two methods:

- **Initialise()**—Sets up the use case adapter and assigns parameters for the upcoming action.
- **Execute()**—Causes the use case adapter to perform its action.

The interoperability adapter creates a JNBridge-generated proxy for the J2EE-based **BLLServiceInterface** object, which is the object that performs the lookup of products by category. The interoperability adapter's constructor creates the proxy, and as part of that action creates the underlying J2EE **BLLServiceInterface** object.

The call to **Initialise()** simply takes a category identifier (an integer), and saves it so that it is available when the command executes. The call to **Execute()** calls the **authenticateCustomer()** method in the **BLLServiceInterface** proxy object, which causes the equivalent method to execute in J2EE, and returns a reference to a J2EE **CustomerData** object.

On the .NET side, this **CustomerData** object is a proxy of the J2EE **CustomerData** object. The remainder of **Execute()** converts the J2EE **CustomerData** object into an equivalent native .NET **CustomerData** object. It does this by iterating through the individual product data in the J2EE **CustomerData** object, extracting the details of that product, and assigning a new native .NET **CustomerRow** object to the native .NET **CustomerData** object.

Note: The namespaces **ndata** and **jdata** represent the longer .NET and J2EE namespaces in order to improve readability and to allow you to recognize and distinguish between .NET-based and J2EE-based objects easily.

```csharp
using System;
using System.Data;
using XBikes.Common.Exceptions;
using XBikes.Common.Interfaces.Architecture;
// namespace of the J2EE BLL Service interface
using xbikes.bll.serviceinterface.j2ee.jnbridge;
// namespace for J2EE version of common data objects
using jdata = xbikes.common.data;
// namespace for .NET version of common data objects
using ndata = XBikes.Common.Schemas;

namespace XBikes.UseCaseInteropAdapters.J2EE.JNBridge
{
    /// <summary>
    /// Use case adapter to authenticate customer information.
    /// </summary>
    public class AuthenticateCustomerInteropAdapter : IUseCaseCommand
    {
        private BLLServiceInterface facade = null;
        /// <summary>
        /// Summary description for AuthenticateCustomerCommand.
        /// </summary>
        public AuthenticateCustomerInteropAdapter()
        {
            try
            {
                facade = new BLLServiceInterface();
            }
            catch (Exception e)
            {
                throw new XBikesInteropException
                    ("[AuthenticateCustomer]: JNBridge Interop
                    Adapter error: ", e);
            }
        }

        private string _email;
        private string _password;

        public void Initialise(object[] parameters)
        {
            _email = (string) parameters[0];
            _password = (string) parameters[1];
        }
        public DataSet Execute()
        {
            try
            {
                // perform the customer authentication
                // on the J2EE side
                // and retrieve the customer data
                jdata.CustomerData cust =
                    facade.authenticateCustomer(_email,_password);
```

(continued)

(continued)

```
                    // copy the Java data into a .NET data object
                    // create the .NET data object
                    ndata.CustomerData ds =
                        new ndata.CustomerData();
                    // create a new row in the .NET data object
                    ndata.CustomerData.CustomersRow cr =
                        ds.Customers.NewCustomersRow();
                    // copy the individual fields from the
                    // J2EE data object to the .NET data object
                    cr.CustomerID = cust.getCustomerID();
                    cr.EmailAddress=cust.getAddress();
                    cr.FullName=cust.getName();
                    cr.Password=cust.getPassword();
                    cr.ZipCode = cust.getZip();

                    // add the data row to the data set
                    ds.Customers.AddCustomersRow(cr);
                    return ds;
    }
                catch (XBikesInteropException intExp)
                {
                    //This will already have been logged on its own tier.
                    //re-throw up the stack for logging at the client.
                    throw (intExp);
                }
                catch (XBikesApplicationException appExp)
                {
                    //This will already have been logged on its own tier.
                    //re-throw up the stack for logging at the client.
                    throw (appExp);
                }
                catch ( Exception e )
                {
                    throw new XBikesInteropException
                        ("[AuthenticateCustomer]: JNBridge Interop
                        Adapter error: ", e);
                }
            }
        }
    }
```

The final part of the configuration the developers carried out is on the .NET side of the XBikes application, where they needed to configure the file that tells the two computers how to communicate. This file is Jnbproxy.config and lives in the WWWroot folder. The developers changed the name **LOCALHOST** to point to the J2EE computer. They also installed Jnbshare.dll and Jnbridgebllproxies.dll in the global assembly cache.

Using Ja.NET for Interoperability

This section shows how you can use Ja.NET to perform bridging between a .NET Web tier application and a J2EE Business tier. Like the previous section on JNBridgePro, it covers the data format choices, how to build the service interface and how to build the interoperability adapters.

Deciding on a Data Format

Ja.NET also has the ability to provide .NET with proxy classes for the Java data classes, allowing you to use these generated data classes throughout your .NET application. For reasons mentioned earlier in this chapter it is more sensible to place the data into a dataset, which can then be used in the .NET Presentation tier. Hence you are likely to perform some data conversion when building the interoperability adapters in .NET.

Building the Service Interface for Ja.NET

Like with JNBridgePro, you could choose to expose an existing service façade to .NET. However, you should protect your code from changes by implementing a layered approach. You can do this by creating another Java class to be your service interface. Because you can return native Java data types to .NET using Ja.NET, this service interface simply calls the appropriate methods on the service façade and returns the resultant data types.

Applications that use Ja.NET for interoperability need Ja.NET runtime components on the J2EE side, and proxy definition libraries (DLLs) on the .NET side. The Java-side runtime component acts as a .NET Framework remoting server, marshalling and unmarshaling parameters, returning values, dispatching methods, and managing the lifecycles of Java objects that .NET references.

Again the developers created the Ja.NET service interface as a Java class. This class passes the method calls across to the existing session bean service façade. This example also shows the **AuthenticateCustomer** use case:

1. The developers created a new **Web Project** called **JaNetBLL**. They added this to the existing **SingleTierXBikes** EAR. Like before, they included **XBikesCommon** and **XBikesBiz** projects as module references.

2. The developers created the contents of the Web project using the **Janetor** tool. This tool creates a WAR that contains the Ja.NET runtime and a configured Web.xml file. After installing the license, they had to configure the host name of the application server, and then export the WAR. They then imported this WAR into the newly created **JaNetBLL** project, overwriting files as needed.

3. To allow the JaNet project to talk to the session bean, the developers created an EJB reference in the Web project to point to the **BusinessServiceFacade** session bean.

4. Finally, they created a Java Class called **BLLServiceInterface** in the **xbikes.bll.serviceinterface.j2ee.janet** package. This class has the same methods as the **BusinessServiceFacade** and simply passes the method calls onto this session bean.

Note: This class is exactly the same as the one detailed in the JNBridge section.

While you can use Ja.NET to generate proxies that access the **BusinessServiceFacade** and the supporting JNDI classes directly, it is more efficient if you perform these operations entirely on the Java side and encapsulate the operations within a wrapper. In other situations, where you cannot change the J2EE code, you might have to access JNDI and EJB classes directly. The section on Using the MSMQ-MQSeries Bridge in Chapter 9, "Implementing Asynchronous Interoperability," shows how to create an adapter that accesses the MQSeries APIs and demonstrates how you could create such an adapter if it were impossible to change the J2EE code.

Building the Interoperability Adapters using Ja.NET

After you construct the service interface that you want your .NET application to consume, you need to generate the proxy assembly for .NET. This assembly contains .NET proxies for the service interface, along with data classes that the service interface uses. For example, if the service interface returns data of the Java type **CustomerData**, the .NET assembly that Ja.NET generates would contain a proxy for this class.

You can use the Ja.NET GUI tools to generate these proxy classes. Select which classes for which you wish to generate proxies and Ja.NET creates them.

You can then add this assembly to your .NET project as a reference, along with the required Ja.NET configuration files, and then consume it like any other .NET class, such as the interoperability adapter. Again, you have to decide upon the level of fine control of the interoperability adapters, either implementing one for each use case, or one for the whole service interface.

Creating the Java Proxy Classes

The first stage in creating the interoperability adapters in XBikes was to generate the proxies for the Java service interface. To do this the developers used the GUI-based proxy generation tool GenNet that is part of Ja.Net.

1. The developers started **GenNet** and added the following folders and Project Utility Jars:

   - C:\xbikes\J2EE-IBM\JaNetBLL\Web ContentWEB-INF\classes
   - C:\xbikes\J2EE-IBM\XBikesCommon
   - C:\Program Files\IBM\WebSphere Studio\runtimes\base_v5\lib\j2ee.jar
   - C:\xbikes\J2EE-IBM\XBikesBiz\ejbModule

2. Next they added the **BLLServiceInterface** class and all the classes in the **xbikes.common.data** package. They changed the data classes to pass by value to improve performance.

3. The developers then saved the generated proxy assembly as JanetBLLEjb.dll with a strong name. The **GenNet** proxy generation tool also generates a remoting configuration file, named Remoting_http.config, containing the .NET Remoting settings that enable communication with the Java components.

Now that they had generated the proxies, the next task was to integrate this into the ASP.NET Presentation tier.

Note: This example focuses on the **AuthenticateCustomer** use case; however the rest follow the same pattern.

Implementing the Interoperability Adapters

The developers opened the .NET XBikes solution and added a new project called **XBikes-UseCaseInteropAdapters-JaNET**. In this project the developers added a new class called **AuthenticateCustomerInteropAdapter** to the **J2EE\JaNET** folder.

Note: The JNBridge and JaNET use case interoperability adapters reside in separate Visual Studio projects from the other XBikes .NET use case interoperability adapters. This avoids conflicts when using JaNET and JNBridge elements within the same project. In a production environment, it is unlikely that you would need both JaNET and JNBridge.

Because the interoperability adapter uses the Ja.Net-generated Java proxies, the developers copied the JanetBLLEjb.dll to the .NET computer and installed it in the GAC. They then added it as a reference to the **XBikes-UseCaseInteropAdapters -JaNET** project.

The **AuthenticateCustomerInteropAdapter** handles the bridging between the .NET Web tier and the J2EE Business tier when authenticating a customer's identity. It implements the **IUseCaseCommand** interface, which means it implements two methods:

- **Initialise()**—Sets up the use case adapter and assigns parameters for the upcoming action.
- **Execute()**—Causes the use case adapter to perform its action.

The interoperability adapter creates a Ja.NET-generated proxy for the J2EE-based **BLLServiceInterface** object, which is the object that performs the authentication of the customer. The interoperability adapter's constructor creates the proxy, and, as part of that action, creates the underlying J2EE **BLLServiceInterface** object.

The call to **Initialise()** simply takes the customers email address and password (both strings), and saves them so that they are available when the command executes. The call to **Execute()** calls the **authenticateCustomer()** method in the **BLLServiceInterface** proxy object, which causes the equivalent method to execute in J2EE, and returns a by value copy of a J2EE **CustomerData** object. This is in accordance with the Ja.NET Best Practices in Chapter 4, "Interoperability Technologies: Point to Point."

On the .NET side, this **CustomerData** object is a proxy of the J2EE **CustomerData** object. The remainder of **Execute()** converts the J2EE **CustomerData** object into an equivalent native .NET **CustomerData** object. It does this by iterating through the individual product data in the J2EE **CustomerData** object, extracting the details of that product, and assigning a new native .NET **CustomerRow** row object to the native .NET **CustomerData** object.

```
using System;
using xbikes.bll.serviceinterface.j2ee.janet;
using xbikes.common.data;
using XBikes.Common.Interfaces.Architecture;
using XBikes.Common.Schemas;
using System.Data;
using XBikes.Common.Exceptions;


namespace XBikes.UseCaseInteropAdapters.J2EE.JaNET
{
    /// <summary>
    /// Class that implements the IUseCaseCommand interface.
    /// This class performs the task of
    /// AuthenticateCustomerInteropAdapter.
    /// It calls into the J2EE Server to get at its BLL Service
    /// Interface
    /// and calls the authenticateCustomer method on the
    /// BLLServiceInterface contained
    /// in the JaNetBLL servlet.
```

(continued)

(continued)

```
/// In actual fact, you could use Ja.NET and the JNDIContext
/// object
/// to directly call the BLL Bean in the app server.
/// For this Case Study, there is an extra layer that has been
/// added, namely
/// that of
/// xbikes.bll.serviceinterface.j2ee.janet.BLLServiceInterface
/// that lives in the JaNetBll servlet.
/// </summary>
public class AuthenticateCustomerInteropAdapter : IUseCaseCommand
{
    private string m_szPassword = "";
    private string m_szEmail = "";

    // the proxy for the BLL service interface object
    private BLLServiceInterface  _facade = null;

    /// <summary>
    /// The constructor for the authenticate customer use case adapter.
    /// </summary>
    public AuthenticateCustomerInteropAdapter()
    {
        try
        {
            // instantiate the BLL service interface .
            _facade = new BLLServiceInterface();
        }
        catch (Exception e)
        {
            throw new
                XBikesInteropException("[AuthenticateCustomerInteropAdapter]:
                                       J2EE JaNET Interop Adapter error: ", e);
        }
    }

    /// <summary>
    /// Sets the parameters for this UseCaseAdapters
    /// </summary>
    /// <param name="parameters"></param>
    public void Initialise(object[] parameters)
    {
        m_szPassword = (string) parameters[0];
        m_szEmail = (string) parameters[1];
    }

    /// <summary>
    /// The Actual Execute Method
    /// </summary>
    /// <returns>DataSet object</returns>
    public DataSet Execute()
    {
        try
```

(continued)

(continued)

```
        {
            // Create the return DataSet Object
            XBikes.Common.Schemas.CustomerData custData =
                    new XBikes.Common.Schemas.CustomerData();

            // Get the EJB Data
            xbikes.common.data.CustomerData ejbCustData =
                    _facade.authenticateCustomer(m_szPassword, m_szEmail);
            // We need a row
            XBikes.Common.Schemas.CustomerData.CustomersRow cr =
                    custData.Customers.NewCustomersRow();
            // Fill in the values
            cr.CustomerID = ejbCustData.getCustomerID();
            cr.EmailAddress = ejbCustData.getAddress();
            cr.FullName = ejbCustData.getName();
            cr.Password = ejbCustData.getPassword();
            cr.ZipCode = ejbCustData.getZip();
            custData.Customers.AddCustomersRow(cr);
            return custData;

        }
        catch (XBikesApplicationException ae)
        {
            throw ae;
        }
        catch (XBikesInteropException ae)
        {
            throw ae;
        }
        catch (System.Runtime.Remoting.RemotingException sre)
        {
            // Is it a problem with the network?
            string message = sre.Message;
            if (message.IndexOf("com.intrinsyc.janet") >= 0)
            {
                throw new XBikesInteropException(sre.Message, sre);
            }
            else
            {
                // or is it an application error?
                throw new XBikesApplicationException(sre.Message, sre);
            }
        }
        catch (Exception eX)
        {
            // generic catch/rethrow
            throw new XBikesApplicationException(eX.Message, eX);
        }

    }
  }
}
```

The final part of the implementing JaNET interoperability adapter is to set up the configuration files. In ASP.NET Web applications, all .NET Remoting configuration settings must be read during the event handler for the **Application_OnStart** event of the web application. JaNET uses .NET Remoting to communicate with the Java components, and the interoperability adapters run as part of the .NET Presentation tier's ASP.NET application. Hence the JaNET configuration settings must also be read in during the event handler for the **Application_OnStart** event of the ASP.NET application. The event handler for the **Application_OnStart** event lives in the Global.asax.cs file of the Web application. This introduces two minor complications to the application architecture:

- If your ASP.NET application communicates with any other components using .NET Remoting, the remoting configuration settings for those components must live in the same file and load at the same time as the **Application_OnStart** event.

- By loading JaNET configuration settings from the **Global.asax.cs** file of the ASP.NET application the interoperability adapter no longer provides complete abstraction.

To accommodate the remoting configuration requirements of the ASP.NET application, the XBikes developers then updated the remoting configuration file, Remoting.config, in **XBikes-Web** with the content from the client section of the Remoting_http.config file that the proxy tool generated.

Note: You can only configure one instance of a type of channel in a .NET Remoting configuration file. Hence you can only have one HTTP channel configured at a time, which can cause issues if you have existing components in your ASP.NET application that use .NET Remoting to communicate. If you already have a channel configured in the Remoting.config file, check that you do not copy the definition of the same type of channel twice when you copy the Ja.NET configuration settings from Remoting_http.config (the generated configuration file) into the Remoting.config file.

If the .NET and J2EE components are on different computers, then you need to ensure the URL specified in the <client> tag of the JaNET configuration settings within the **Remoting.config** file contains the name of the computer hosting the J2EE components.

Summary

This chapter looked at how the developers implemented interoperability in the sample XBikes application. You saw how to implement an ASP.NET application in the Presentation tier and then connect this to an existing J2EE Business tier. You saw how to implement use case adapters, service interfaces and service façades to do this. You also covered how to use runtime bridges to connect J2EE and .NET where Web services are not suitable.

References

For more information about GLUE
http://www.themindelectric.com/

- or -

http://www.webmethods.com/

8

Integrating .NET in the Business Tier

Introduction

Chapter 7, "Integrating .NET in the Presentation Tier," described how to integrate a .NET Framework Presentation tier with a J2EE Business tier and how to define Java service interfaces that encapsulate J2EE business service façades. It then covered the design of .NET Framework interoperability adapters so that .NET Framework applications, such as ASP.NET Web Forms, can invoke the Java service interfaces.

This chapter is the reverse of Chapter 7; it describes how to integrate a J2EE Presentation tier with a .NET Framework Business tier. It includes two sections that define different ways to achieve this interoperability:

- **Using Web Services for Interoperability**—This section describes how to define .NET Framework Web service (WS) service interfaces to encapsulate .NET Framework business service façades. It then describes how to design Java interoperability adapters to enable Java code, such as a J2EE Presentation tier to invoke the .NET Framework WS service interfaces.

- **Using Ja.NET for Interoperability**—This section describes how to use Ja.NET to enable a J2EE Presentation tier to access .NET Framework business service façades through the use of .NET Remoting.

For each of these approaches, this chapter describes how to address the following technical issues:

- Determining data exchange formats and types.
- Designing and building the service interface.
- Designing and building the interoperability adapters.

The following sections briefly summarize how you can resolve these technical issues in the Web services and Ja.NET scenarios. The chapter then provides detailed descriptions of each scenario and describes what the XBikes developers did in the sample application.

Determining Data Exchange Formats and Types

As Chapter 7 illustrates, one of the keys to interoperability is to define and use consistent data exchange formats and data types in the .NET Framework and Java applications. This chapter describes how to expose data formats and data types from the .NET Framework Business tier and how to consume these data formats and data types in the J2EE Presentation layer.

A good way to achieve consistency is to define XML Schemas to represent your data types. You can then generate .NET Framework and Java classes that are compatible with the XSD types and use XML serialization to convert between XML data and objects in memory. This approach is particularly suitable when you use Web services as the interoperability mechanism, because Web services always exchange data in XML format (enclosed in a SOAP envelope).

When you use .NET Remoting as the interoperability mechanism, Ja.NET allows you to expose most .NET Framework data types to Java. You can therefore pass actual .NET Framework objects between the J2EE Presentation tier and the .NET Framework Business tier.

For a detailed discussion about data exchange factors, see Chapter 3, "Interoperability Fundamentals."

Designing and Building the Service Interface

As described in Chapter 7, the role of the service interface is to expose the functionality of the business service façade so that other parts of the application can access it.

Chapter 6, "Implementing Interoperability Design Elements," described how the developers implemented the XBikes business service façade in .NET Framework. In your application, this could be either a serviced component or an ordinary .NET Framework class. The service interface exposes this .NET Framework functionality to the J2EE Presentation tier. The J2EE Presentation tier can call into the service interface, and then the service interface relays the calls on to the .NET Framework business service façade.

Depending on your implementation details, the service interface might need to manipulate data before it is passed into the business service façade, and it might also need to manipulate returned values from the business service façade.

Designing and Building the Interoperability Adapters

Interoperability adapters change the data from your applications into a suitable format for interoperability. They also hide the implementation details of the interoperability technique from the connected applications.

You should create interoperability adapters based on the design of the service interface and the level of fine control that you require. You may choose either to build an interoperability adapter for each use case or implement a single interoperability adapter for each service. The interoperability adapters may have to change the structure of the data before returning it to the calling application.

In the XBikes application, the developers created an interoperability adapter for each use case. This choice allows selection of the interoperability technology at the use case level, showing how different use cases can execute through different interoperability adapters. For example, the **AuthenticateCustomer** use case could execute in the .NET Business tier, whereas the **GetCategories** use case calls into the J2EE Business tier.

Using Web Services for Interoperability

Web services are the recommended interoperability technique, unless performance or other considerations require a binary solution. This section looks at how you can use Web services to implement interoperability. It covers the data format choices, how to build the service interface by using .NET Framework Web services, and how to build the J2EE interoperability adapters.

Deciding on a Data Format

As Chapter 7 observed, it is a good idea for Web services to use primitive XSD data types such as strings and integers instead of using complex XSD data types. All Web service stacks support the primitive XSD data types, so using these data types promotes flexibility and simplifies client access.

If you use primitive data types and need to return something more complex, such as an order, you can package the data as a string. The best solution for this is to populate a string with an XML representation of the data. This XML encoding should follow an agreed schema.

If your communicating applications use compatible Web services stacks, then you can use complex data types to link components rather than serializing into an XML string. While there is currently no guarantee of interoperability between all manufacturers' Web stacks, this situation should change as more Web stack implementations start to follow industry guidelines.

Note: There is little performance difference between passing .NET Framework data types directly and serializing them and passing them as strings, because the Web service has to serialize the .NET Framework data into XML anyway.

In the XBikes application, the J2EE and .NET Framework developer teams decided on a common data format for the Web services. They created an XML Schema from this design, which both teams then used to create the appropriate classes and mapping files.

Building the Service Interface in .NET Framework

You perform the following two tasks to build the service interface in .NET Framework:

- Define .NET Framework data types based on an XML Schema.
- Create .NET Framework Web services.

The following sections describe how to perform these tasks.

Defining .NET Framework Data Types based on an XML Schema

To enable .NET Framework applications to present data for consumption by Java applications, it is a good idea to define .NET Framework classes that you can serialize as XML strings. You can use the Xsd.exe tool in the .NET Framework SDK to generate .NET Framework classes from existing XML Schemas. When instances of these classes are serialized to XML, they generate the correct XML structure as defined by the XML Schemas.

You can use the Xsd.exe tool in one of two ways, depending on how you want to represent data within your .NET Framework application:

- Use the **/dataset** switch to generate .NET Framework typed dataset classes.
- Use the **/class** switch to generate normal .NET Framework classes.

The XBikes developers used the Xsd.exe tool with the **/dataset** switch to generate .NET Framework typed dataset classes. The following code sample shows how the XBikes developers generated a typed dataset class for the **CustomerData** type. To do this, they opened a Visual Studio .NET 2003 command prompt and ran the following command (note that the **/namespace** switch specifies the .NET Framework namespace of the generated classes).

```
xsd CustomerData.xsd /dataset /namespace:xbikes.common.schemas
```

Typed dataset classes inherit from the **System.Data.DataSet** class and have named inner types and type-safe properties that map directly to the XML structure that the XML Schema defines. Typed dataset classes are serializable by default. However, if you serialize a typed dataset using the **XMLSerializer** class in .NET Framework, the serialized XML output does not conform to the XML Schema that you used to generate the typed dataset. Instead, it contains an XML representation of the typed dataset object itself, including .NET Framework-specific information such as the inner types and type-safe properties. You cannot use this method to exchange data in an interoperability scenario as the Java client does not know how to deserialize the .NET Framework-specific XML format of the serialized typed dataset.

To get around this issue, you can use the typed dataset's **GetXml** method. Typed datasets have a **GetXml** method, which returns the data contained in a dataset object in an XML formatted string. The format of the XML string the **GetXml** method returns matches the one specified by the XML Schema that defines the typed dataset. You can then exchange this XML string with Java clients that can then deserialize it into a corresponding Java class.

If you are not using datasets in your .NET Framework application, you can use the **/class** switch with Xsd.exe to generate normal .NET Framework classes as shown in the following example, which again illustrates the **CustomerData** custom data class.

```
xsd CustomerData.xsd /class /namespace:MyNamespace
```

The generated classes contain public fields corresponding to the structure defined by the XML Schema. It is a good idea to make the fields private and define public properties to get and set the fields. The following sample code shows how the generated classes appear after making these changes.

```
using System;
using System.Xml.Serialization;

namespace MyNamespace
{
  [System.Xml.Serialization.XmlTypeAttribute(
          Namespace="http://xbikes.com/CustomerData.xsd")]
  [System.Xml.Serialization.XmlRootAttribute(
          Namespace="http://xbikes.com/CustomerData.xsd", IsNullable=false)]
  public class CustomerData
  {
    private CustomerDataCustomers[] Items;

    [System.Xml.Serialization.XmlElementAttribute("Customers")]
    public CustomerDataCustomers[] customers
    {
      set { Items = value; }
      get { return Items;  }
    }
  }
```

(continued)

(continued)

```
[System.Xml.Serialization.XmlTypeAttribute(
        Namespace="http://xbikes.com/CustomerData.xsd")]
public class CustomerDataCustomers
{
  private int    _CustomerID;
  private string _FullName;
  private string _EmailAddress;
  private string _Password;
  private string _ZipCode;

  public int CustomerID
  {
    set { _CustomerID = value; }
    get { return _CustomerID;  }
  }

  public string FullName
  {
    set { _FullName = value; }
    get { return _FullName;  }
  }

  public string EmailAddress
  {
    set { _EmailAddress = value; }
    get { return _EmailAddress;  }
  }

  public string Password
  {
    set { _Password = value; }
    get { return _Password;  }
  }

  public string ZipCode
  {
    set { _ZipCode = value; }
    get { return _ZipCode;  }
  }
 }
}
```

The next set of sample code shows how to create and serialize an instance of the **CustomerData** class. **XmlSerializer** is a standard .NET Framework class in the **System.Xml.Serialization** namespace, and it allows you to serialize and deserialize objects to and from XML format.

```
using System;                    // For the Console class
using System.Xml.Serialization;  // For the XmlSerializer class
using System.IO;                 // For the StringReader and StringWriter classes
using System.Text;               // For the StringBuilder class
using MyNamespace;               // For CustomerData and CustomerDataCustomers

class SerializationExample
{
  static void Main(string[] args)
  {
    // Create and initialise a customer
    CustomerDataCustomers customer = new CustomerDataCustomers();
    customer.FullName = "someone";
    customer.EmailAddress = "someone@microsoft.com";
    customer.CustomerID = 1008;
    customer.Password = "secret";
    customer.ZipCode = "91210";

    // Create a customer collection, containing a single customer
    CustomerData cd = new CustomerData();
    cd.customers = new CustomerDataCustomers[] { customer };

    // Serialize the customer collection to an XML string
    XmlSerializer ser = new XmlSerializer(typeof(CustomerData));
    StringBuilder sb = new StringBuilder();
    StringWriter writer = new StringWriter(sb);
    ser.Serialize(writer, cd);
    writer.Close();

    // Output the XML string that represents the customer collection
    Console.Write(sb.ToString());
  }
}
```

The result is that when the **CustomerData** object is serialized to XML, the XML data has exactly the correct format as specified by the XML Schema.

Creating the .NET Framework Web Service

The next task is to create a .NET Framework Web service to provide a service interface that encapsulates the .NET Framework business service façade.

Visual Studio .NET and the .NET Framework make it extremely easy to create Web services. When you create an ASP.NET Web service project in Visual Studio .NET, the project contains a single Web service. The Web service comprises an .asmx file (for example, MyWebService.asmx) and a code-behind file (for example, MyWebService.asmx.cs). The code-behind file contains a class that inherits from **System.Web.Services.WebService**, and it can contain a series of methods annotated with the **[WebMethod]** attribute.

You must define a separate Web service method for each business method that you want to expose from the **BusinessServiceFacade**. To simplify interoperability, the Web service methods should convert the return values from the **BusinessServiceFacade** methods into XML-formatted strings. Use one of the following techniques to perform this conversion:

- If you are using .NET Framework datasets to represent data, you can call **GetXml** to convert the dataset into an XML string.

- If you are using normal .NET Framework classes to represent data, you must use the **XmlSerializer** to obtain the XML string representation for your objects.

The flow of logic in any of the Web service methods is as follows:

1. The application calls the Web service method.
2. The Web service method creates the **BusinessServiceFacade** object.
3. The Web service method calls the appropriate method on the **BusinessServiceFacade**, passing the converted data.
4. If the **BusinessServiceFacade** method returns data, the Web service method converts this data to a string by using the helper class.
5. The Web service method returns the string representation of the data back to the calling application.

Figure 8.1 shows this in action.

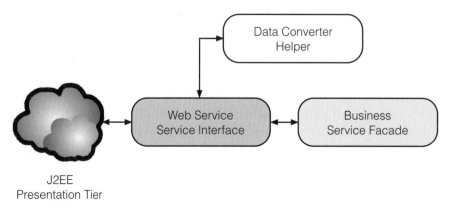

Figure 8.1

Implementing a .NET Framework service interface for the .NET Framework business service façade

The following procedure describes how the XBikes developers created a .NET Framework Web service service interface to expose the business service façade in the Business tier of the .NET Framework version of XBikes:

1. The developers created a new ASP.NET Web service project named **XBikes-BLL-WSServiceInterface**.

2. They removed the default Service1.asmx file and replaced it with a new Web service named BLLWSServiceInterface.asmx. The developers annotated the Web service class with a **[WebService]** attribute as follows.

```
[WebService(Namespace="http://XBikes.com/BLLWSServiceInterace/")]
public class BLLWSServiceInterface : System.Web.Services.WebService
{
    // Members...
}
```

3. The team added Web service methods to the Web service class, with the correct method signatures for each of the methods exposed by the existing business service façade. However, instead of each method accepting or returning datasets as parameters, the developers changed the data type exchanged to "string."

```
[WebService(Namespace="http://XBikes.com/BLLWSServiceInterace/")]
public class BLLWSServiceInterface : System.Web.Services.WebService
{
    [WebMethod]
    public string AuthenticateCustomer(string email, string password)
    {}

    [WebMethod]
    public string GetCategories()
    {}

    [WebMethod]
    public string GetProductsByCategory(int CategoryID)
    {}

    [WebMethod]
    public string GetSearchResults(string keyword)
    {}

    [WebMethod]
    public void PlaceOrder(string order)
    {}

    [WebMethod]
    public string GetCustomerOrders(int customerID)
    {}
}
```

4. The team added code to each of the Web service methods to call the business service façade methods. The following code sample shows how this was done for the **GetCategories** method in the Web service service interface. The developers called the **GetXml** method of the **CategoriesData** object returned from the business service façade to convert the data into an XML formatted string, which the WS service interface returns to its caller.

```
[WebMethod]
public string GetCategories()
{
  try
  {
    // Create a business service façade (BSF) object
    BusinessServiceFacade bsf = new BusinessServiceFacade();

    // Call the GetCategories method on the BSF object
    CategoriesData cd = bsf.GetCategories();

    // Convert the CategoriesData dataset into XML, and return it
    return cd.GetXml();
  }
  catch (XBikesInteropException intExp)
  {
    //.. Error handling code
  }
}
```

5. According the WS-I Basic Profile 1.0, Web services should support the SOAP protocol but not the HTTPGet or HTTPPost protocols. To remove support for the protocols from the Web service, the XBikes developers added the following code to the **<system.web>** section of the Web.config file for the Web service.

```
<webServices>
  <protocols>
    <remove name="HttpGet" />
    <remove name="HttpPost" />
  </protocols>
</webServices>
```

To test the Web service, the developers built and ran the Web service project in Visual Studio .NET 2003. When you run an ASP.NET Web service project, a test page appears automatically in the browser. The test page contains hyperlinks that allow you to invoke each of the Web service methods. The test page also has text boxes for you to enter input values if necessary. After you invoke a Web service method, another browser window opens showing the XML response from the Web service method.

Note: Although the XBikes sample application is not fully WS-I Basic Profile 1.0 compliant, the developers used toolkit capability, available at the time of development, to come as close as possible to Basic Profile compliance.

Creating the Interoperability Adapters in J2EE

Earlier sections described how to create the Web service service interface in .NET Framework; after that is created, you can proceed to build the J2EE interoperability adapters. This section describes how. The procedures to do this are as follows:

● Build the Java data classes based on the XML Schema.

● Build a Web service proxy using the tools provided by your Web services stack.

● Create an adapter for either the entire service interface, or one for each use case.

Note: In XBikes, the developers created an adapter for each use case.

The interoperability adapter calls the proxy, which then calls the Web service. The adapter also has to convert any Java data to and from the correct string/XML format based on the XML Schema.

The logic flow for an adapter is as follows:

1. The application calls the adapter method.

2. The adapter method converts any complex data to an XML string representation.

3. The adapter method creates an instance of the Web service proxy.

4. The adapter method calls the appropriate method in the Web service proxy.

5. If the proxy returns data, the adapter method converts it into the correct Java format if necessary.

6. The adapter method returns the data back to the calling application.

Figure 8.2 shows this in operation.

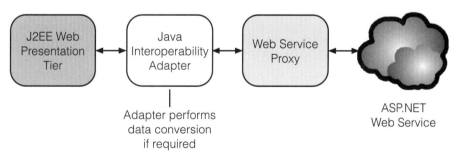

Figure 8.2
Web service proxy operation with J2EE applications

The tasks to build the Java adapters are the following:

1. Create the Java data types and XML mapping from the XML Schema.
2. Create the Java Web service proxies from the WSDL for the .NET Framework Web service.
3. Create the Java adapters to convert Java data and call the .NET Framework Web service.

The following sections describe how to perform these tasks.

Creating Java Data Types and XML Mapping from the XML Schema

Most Java XML products provide tools that allow you to create Java data types based on an XML Schema. Typically, these tools also create a mapping file that maps each field in the Java class to an element or attribute in the XML Schema.

Note: If your existing Java data types are already consistent with an XML Schema, you do not have to define intermediary Java classes. Simply define a mapping file that maps Java fields directly to elements and attributes in the XML Schema.

After you define the XSD-based Java classes, the next step is to write code that copies data from your original Java objects into objects of the XSD-based classes. You must then write code to serialize the XSD-based objects into an XML formatted string.

It is a good idea to put the serialization code into a *helper* class, and this is what the XBikes developers did. The **helper** class requires two methods for each type of data you want to write to a string or read from a string; the methods take a single parameter for the type of data you want to convert and return a single value of the converted type. The following method signatures show how to convert an **Order** object to and from an XML formatted string.

```
public static String orderToString(Order o);
public static Order StringToOrder(String o);
```

The following steps illustrate how the XBikes developers created XSD-based Java classes from the CustomerData.xsd XML Schema described earlier in this chapter. The XBikes developers used GLUE to generate the XSD-based Java classes, and to create mapping files so that GLUE can serialize and deserialize Java objects to and from XML. The steps were:

1. The developers created Java classes based on the CustomerData.xsd schema, using the schema2java tool provided by GLUE.

```
schema2java CustomerData.xsd -g -p xbikes.common.dataconverters.customers
```

2. The **schema2java** command generated two Java files, CustomerData_TYPE.java and Customers_TYPE.java. The XBikes developers added these files to the Java project, placing them in the common package for easy access. The package destination was **xbikes.common.dataconverters.customers**.

3. The **schema2java** command also generated a CustomerData.map file, which the GLUE serializer uses to map the fields to the correct XML elements and attributes. The XBikes developers copied this map file into the XBikesWeb\Web Content \WEB-INF\maps folder, which is where GLUE expects to find map files for XML serialization.

4. Because GLUE is the chosen environment, the team added the Glue.jar file to the build path.

5. Next, the developers wrote a **Helper** class to perform the conversion between Java data and strings. They named the new class **CustomerConverter**, and added it to the **xbikes.common.dataconverters** package.

6. The developers added two methods to the **CustomerConverter** class, one to convert an XML string into a Java object, and the other to convert a Java object into an XML string. These methods use the GLUE serializer to read and write XML data from XSD-based **CustomerData_TYPE** and **Customers_TYPE** objects.

   The **CustomerData_TYPE** and **Customers_TYPE** data types exist solely to allow XML data to be serialized and deserialzed as Java objects; the rest of the J2EE application uses an existing Java class named **CustomerData**. Therefore the conversion methods in **CustomerConverter** are expressed entirely in terms of the **CustomerData** class, and they perform internal conversions between this data type and **CustomerData_TYPE** and **Customers_TYPE**.

   The following code listing shows the completed **CustomerConverter** class.

```
package xbikes.common.dataconverters;
import java.io.StringWriter;
import xbikes.common.data.CustomerData;
import xbikes.common.dataconverters.customers.CustomerData_TYPE;
import xbikes.common.dataconverters.customers.Customers_TYPE;
import xbikes.common.exceptions.XBikesInteropException;
import electric.xml.Document;
import electric.xml.io.IReader;
import electric.xml.io.IWriter;
import electric.xml.io.literal.LiteralReader;
import electric.xml.io.literal.LiteralWriter;
public final class CustomerConverter
{
    private static final String WRITER = "CustomerData";
    private static final String NAMESPACE =
        "http://tempuri.org/CustomerData.xsd";
```

(continued)

(continued)

```java
public static CustomerData stringToCustomerData(String xml) throws
    XBikesInteropException
{
    try
    {
        // Need to convert the string into xml
        Document d = new Document(xml);
        IReader reader = new LiteralReader(d);
        CustomerData_TYPE myCustomer =
            (CustomerData_TYPE)
            reader.readObject(CustomerData_TYPE.class);
        Customers_TYPE customer = myCustomer.getCustomers();
        CustomerData cd = new CustomerData();
        cd.setAddress(customer.getEmailAddress());
        cd.setCustomerID(customer.getCustomerID());
        cd.setName(customer.getFullName());
        cd.setPassword(customer.getPassword());
        cd.setZip(customer.getZipCode());
        return cd;
    }
    catch (Exception e)
    {
        System.out.println(e.getMessage());
        throw new XBikesInteropException(e.getMessage());
    }
}
public static String customerDataToString(CustomerData cd) throws
    XBikesInteropException
{
    try
    {
        // Move the data from the internal java classes into those
        // generated by the schema tool
        Customers_TYPE customer = new Customers_TYPE();
        customer.setCustomerID(cd.getCustomerID());
        customer.setEmailAddress(cd.getAddress());
        customer.setFullName(cd.getName());
        customer.setPassword(cd.getPassword());
        customer.setZipCode(cd.getZip());
        CustomerData_TYPE customerData = new CustomerData_TYPE();
        customerData.setCustomers(customer);
        // Write the object to a string, via the LiteralWriter /
        // Document and StringBuffer
        IWriter writer = new LiteralWriter(WRITER);
        writer.writeObject(customerData);
        writer.writeNamespace("", NAMESPACE);
        Document d = writer.getDocument();
        String sCustomerData = "";
        StringWriter sw = new StringWriter();
        d.write(sw);
```

(continued)

(continued)

```
            sCustomerData = sw.getBuffer().toString();
            return sCustomerData;
        }
        catch (Exception e)
        {
            System.out.println(e.getMessage());
            throw new XBikesInteropException(e.getMessage());
        }
    }
}
```

The conversion methods in the **CustomerConverter** class allow **CustomerData** objects to be converted to and from the XML format defined by the **CustomerData.xsd** schema.

Creating Java Web Service Proxies

The next task is to generate the Java proxy classes for the .NET Framework Web service. Most Web service stacks provide a tool named wsdl2java (or similar), to generate Java proxy classes from WSDL.

The following steps describe how the XBikes developers used GLUE to generate Java proxy classes for the .NET Framework Web service:

1. The developers used the Wsdl2java tool in GLUE to generate Java proxy classes and associated helper classes for the .NET Framework Web service.

   ```
   wsdl2java
   http://localhost/XBikes-BLL-WSServiceInterface/BLLWSServiceInterface.asmx?wsdl
   -p xbikes.usecaseintropadapters.net.ws
   ```

   This command generated a **BLLWSWebServiceInterfaceHelper** Java class and an **IBLLWSServiceInterfaceSoap** Java interface These Java types were located in **xbikes.usecaseinteropadapters.net.ws** Java package.

2. The developers added the **BLLWSWebServiceInterfaceHelper** Java class and the **IBLLWSServiceInterfaceSoap** Java interface to the J2EE **XBikesWeb** project.

The Web service proxies enable the J2EE presentation layer to invoke Web service methods upon the .NET Framework Web service.

Creating the J2EE Interoperability Adapters

Now that you have the Java data classes and Web service proxies, you can define the interoperability adapters for the J2EE application. You can either define a single adapter for each Web service or define a separate adapter for each use case, depending upon the level of fine control you require. The XBikes developers created an adapter for each use case to give maximum flexibility.

The XBikes use cases follow the Command pattern. Each adapter class implements an interface named **IUseCaseCommand** and provides **initialise** and **execute** methods:

- **initialise**—Sets up the use case adapter and assigns parameters for the upcoming action.

- **execute**—Causes the use case adapter to perform its action.

Adapter classes are named after the command that they adapt. For example, **AuthenticateCustomerCommandAdapter** is the adapter class for the **AuthenticateCustomerCommand** command. The following code listing shows how the XBikes developers implemented the **AuthenticateCustomerCommandAdapter** adapter class.

```
package xbikes.usecaseinteropadapters.j2ee.ws;
import javax.naming.InitialContext;
import javax.naming.NamingException;
import javax.rmi.PortableRemoteObject;

import xbikes.bll.facade.BusinessServiceFacadeHome;
import xbikes.common.data.CustomerData;
import xbikes.common.data.ValueObject;
import xbikes.common.dataconverters.CustomerConverter;
import xbikes.common.interfaces.architecture.IUseCaseCommand;
public class AuthenticateCustomerCommandAdapter implements IUseCaseCommand
{
    private String email;
    private String password;
    /**
     * Constructor for AuthenticateCustomerCommandAdapter.
     */
    public AuthenticateCustomerCommandAdapter()
    {
        super();
        this.email = "";
        this.password = "";
    }
    /**
     * @see xbikes.common.interfaces.architecture.IUseCaseCommand#execute()
     */
    public ValueObject execute() throws Exception
    {
        IBLLWSServiceInterface service;
        service = BikesWebServiceHelper.bind();
        String xml = service.authenticateCustomer(email, password);
        CustomerData cd = CustomerConverter.stringToCustomerData(xml);
        return cd;
    }
```

(continued)

(continued)

```
public ValueObject execute(String pEmail, String pPassword) throws Exception
{
    this.email = pEmail;
    this.password = pPassword;
    return this.execute();
}
/**
 * @see
 xbikes.common.interfaces.architecture.IUseCaseCommand#initialise(Object[])
 */
public void initialise(Object[] params)
{
    this.email = params[0].toString();
    this.password = params[1].toString();
}

}
```

This section described how to create interoperability adapters in Java and service interfaces in .NET that use Web services to interoperate. The next sections describe how to implement interoperability adapters and service interfaces using Ja.NET to provide higher performance interoperability solutions.

Using Ja.NET for Interoperability

This section shows how you can use Ja.NET to perform bridging between a Java (JSP) Web tier and a .NET Framework Business tier. It describes the data format choices, how to create the service interface, and how to build the interoperability adapters.

Deciding on a Data Format

Ja.NET implements pure .NET Remoting, allowing you to expose any .NET Framework data type to Java. However, you are advised not to expose datasets to .NET Remoting clients directly for the following reasons:

- The current implementation of the .NET Framework **DataSet** class does not offer optimum performance for serialization and deserialization. This is a known issue, and Microsoft plans to address this in future releases of the .NET Framework.

- Typed datasets include inner classes, but the current version of Ja.NET does not support serialization of inner classes. This will be supported soon in a service release of the Ja.NET runtime.

If your .NET Framework application uses typed datasets, the recommended approach for exchanging data is to generate a set of simple custom data classes from the same XML Schema (XSD file) as the typed datasets. This can be done using the technique shown earlier in the chapter for generating a regular class from an XSD file.

These simple classes contain the data within the dataset classes, but their design improves serialization performance. Also, you can pass the simple classes using Ja.NET because they do not contain any inner-classes.

Building the Service Interface for Ja.NET

Ja.NET is a pure Java implementation of the .NET Remoting protocol, so you do not have to write any special code or runtime libraries when you expose .NET Remoting objects to Java applications.

As the previous section covers, the XBikes developers could not return dataset objects from the .NET Framework service interface. So the developers took the following steps to overcome the difficulties with datasets:

1. They created a set of simple custom data classes for the .NET Framework dataset classes. The simple classes contain the data within the dataset classes but are optimized for performance (for more information, see Ja.NET best practices in Chapter 4, "Interoperability Technologies: Point to Point").

2. The developers created a wrapper interface around the .NET Framework business service façade to return the simple classes instead of the dataset classes.

Figure 8.3 shows how Ja.NET uses pure .NET Remoting to achieve interoperability between the J2EE Presentation tier and the .NET Framework Business tier.

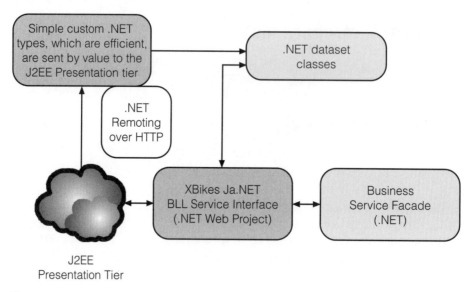

Figure 8.3

Implementing a custom .NET Framework service interface for the .NET Framework business service façade

The following steps describe how the XBikes developers defined a custom service interface to expose the .NET Framework business service façade to Ja.NET:

1. The developers created a new Web project in Visual Studio .NET named **XBikes-BLL-JaNetServiceInterface**.

2. The developers created a series of .NET Framework simple custom data classes, such as the **CustomerData** class shown in the next step; these classes are similar to the corresponding data classes in Java. The developers placed these classes in a folder named **JaNetWireDataTypes**.

```
using System;

namespace XBikes.BLL.ServiceInterface.Net.JaNet
{
    /// <summary>
    /// Wrapper class for DataSet CustomerData class
    /// Merely contains the intrinsic values of the DataSet
    /// It is sent over the wire by value, and is more efficient than
    /// sending the whole DataSet
    /// </summary>
    ///
    [Serializable()]
    public class CustomerData
    {
        /// <summary>
        /// Constructor
        /// </summary>
        public CustomerData()
        {
        }

        private int customerID;

        private string name;

        private string address;

        private string password;

        private string zip;

        /// <summary>
        /// Gets Customer ID
        /// </summary>
        /// <returns>Customer ID</returns>
        public int getCustomerID()
        {
            return customerID;
        }
    }
```

(continued)

(continued)

```
/// <summary>
/// Gets Customer ID
/// </summary>
/// <param name="customerID">Customer ID</param>
public void setCustomerID(int customerID)
{
    this.customerID = customerID;
}

/// <summary>
/// Gets Name
/// </summary>
/// <returns>Name</returns>
public string getName()
{
    return name;
}

/// <summary>
/// Sets Name
/// </summary>
/// <param name="name">Name</param>
public void setName(string name)
{
    this.name = name;
}

/// <summary>
/// Gets Address
/// </summary>
/// <returns>Address</returns>
public string getAddress()
{
    return address;
}

/// <summary>
/// Sets Address
/// </summary>
/// <param name="address">Address</param>
public void setAddress(string address)
{
    this.address = address;
}
```

(continued)

(continued)

```
        /// <summary>
        /// Gets Password
        /// </summary>
        /// <returns>Password</returns>
        public string getPassword()
        {
            return password;
        }

        /// <summary>
        /// Sets Password
        /// </summary>
        /// <param name="password">Password</param>
        public void setPassword(string password)
        {
            this.password = password;
        }

        /// <summary>
        /// Gets Zip
        /// </summary>
        /// <returns>Zip</returns>
        public string getZip()
        {
            return zip;
        }

        /// <summary>
        /// Sets Zip
        /// </summary>
        /// <param name="zip">Zip</param>
        public void setZip(string zip)
        {
            this.zip = zip;
        }
    }
}
```

3. Next the developers created a .NET Framework class named
   BLLJaNetServiceInterface to perform the conversion between .NET Framework
   dataset classes and the simple classes. **BLLJaNetServiceInterface** inherits from
   System.MarshalByRefObject because it is a marshal-by-reference data type.
   The following code listing shows the **AuthenticateCustomer** method for
   BLLJaNetServiceInterface class.

```
using System;
using XBikes.BLL.Facade;
using XBikes.Common.Exceptions;
using XBikes.Common.Schemas;
using System.Collections;
using System.EnterpriseServices;
```

(continued)

(continued)

```
namespace XBikes.BLL.ServiceInterface.Net.JaNet
{
    /// <summary>
    /// Class that wraps the BLL Business Service Facade.
    /// This class is a custom wrapper and does NOT implement the
    /// IBLLServiceFacade interface, as that interface deals directly with
    /// the DataSet classes.
    /// The DataSet classes currently have performance issues when being
    /// serialized over the wire. As well the current version of Ja.NET (1.5.0)
    /// does not handle the serialization of inner classes. The future version
    /// of the DataSet classes will have greatly improved performance. As well,
    /// Ja.NET will support inner class serialization in the new future.
    /// </summary>
    public class BLLJaNetServiceInterface : System.MarshalByRefObject
    {
        /// <summary>
        /// Constructor - No Action
        /// </summary>
        public BLLJaNetServiceInterface()
        {

        }
        /// <summary>
        /// This is the wrapped version of the AuthenticateCustomer
        /// method in the
        /// standard IBLLServiceFacade method. Converts the DataSet
        /// CustomerData object
        /// the more remoting friendly wrapper version.
        /// </summary>
        /// <param name="email">The email of the user</param>
        /// <param name="password">Password of the User</param>
        /// <returns>Wrapped Version of Customer Data</returns>
        public XBikes.BLL.ServiceInterface.Net.JaNet.CustomerData
                AuthenticateCustomer(string email, string password)
        {
            try
            {
                // Create a return type object
                XBikes.BLL.ServiceInterface.Net.JaNet.CustomerData ejbCustData =
                    new XBikes.BLL.ServiceInterface.Net.JaNet.CustomerData();

                // Use the .Net Business Service Facade and
                // get a Data Set customer object
                BusinessServiceFacade bsf = new BusinessServiceFacade();
                XBikes.Common.Schemas.CustomerData custData =
                    (XBikes.Common.Schemas.CustomerData)
                    bsf.AuthenticateCustomer(email, password);
```

(continued)

(continued)

```
            //Check if authentication failed by looking for
            //an empty CustomerData dataset.
            if (custData.Customers.Count != 0)
            {
                // Fill in the wrapper object with values
                // from the DataSet object
                ejbCustData.setCustomerID(custData.Customers[0].CustomerID);
                ejbCustData.setName(custData.Customers[0].FullName);
                ejbCustData.setAddress(custData.Customers[0].EmailAddress);
                ejbCustData.setZip(custData.Customers[0].ZipCode);
            }
            else
            {
                //do nothing - leave ejbCustData empty
            }
            return ejbCustData;
        }
        catch (XBikesApplicationException ae)
        {
            throw ae;
        }
        catch (XBikesInteropException ae)
        {
            throw ae;
        }
        catch (System.Runtime.Remoting.RemotingException sre)
        {
            // Is it a problem with the network?
            string message = sre.Message;
            if (message.IndexOf("com.intrinsyc.janet") >= 0)
            {
                throw new XBikesInteropException(sre.Message, sre);
            }
            else
            {
                // or is it an application error?
                throw new XBikesApplicationException(sre.Message, sre);
            }
        }
        catch (Exception eX)
        {
            // generic catch/rethrow
            throw new XBikesApplicationException(eX.Message, eX);
        }


    }
}
```

4. Finally the XBikes developers modified the **Web.config** file to expose the service for .NET Remoting. The developers chose to host the .NET Remoting component in IIS, using HTTP as the transport but with binary formatting for performance. The **<system.runtime.remoting>** section of the **Web.config** file is shown in the following code sample.

```
<system.runtime.remoting>
  <application>
    <service>
      <activated
         type="XBikes.BLL.ServiceInterface.Net.JaNet.BLLJaNetServiceInterface,
              XBikes-BLL-JaNetServiceInterface" />
    </service>
    <channels>
      <!-- <channel port="<JaNet Port From Janetor>" ref="tcp"/>      -->
      <!-- IMPORTANT:  COMMENT OUT THE FOLLOWING IF UNDER .NET 1.0!!!  -->
      <!-- and uncomment the statement above                          -->
      <channel ref="http">
        <serverProviders>
          <formatter ref="binary" typeFilterLevel="Full"/>
        </serverProviders>
      </channel>
      <!-- END .NET 1.1 SPECIFIC  -->
    </channels>
  </application>
</system.runtime.remoting>
```

Creating the Interoperability Adapters using Ja.NET

After you construct and expose the service interface, the next step is to create the interoperability adapters in J2EE.

Because Ja.NET implements pure .NET Remoting, you must define a Java proxy class that the J2EE application can call to consume the exposed .NET Framework service interface. You can use graphical tools provided by Ja.NET to create this proxy class. After you have created the proxy class, it is a simple task to define the Java interoperability adapters.

The following steps describe how the XBikes developers created the interoperability adapters using Ja.NET:

1. The developers used the GenNet tool to create Java proxy classes for selected .NET Framework assemblies. GenNet generated a set of Java source files, which the developers compiled and added to JanetNetBllProxies.jar. The developers also added Janet.jar to the same folder as JanetNetBllProxies.jar.

2. The developers used the Janetor tool to configure the location of the .NET Framework client. This is the Java equivalent of defining .NET Remoting configuration files.

3. The developers created a new package named
   xbikes.usecaseinteropadapters.net.janet in the **XBikesWeb** project, and they
   added the use case adapter classes. Each adapter class makes a call into the proxy
   JAR file to communicate with a particular .NET Framework service. The code for
   the **AuthenticateCustomerCommandAdapter** adapter class is shown in the
   following code sample.

```
package xbikes.usecaseinteropadapters.net.janet;

import xbikes.common.data.CustomerData;
import xbikes.common.data.ValueObject;
import xbikes.common.interfaces.architecture.IUseCaseCommand;

import XBikes.BLL.ServiceInterface.Net.JaNet.*;

public class AuthenticateCustomerCommandAdapter implements IUseCaseCommand
{
  // Values required when the command is executed
  private String email;
  private String password;

  // Constructor
  public AuthenticateCustomerCommandAdapter() throws Exception
  {
    email = "";
    password = "";
  }

  // Set up the use case adapter and assign parameters for the upcoming action
  public void initialise(Object[] params)
  {
    this.email = params[0].toString();
    this.password = params[1].toString();
  }

  // Execute the command, using the email and password instance variables
  public ValueObject execute() throws Exception
  {
    // Invoke the AuthenticateCustomer method on the remote object
    BLLJaNetServiceInterface rf = new BLLJaNetServiceInterface();
    XBikes.BLL.ServiceInterface.Net.JaNet.CustomerData cdr =
                              rf.AuthenticateCustomer(email, password);

    System.out.println("AuthenticateCustomerCommandAdapter: " +
                  ".NET Framework remoting object returned details " +
                  "for Customer: " + cdr.getname() + ".");
```

(continued)

(continued)

```
        // Return a Java CustomerData object
        return new CustomerData(cdr.getcustomerID(),
                                cdr.getname(),
                                cdr.getaddress(),
                                password,
                                cdr.getzip());
    }

    // Execute the command, using specific email and password values
    public ValueObject execute(String pEmail, String pPassword) throws Exception
    {
      this.email = pEmail;
      this.password = pPassword;
      return this.execute();
    }
  }
}
```

The **AuthenticateCustomerCommandAdapter** adapter class provides a bridge from the J2EE Presentation tier and the .NET Framework Business tier.

Summary

This chapter included practical examples of how to integrate a J2EE Presentation tier with a .NET Framework Business tier. It showed two different interoperability techniques, those of Web services and of .NET Remoting using a runtime bridge. Web services are the preferred mechanism in most situations, but .NET Remoting with a runtime bridge is more appropriate if you require faster communication rates or want to use a binary interoperability mechanism.

9

Implementing Asynchronous Interoperability

Introduction

Implementing asynchronous interoperability is the third interoperability scenario introduced in Chapter 1, "Introduction," involving the connection of .NET Framework components to message queuing components in the Data tier. Asynchronous interoperability covers situations where you want a client application to be able to make a call to another tier or process. Having made the call, the client can then continue to operate while the remote component processes the request rather than wait for the result.

Using asynchronous operations only makes sense for tasks that are amenable to this style of operation. In the sample XBikes application, the process of placing an order is a good candidate for using message queues and is recommended best practice for business to consumer e-commerce applications.

The main focus of this chapter is on connecting to IBM WebSphere MQ. Another section reviews the MSMQ-MQSeries Bridge that ships with Microsoft Host Integration Server (HIS) and provides a bridge between Microsoft Message Queuing (MSMQ) and IBM WebSphere MQ (formerly known as MQSeries).

The section on JNBridgePro covers how you can generate Java proxy assemblies that bridge the connection between the .NET Framework Business tier components and WebSphere MQ. The chapter finishes with a section that shows the same technique using Ja.NET.

Determine Data Exchange Formats and Data Types

Like with the other interoperability technologies, you first have to decide upon a data format that both .NET Framework and Java can understand. This choice is dependent on a number of factors:

- How are you going to integrate with the message queues?
- Are you using a bridging product to wrap message queue functionality?
- Are you using the MSMQ-MQSeries Bridge?

Your choice of data exchange format and data types depends on which integration technology you use:

- If you are using one of the bridging products to wrap the message queue functionality, you are likely to use the same data exchange format and data types as you used for point-to-point communication.
- If you use the MSMQ-MQSeries Bridge, you have to implement a similar strategy to Web services. In order to allow objects to be read from and written to the message queues you must serialize these XML documents into strings. XML-formatted strings preserve the richness of information contained in .NET Framework or Java objects and they overcome the interoperability difficulties that arise when exchanging real objects.

This chapter describes each of these options.

Designing and Building the Service Interface

When using message queuing for asynchronous interoperability, there are no direct calls into service interfaces across technological boundaries. Instead, the role of service interfaces is more like "message consumers." The service interface is an application that monitors and picks up messages from a queue, unpacks the data, and sends it to the existing façade or application that processes the message.

Both .NET Framework and J2EE provide built-in support for activation of components from messages (queued components in .NET Framework and message-driven beans in J2EE). However, there are differences in the required message structure in each case, so this approach is not feasible when you require interoperability between .NET Framework and J2EE. Instead you write a service interface yourself that consumes messages and passes them on to the appropriate service façade.

Building a message consumer is an easy task. Regardless of the technology that you use to write the message, the technique for consuming the message is the same. You need to create a client application or service that polls for messages on the queues and reads any messages found. The data you extract from the message is then either already in the correct format (if it uses the bridging technologies) or requires de-serializing from an XML string back into the correct data class using the techniques described for Web services in Chapters 7 and 8.

Figure 9.1 shows the role of service interfaces in asynchronous communications.

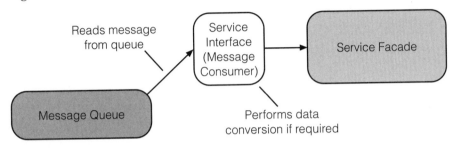

Figure 9.1
The role of service interfaces in asynchronous communications

After the data is back into the correct format, all you need is a method call into the appropriate service façade.

Designing and Building the Asynchronous Interoperability Adapters

Building the asynchronous interoperability adapters is a similar process to building a synchronous adapter, except that instead of making calls to the correct service interface, you place a message in a message queue. Again, depending on the technology in use, you may have to manipulate the data, either by converting it into the Java data proxies or by serializing it into a string as XML.

Figure 9.2 shows the role of interoperability adapters in asynchronous communications.

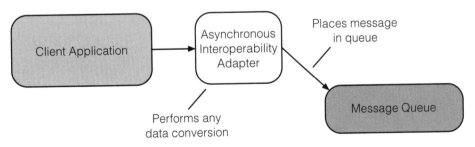

Figure 9.2
The role of interoperability adapters in asynchronous communications

How the message joins the message queue depends upon the technology used. For bridging products that wrap the JMS functionality, you can place the messages in the queue using **ObjectMessage** types; otherwise, you have to use text-based message types.

Using the MSMQ-MQSeries Bridge

If you are familiar with code that writes messages from .NET Framework to MSMQ and have experience of writing JMS code to work with WebSphere MQ, enabling interoperability using the MSMQ-MQSeries Bridge is straightforward.

MSMQ-MQSeries Bridge requires two computers, the first with the following configuration:

- Windows 2000 or Windows 2003
- Active Directory
- MSMQ-MQSeries Bridge
- MSMQ (with routing support)
- WebSphere MQ client

The second computer should have Windows 2000 installed as a member server and should be running WebSphere MQ.

You need to configure the computer running WebSphere MQ as the foreign computer in MSMQ. Do this by creating a foreign site under the Services/MsmqServices node in Active Directory Sites and Services, add a new MSMQ routing link to link the local site (usually Default-First-Site-Name) to the foreign site, add the MSMQ computer as the local site gate, and then add the MQ Series computer as a foreign computer to the foreign site.

For more information about the details of configuring MSMQ foreign sites, see "Configuring cross-platform messaging" on TechNet.

For more information about how to configure and use the MSMQ-MQSeries Bridge, see "Chapter 13 — MSMQ-MQSeries Bridge Configuration Guide" on TechNet.

Consider the scenario where you are reading WebSphere MQ messages using JMS. Originally, those messages came from MSMQ and passed over the bridge. In this case, there should be no message consumption problems providing you change the WebSphere MQ JMS configuration. To implement this interoperability scenario, set the Queue Configuration for WebSphere MQ's **targetClient** to **MQ**, not **JMS**. If you do not make this change, WebSphere MQ expects a JMS headed message, which .NET Framework cannot generate.

Note: Do not configure **targetClient** on existing queues, because the change may cause existing JMS applications to fail. Always create a new message queue exclusively for interoperability purposes.

In the reverse direction, providing you change the **targetClient** to MQ, you can generate messages from JMS and then pass them over the bridge and consume them in a .NET Framework application.

Configuring the Message Queues

To enable interoperability through the MSMQ-MQSeries Bridge, you need to create two queues for each direction in which you want to send messages. You need to define local queues for receiving messages and remote queues for sending messages. You also have to configure the bridge correctly.

Figure 9.3 shows how you might set up two queues for each direction you want to send messages between .NET Framework and Java.

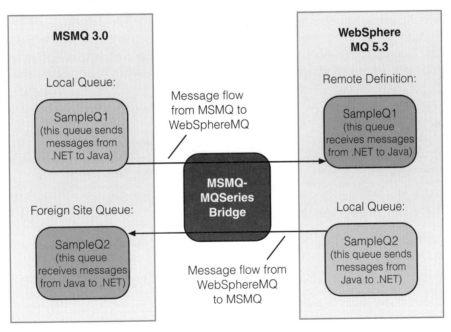

Figure 9.3
Logical representation of the MSMQ-MQSeries Bridge connecting MSMQ and MQ Series

Start by defining the MSMQ queues. You add a local queue to the computer running the bridge and a remote queue on the foreign computer.

Next, using the MSMQ-MQSeries Bridge Manager, you add a MQI channel which points to the computer running WebSphere MQ. This creates four message pipes, two transactional and two non-transactional, that route messages between the two queuing systems. After you have created these, you need to export both the client and server definitions. Copy these files to the WebSphere MQ computer, and then import them using the **runmqsc** command. This command configures the transmission queues and keeps the channels synchronized across the bridge.

The next step is to create a local and remote queue in WebSphere MQ. Configure the remote queue to point to the MSMQ queue through the bridge. Do this by configuring the remote queue manager name and transmission queue name to point to the objects that the import created.

Finally, you need to copy the WebSphere MQ Client Channel Table file from the computer running WebSphere MQ to the MSMQ computer and configure the **MQCHLLIB** and **MQCHLTAB** environment variables to point to this file.

Selecting a Data Format

When sending messages on queues using the MSMQ-MQSeries Bridge, you must ensure that the receiving end can consume the message data. The only realistic way of sending complex data between J2EE and .NET Framework is to serialize the data into an XML-formatted string. Additionally, WebSphere MQ supports sending **TextMessages**, where you load up the body with a string containing the XML data you want to send. MSMQ also allows you to send simple messages containing an XML-formatted string.

Note: It is not feasible to use other data types because of binary serialization differences between .NET Framework and J2EE as discussed in Chapter 3, "Interoperability Fundamentals."

Creating the Message Consumer

This guide has already covered how the Message Consumer is an application that you create to poll and read messages from a queue and place them into the resource façade. Because you are using the bridge, you work with XML-formatted strings. Therefore, you have to reconstruct the data from the XML string before you can use it to call methods on the resource façade. The next two sections consider how to do this on the two platforms.

Creating the .NET Framework Message Consumer

As described in Chapter 5, "Interoperability Technologies: Resource Tier "the .NET Framework message consumer reads from an MSMQ queue. After you read the contents of the message you must reconstruct the data. For techniques about how to do this, see the "Web Services" section of Chapter 7, "Integrating .NET in the Presentation Tier."

The following code sample shows how to read a message from MSMQ and the data you use to build the correct .NET Framework data type.

```
MessageQueue q = new MessageQueue(_queueName);
q.Formatter = new XmlMessageFormatter( new Type[] {typeof(String)} );
Message order = q.Receive(0);
string xml = (string) order.Body();
StringReader sr = new StringReader(xml);
OrderData ds = new OrderData();

// Load result string back into an OrderData-typed DataSet
ds.ReadXml(sr);
```

Note: The preceding sample uses the **OrderData** custom data type from XBikes. However, the XBikes application does not implement this code.

Creating the J2EE Message Consumer

The J2EE message consumer reads from WebSphere MQ, which you can build using either the MQI Java classes or JMS. After you read the message, you have to reconstruct the Java data from the XML string. For techniques about how to do this, see the "Web Services" section of Chapter 8, "Integrating .NET in the Business Tier."

The following code sample shows how you can read a message from WebSphere MQ and the data you use to build the correct J2EE data type.

```
String connectionName = "XBikesQFC";
InitialContext ic = new InitialContext();
QueueConnectionFactory factory =
        (QueueConnectionFactory) ic.lookup(connectionName);
QueueConnection connection = factory.createQueueConnection();
QueueSession session =
connection.createQueueSession(false, Session.AUTO_ACKNOWLEDGE);
Queue queue = (Queue) ic.lookup(queueName);
QueueReceiver receiver = session.createReceiver(queue);
connection.start();

TextMessage message = (TextMessage) receiver.receive();
String orderXML = message.getText();
OrderData order = OrderConverter.stringtoOrderData(orderXML);
DalServiceFacade facade = getFacadeHome().create();

return facade.saveOrder(order);
```

Note: The preceding sample uses the **OrderData** custom data type, and the **OrderConverter** class from XBikes. However, the XBikes application does not implement this code.

Creating the Interoperability Adapter

Following the techniques already discussed in this guide, it is recommended that you create an asynchronous interoperability adapter to provide access to the asynchronous communication channel. This adapter serializes the data for the message into an XML formatted string.

Creating the .NET Framework Asynchronous Interoperability Adapter

The .NET Framework application sends a message to MSMQ, so you can use the .NET Framework classes to do this, as discussed in Chapter 5. Because the final destination of the message is to WebSphere MQ, you must write the message as a string.

If you are using datasets, you can extract the XML using the **GetXml()** method. You can then place the XML string in the MSMQ message queue as the following code example shows.

```
string xml = order.GetXml();
MessageQueue q = new MessageQueue(_queueName);
q.Send(xml);
```

Note: The preceding sample uses the **OrderData** class from the **order** object that appears in the XBikes application. However the XBikes application does not implement this code.

Creating the J2EE Asynchronous Interoperability Adapter

The J2EE application sends a message to WebSphere MQ, so you can use the JMS classes (or MQI) to send the message. Again, because the final message destination is MSMQ, you must create a string message rather than writing an object.

For the background and code for serializing Java data to an XML string, see the "Web Services" section of Chapter 7. To send the message, you can use JMS code similar to the following example.

```
InitialContext ic = new InitialContext();
QueueConnectionFactory factory =
    (QueueConnectionFactory) ic.lookup("XBikesQCF");
QueueConnection connection = factory.createQueueConnection();
QueueSession session =
    connection.createQueueSession(false, Session.AUTO_ACKNOWLEDGE);
Queue queue = (Queue) ic.lookup("XBikesQ");
QueueSender sender = session.createSender(queue);
sender.setDeliveryMode(DeliveryMode.NON_PERSISTENT);
sender.setPriority(4);
sender.setTimeToLive(0);
connection.start();
```

(continued)

(continued)

```
// Use a text message
TextMessage message = session.createTextMessage();

// Convert the order to a string
String sorder = OrderConverter.orderListDataToString(orderObject);
message.setText(sorder);
sender.send(message);
```

Note: The preceding sample uses the **OrderData** and **OrderConverter** classes from XBikes. However, the XBikes application does not implement this code.

Now that how to implement the MSMQ-MQSeries Bridge has been described, it is time to look at runtime bridges for asynchronous interoperability.

Using JNBridgePro

Chapter 4, "Interoperability Technologies: Point to Point," shows how JNBridgePro lets you create .NET Framework proxies for Java classes. These .NET Framework proxies allow your .NET Framework application to interact with the native Java classes. One technique of providing asynchronous interoperability is to create proxy classes for the JMS classes on Java. This technique provides the ability to make JMS message calls from .NET Framework. This solution is somewhat different to those discussed so far, because .NET Framework would not be directly interacting with the message queues; it would be communicating through Java. Therefore, you need a running J2EE application server to provide .NET Framework with JMS access.

Figure 9.4 shows the role of JNBridge in asynchronous communications.

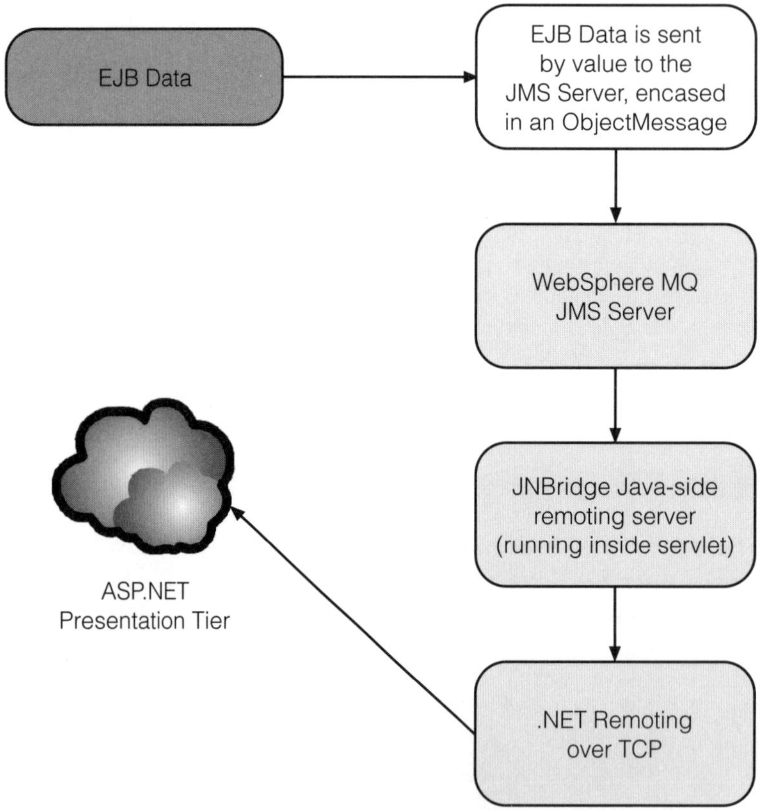

Figure 9.4
The role of JNBridge in asynchronous communications

Note: Because JNBridgePro wraps JMS, there is no special configuration required other than configuring the JMS support for WebSphere MQ.

Deciding on a Data Format for JNBridgePro

JNBridgePro wraps the JMS functionality, allowing you to place a Java object directly into the message queue. The only task from a data perspective is to create a .NET Framework proxy of the Java data object, populate this with the data from .NET Framework, and then use this object to write the message.

Creating the Message Consumer for JNBridgePro

Because the JNBridgePro adapter places a JMS message in WebSphere MQ, you can use standard JMS code for reading the message. JMS with a JNBridgePro wrapping determines the format of the message you read, so there is no need to change the data that you can send directly to the resource application. The following code example shows how to read the message from JMS.

```
InitialContext ic = new InitialContext();
QueueConnectionFactory factory = (QueueConnectionFactory)
ic.lookup(connectionName);

QueueConnection connection = factory.createQueueConnection();
QueueSession session =
connection.createQueueSession(false, Session.AUTO_ACKNOWLEDGE);
Queue queue = (Queue) ic.lookup(queueName);
QueueReceiver receiver = session.createReceiver(queue);
connection.start();

ObjectMessage message = (ObjectMessage) receiver.receive();
order = (OrderData) message.getObject();
DalServiceFacade facade = getFacadeHome().create();

return facade.saveOrder(order);
```

Creating the Asynchronous Interoperability Adapter for JNBridgePro

To create the asynchronous interoperability adapter, you need to expose the JMS classes from J2EE into the .NET Framework application. You can do this using the JNBridgePro proxy generation tool, in the same way that you used it to achieve interoperability as described in Chapter 7.

To create the proxy, add the **j2ee.jar**, **jndi.jar**, and **jms.jar** packages as well as any application-specific data classes you require to the JNBridgePro **classpath**. You must create proxies for the following classes:

- **javax.naming.InitialContext**
- **javax.naming.NamingException**
- **javax.jms.QueueConnectionFactory**
- **javax.jms.QueueConnection**
- **javax.jms.QueueSession**
- **javax.jms.Session**
- **javax.jms.Queue**
- **javax.jms.QueueSender**
- **javax.jms.ObjectMessage**

- javax.jms.JMSException
- javax.jms.DeliveryMode
- javax.jms.InvalidDestinationException

In the XBikes sample application, this list also included the classes from the **xbikes.common.data** package.

After you generate the proxy and configure the .NET Framework application, the .NET Framework interoperability adapter calls the proxy classes in a similar way that the J2EE application would use them. The following code sample shows how to create a new JMS message in WebSphere from .NET Framework.

```
InitialContext ic = new InitialContext();
QueueConnectionFactory factory =
(QueueConnectionFactory) ic.lookup(connectionName);

QueueConnection connection = factory.createQueueConnection();
connection.start();
QueueSession session =
connection.createQueueSession(false,    SessionConstants.AUTO_ACKNOWLEDGE);
javax.jms.Queue queue = (javax.jms.Queue) ic.lookup(queueName);
QueueSender sender = session.createSender(queue);

ObjectMessage message = session.createObjectMessage(order);
sender.send(message);
```

Note: This it is almost identical to sending a JMS message from Java, but the language is C#.

The next section covers the same techniques but using Ja.NET instead of JNBridgePro.

Using Ja.NET

Chapter 4 shows how Ja.NET lets you to define .NET Framework proxy classes for Java classes, to enable .NET Framework applications to access Java classes. In a similar way, you can define .NET Framework proxy classes for the Java JMS classes to enable .NET Framework applications to make JMS message calls. This solution is somewhat different to those discussed so far, because the .NET Framework application is communicating through Java rather than interacting directly with the message queues. This implementation requires that you run a J2EE application server to provide .NET Framework with JMS access.

At first sight, this looks the same as the JNBridgePro solution; however, Ja.NET comes supplied with a ready-built JMS proxy. This is because all JMS invocations are implemented through interfaces. Hence you do not need to create a proxy yourself when you use Ja.NET.

Figure 9.5 shows the role of Ja.NET in asynchronous communications.

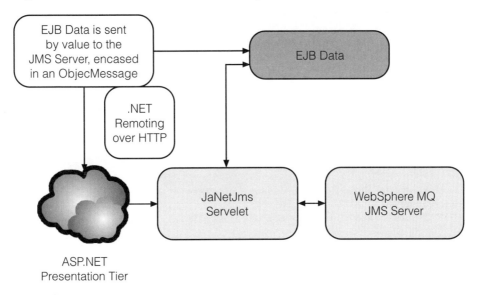

Figure 9.5
The role of Ja.NET in asynchronous communications

Again, you need to configure message queues and decide on a data format.

Configuring the Message Queues

Because Ja.NET provides a wrapper for JMS, there is no special configuration required. However, you still need to configure WebSphere MQ for JMS support.

Deciding on a Data format for Ja.NET

Because Ja.NET wraps the JMS functionality, you can place a Java object directly into the message queue. The only task from a data perspective is to create a .NET Framework proxy of the Java data object, populate this with the data from .NET Framework, and then use this object to write the message.

Creating the Message Consumer for Ja.NET

Because the Ja.NET adapter places a JMS message in WebSphere MQ, you can use standard JMS code for reading the message. The message is in JMS format with a Ja.NET wrapper, so there is no need to change the data. Thus you can send it directly to the resource application. The following code sample shows how to read the message from JMS.

```
InitialContext ic = new InitialContext();
QueueConnectionFactory factory = (QueueConnectionFactory)
ic.lookup(connectionName);

QueueConnection connection = factory.createQueueConnection();
QueueSession session =
connection.createQueueSession(false, Session.AUTO_ACKNOWLEDGE);
Queue queue = (Queue) ic.lookup(queueName);
QueueReceiver receiver = session.createReceiver(queue);
connection.start();

ObjectMessage message = (ObjectMessage) receiver.receive();
order = (OrderData) message.getObject();
DalServiceFacade facade = getFacadeHome().create();

return facade.saveOrder(order);
```

The next section looks at creating the asynchronous interoperability adapter.

Creating the Ja.NET Asynchronous Interoperability Adapter

To create this adapter, use the prepackaged JMS proxy that ships with Ja.NET 1.5. This proxy is strong named so you can use it from within a COM+ context without problems. You also have to create proxy classes for any Java data types you want to access from .NET Framework. Remember to package the data into the Java classes before placing the message in the queue.

Note: Chapter 7 contains details for generating proxies for Ja.NET.

The following code sample shows how to send a message from .NET Framework to a JMS queue using Ja.NET.

```
JNDIContext context = new JNDIContext();
object o = context.Lookup("javax.jms.QueueConnectionFactory", "XBikesQCF");
javax.jms.QueueConnectionFactory factory =
    (javax.jms.QueueConnectionFactory) o;
QueueConnection connection = factory.createQueueConnection();
QueueSession session =
    connection.createQueueSession(false, SessionConstants.AUTO_ACKNOWLEDGE);
javax.jms.Queue queue =
(javax.jms.Queue) context.Lookup("javax.jms.Queue", "XBikesQ");
QueueSender qSender = session.createSender(queue);
qSender.setDeliveryMode(DeliveryMode.NON_PERSISTENT);
qSender.setPriority(4);
qSender.setTimeToLive(0);
connection.start();

ObjectMessage message = (ObjectMessage)session.createObjectMessage();
message.setObject(ejbOrder);
qSender.send(message);
```

Again, this is almost identical to sending a JMS message from Java, but the language is C#.

Summary

This chapter described mechanisms for connecting from a .NET Framework Business tier to a Java environment using asynchronous connections to message queuing components. It also covered configuring runtime bridges to make the connection and using proxies with both JNBridgePro and Ja.NET.

References

For more information about the details of configuring MSMQ foreign sites
See "Configuring cross-platform messaging"
*http://www.microsoft.com/technet/treeview/default.asp?url=/technet/prodtechnol
/windowsserver2003/proddocs/standard/msmqconcepts/sag_msmqconcepts_admforeign.asp*

For more information about how to configure and use the MSMQ-MQSeries Bridge
See "Chapter 13—MSMQ-MQSeries Bridge Configuration Guide"
*http://www.microsoft.com/technet/treeview/default.asp?url=/technet/prodtechnol/host/reskit
/part3/hisrkc13.asp?frame=true*

Appendix A

Installing XBikes on J2EE

Introduction

There are several ways to deploy the J2EE version of XBikes. This appendix describes the following common deployment scenarios:

- Deploying XBikes on WebSphere Application Developer Studio 5.0
- Deploying XBikes on WebSphere Application Server 5.0 on a Single Computer
- Deploying XBikes on WebSphere Application Server 5.0 on Multiple Computers

This appendix also includes a section on changing interoperability methods, so that you can see how to configure the different use case adapters to change the interoperability methods that you use.

To assist with the descriptions of what the XBikes developers did in Chapters 7 to 9, this appendix provides two installation methods:

- Automated
- Manual

The automated installation runs from a Microsoft Windows Installer (.msi) file, installing and configuring the XBikes application. However, the manual installation steps let you work through the complete process of deploying the J2EE version of XBikes.

Note: The manual installation is recommended for those with some experience of J2EE applications and IBM WebSphere products.

Deploying XBikes on WebSphere Application Developer Studio 5.0

Using WebSphere Application Developer Studio 5.0 to run the XBikes sample code requires you to install and configure the following software on a single computer:

- Windows 2000 Server with Service Pack 3 or later in Workgroup mode
- Microsoft SQL Server 2000 with mixed mode security and Service Pack 3
- Microsoft JDBC Driver for Microsoft SQL Server 2000
- A default installation of IBM WebSphere Application Developer Studio 5.0
- A custom installation of IBM WebSphere MQ 5.3 (described in the following section)
- A default installation of GLUE 4.1.2 Professional

Note: You must install a valid GLUE license file into Glue.jar. See the GLUE documentation for help.

Configuring IBM WebSphere MQ 5.3

When setting up IBM WebSphere MQ, ensure you select a custom install and add support for Java Messaging. To do this, complete the following steps.

▶ **To install IBM WebSphere MQ**

1. Open Windows Explorer, and then double-click **WebSphereMQ_t_en_us.exe**. The **WebSphere MQ (Evaluation Copy)** dialog box appears. Click **Next**.

2. The **Location to Save Files** page prompts you for a folder into which you want to extract the installation files. Note that this is not the directory into which you install IBM WebSphere MQ. The default folder is C:\Program Files\IBM\Source \WebSphere MQ t_en_us. Either accept the default value, enter a new directory, or click the **Change** button and browse for a directory.

3. Click **Next** to continue. The installation process extracts the WebSphere MQ installation files into the directory you specified.

4. In the dialog box that appears after the installation files are extracted, click **Yes**.

5. The WebSphere MQ Installation Launchpad appears. Click **Software Prerequisites**.

6. The Launchpad checks your system for prerequisite software. Check that the check boxes next to each required component are selected. However, note that the installation routine can fail to detect the presence of a supported Java Runtime Environment 1.3 or later.

7. Click **Network Prerequisites** and check that your computer meets the requirements. If the computer is in Workgroup mode, you can click **No**.

8. Click **WebSphere MQ Installation** and check the pre-installation status. If you are certain you have already installed a Java Runtime Environment 1.3 or later, you can ignore any warnings about that component.

9. Click the **Launch WebSphere MQ Installer** button. The **WebSphere MQ Installation Wizard** appears. Click **Next**.

10. On the **License Agreement** page, click the option to accept the terms in the license agreement, and then click **Next**.

11. On the **Setup Type** page, click **Custom**, and then click **Next**.

12. Accept the default installation folder of C:\Program Files\IBM\WebSphere MQ for the program files, and then click **Next**.

13. Accept the default installation folder of C:\Program Files\IBM\WebSphere MQ\ for the data files, and then click **Next**.

14. Accept the default installation folder of C:\Program Files\IBM\WebSphere MQ \log\ for the log files, and then click **Next**.

15. On the **Features** page, click the red cross next to **Java Messaging**, click **Install this feature**, and then click **Next**.

16. The **Ready to Install WebSphere MQ** page appears. Check that the settings are correct, and then click **Install**.

17. A dialog box asks if you have purchased sufficient license units to install IBM WebSphere on this computer. If you are using the evaluation version of WebSphere MQ, click **Yes**.

18. After the installation process completes, click **Finish**.

19. When the Prepare WebSphere MQ Wizard appears, click **Next**.

20. On the **WebSphere MQ Network Configuration** page, click **No**. This assumes that your computer is a member of a Workgroup. Click **Next**. The WebSphere MQ Service starts.

21. Click the **Setup the Default Configuration** link.

22. When the Default Configuration Wizard appears, click **Next**.

23. The next page gives you basic information on what you are doing. Click **Next**.

24. On the **Select Options** page, leave the options for **Allow remote administration of the queue manager** and **Join the queue manager to the default cluster** selected. Click **Next**.

25. On the **Join Default Cluster** page, select the option for **Yes, make it the repository for the cluster**. Click **Next**.

Note: If you are using a computer that gets its IP address dynamically, a message may appear that asks if another computer with a fixed IP address is available to hold the repository. If this message appears, click **No**.

---

26. The **Repository Location** page confirms that the current computer holds the repository for the cluster. Click **Next**.

27. On the **Default Configuration Summary** page, check that the settings are correct, and then click **Finish**.

28. WebSphere MQ then sets up the default configuration. The **WebSphere MQ Default Configuration** dialog box appears, showing the **Queue Manager** and **Default Cluster Membership** details. Click **Close**.

29. On the **Prepare WebSphere MQ Wizard** page, click **Next**.

30. On the **Completing the Prepare WebSphere MQ Wizard** page, clear all check boxes, and then click **Finish**.

This completes the installation and configuration of IBM WebSphere MQ.

Creating the XBikesQ Queue

To create the message queue that XBikes uses, complete the following steps.

▶ **To create the XBikes message queue**

1. Start WebSphere MQ Explorer by clicking **Start**, pointing to **All Programs**, pointing to **IBM WebSphere MQ**, and then clicking **WebSphere MQ Explorer**.

2. Expand **WebSphere MQ**, expand **Queue Managers**, and then expand **QM_<machine name>** (where <machine name> is the name of your computer).

3. Right-click **Queues**, point to **New**, and then click **Local Queue**.

4. In the **Queue Name** box, type **XBikesQ**, and then click **OK**.

5. In the **WebSphere MQ** dialog box, click **Don't Share in Cluster**. The **WebSphere MQ** dialog box closes.

6. Close WebSphere MQ Explorer.

Installing the XBikes Sample Code

To install the XBikes sample code for the J2EE platform, complete the following steps.

Note: Check again that your system meets the prerequisites listed at the beginning of this section. For example, failure to install a component such as Microsoft SQL Server results in the database tables not installing.

▶ **To install the XBikes application and the XBikes database**

1. Open Windows Explorer, and then double-click **Xbikesj2ee.msi**. In the **Welcome to the XBikes J2EE Setup Wizard** page, click **Next**.

2. On the **Installation Options** page, make sure **Single Tier** is selected, and then click **Next**.

3. On the second **Installation Options** page, make sure the **Install Source Code** and **Install Database** check boxes are selected and the **Install to WebSphere Application Server 5.0 (uncheck for single tier WSAD only)** check box is not selected, and then click **Next**.

4. On the **Confirm Installation** page, click **Next** to begin the installation. The installation copies the XBikes sample code and installs the XBikes database.

5. When the installation is complete, click **Close**.

Configuring the JMS Queues

To configure the JMS entries for the XBikes queues, complete the following steps.

▶ **To configure the XBikes JMS queues for WebSphere Application Developer Studio 5.0**

1. Start WebSphere Application Developer Studio 5.0 by clicking **Start**, pointing to **All Programs**, pointing to **IBM WebSphere Studio**, and then clicking **Application Developer 5.0**.

2. In the **WebSphere Studio** dialog box, change the workspace to **C:\Xbikes \J2ee-ibm**, and then click **OK**.

3. The J2EE–IBM WebSphere Studio Application Developer window appears. In the left pane under **J2EE Navigator**, right-click **XBikesWeb**, and then click **Run on Server**.

4. In the **Server Selection** dialog box, click **Use an existing server**, and then click **Next**.

5. In the **Select Tasks** dialog box, ensure that both check boxes are not selected, and then click **Finish**.

6. Ensure that the WebSphere server is started with WebSphere Studio.

7. Open Internet Explorer and navigate to http://localhost:9090/admin/. This opens the Web server administration tool.

8. In the **User ID** box, type **Admin**, and then click **OK**.

9. Expand **Resources**, and then click **WebSphere MQ JMS Provider**.

10. In the right pane, select **Server** for the scope, and then click **Apply**.

11. Under **Additional Properties**, click **WebSphere MQ Queue Connection Factories**, and then click **XBikesQCF**.

12. In the **Queue Manager** field under **General Properties**, change the value to the exact name of the Queue Manager on your computer, and then click **OK** under **General Properties**.

Note: If you do not know the name of the Queue Manager, open the WebSphere MQ Explorer by clicking **Start**, pointing to **Programs**, pointing to **IBM WebSphere MQ**, and then clicking **WebSphere MQ Explorer**. Expand **WebSphere MQ**, and then expand **Queue Managers**. The name of the Queue Manager displays.

---

13. In the left pane, click **WebSphere MQ JMS Provider**.

14. Under **Additional Properties** in the right pane, click **WebSphere MQ Queue Destinations**, and then click **XBikesQ**.

15. Under **General Properties**, locate the **Base Queue Manager Name** field. As in step 9, enter the name of your Queue Manager in the form of "QM_<machine name>" (without the quotation marks). Note that this value is case-sensitive. At the bottom of the **General Properties** section, click **OK**.

16. Under **Messages** in the right pane, click **Save**, and then click **Save** under **Save to Master Configuration**.

17. Click **Logout**, and then close Internet Explorer.

18. Restart your WebSphere server for the changes to take effect.

Running XBikes

To execute XBikes within WebSphere Application Developer Studio, complete the following steps.

▶ **To execute the XBikes application within WebSphere Application Developer Studio**

1. Start WebSphere Application Developer Studio 5.0 by clicking **Start**, pointing to **All Programs**, pointing to **IBM WebSphere Studio**, and then clicking **Application Developer 5.0**.

2. In the **WebSphere Studio** dialog box, change the workspace to **C:\Xbikes \J2ee-ibm**, and then click **OK**.

3. The J2EE–IBM WebSphere Studio Application Developer window appears. In the left pane under **J2EE Navigator**, right-click **XBikesWeb**, and then click **Run on Server**.

4. In the **Server Selection** dialog box, click **Use an existing server**, and then click **Next**.

5. In the **Select Tasks** dialog box, ensure that both check boxes are not selected, and then click **Finish**.

6. After the server starts, the XBikes application appears in the WebSphere Studio Internal Web browser window.

The XBikes Web application allows you to browse bikes by type, order bikes, change quantities, and check out your order.

Using WebSphere Studio Application Developer 5.1 with XBikes

If you want to use WebSphere Studio Application Developer 5.1 instead of version 5.0, you have to make some changes to the project. Use the following steps as a guide to resolve the configuration problems encountered when using version 5.1. You also have to install fix pack CSD05 for WebSphere MQ. For more information about the fix pack, including download information, see "WebSphere MQ Support, Service Summary for Windows NT and Windows 2000" on the IBM Web site (*http://www-3.ibm.com/software/integration/mqfamily/support/summary/wnt.html*).

▶ **To configure the XBikes application for WebSphere Studio 5.1**

1. Start WebSphere Application Developer Studio 5.1 by clicking **Start**, pointing to **All Programs**, pointing to **IBM WebSphere Studio**, and then clicking **Application Developer 5.1**.

2. In the **WebSphere Studio** dialog box, change the workspace to **C:\Xbikes \J2ee-ibm**, and then click **OK**.

3. In the **Different Workspace Version** dialog box, click **OK**.

4. When the project is fully loaded in Studio, click **Rebuild All** on the **Project** menu. A number of build errors will display in the Task window.

▶ **To correct the build errors**

1. Right-click **XBikesResourceInteropFactory**, and then click **Properties**. The **XBikesResourceInteropFactory Properties** dialog box appears.

2. In the left pane of the **Properties** dialog box, click **Java Build Path**, and then click the **Libraries** tab.

3. Remove J2EE.jar from the **JAR's and class folders on the build path** list by highlighting **J2EE.jar** and clicking **Remove**.

4. Click **Add External JARs**. The **JAR Selection** dialog appears.

5. Navigate to the C:\Program Files\IBM\WebSphere Studio\Application Developer\v5.1\runtimes\base_v5\lib\ folder, click **J2EE.jar**, and then click **Open**.

6. Click **OK** to close the **Properties** dialog box.

7. Right-click **XBikesUseCase**, and then click **Properties**. The **XBikesUseCase Properties** dialog box appears.

8. In the left pane of the **Properties** dialog box, click **Java Build Path**, and then click the **Libraries** tab.

9. Remove **J2EE.jar** from the **JAR's and class folders on the build path** list by highlighting **J2EE.jar**, and then clicking **Remove**.

10. Click **Add External JARs**. The **Jar Selection** dialog appears.

11. Navigate to the C:\Program Files\IBM\WebSphere Studio \Application Developer\v5.1\runtimes\base_v5\lib\ folder, click **J2EE.jar**, and then click **Open**.

12. Click **OK** to close the **Properties** dialog box.

13. In the upper left pane, click **J2EE Hierarchy**.

14. Expand the **servers** node and check that **ServerOne** is listed. If ServerOne is **not** listed under the Servers node, do the following:

   a. Right-click **Servers**, and then click **Create a New Server and Server Configuration**. The **Create a New Server and Server Configuration** dialog box appears.

   b. In the **Server Name** field, enter **TestServer**, and then click **Finish**.

   c. In the **J2EE Hierarchy** view, expand **Servers**, and then right-click **TestServer**.

   d. Click **Switch Configuration**, and then click **WebSphere v5.0 Server Configuration**.

15. In the **J2EE Hierarchy** view, expand **EJB Modules**, and then expand **Maps**.

16. Right-click **XBikes:MSSQLServer_V7_1**, and then click **Delete Map Resource**. The **Delete Map Options** dialog box appears.

17. Make sure the **Map** and **Schema** check boxes are selected, and then click **OK**. The **Delete Map Options** dialog box closes.

18. Right-click **XBikesDal**, click **Generate**, and then click **EJB to RDB mapping**. The **EJB to RDB Mapping** dialog box appears.

19. Make sure the **Create a new backend folder** check box is selected, and then click **Next**.

20. Select the **Meet in the middle** radio button, and then click **Next**.

21. Select the **Use Existing Connection** checkbox, verify that **XBikes** is selected in the **Existing Connection** drop-down box, and then click **Next**.

22. From the **Import Table** list, select the **dbo.Categories, dbo.Customers, dbo.OrderDetails**, and **dbo.Orders dbo.Products** tables; then click **Next**.

23. Select **Match By Name**, and then click **Finish**. The **Mapping** file opens in the main window.

24. In the **Enterprise Beans** pane, click **CategoriesDataAdapter**.

25. In the **Tables** pane, right-click the **Categories** table, and then click **Match By Name**.

26. Repeat steps 24 and 25 for the **CustomerDataAdapter, ProductsDataAdapter, OrderDataAdapter**, and **OrderDetailsDataAdapter** tables.

27. Save and close the **Mapping** file. At this point, all build errors should be removed from the project.

28. Right-click **XBikesDAL**, click **Generate**, and then click **Deployment and RMIC code**. The **Generate Deployment and RMIC Code** dialog box appears.

29. Click **Select All**, and then click **Finish**.

30. Expand the **Servers** node in the **J2EE Hierarchy** view, right-click **TestServer**, and then click **Start**.

31. Reconfigure the Queue Manager settings using the Web admin tool. For instructions, see **Configuring the JMS Queues** earlier in this appendix.

32. Restart the WebSphere server and test.

Deploying XBikes on WebSphere Application Server 5.0 on a Single Computer

Before you begin, install and configure the following software on a single computer in the following order:

1. Windows 2000 Server with Service Pack 3 or higher in Workgroup mode

2. Microsoft SQL Server 2000 with mixed mode security and Service Pack 3

3. Microsoft JDBC Driver for Microsoft SQL Server 2000

4. A custom installation of WebSphere Application Server 5.0 (described in the following section)

5. IBM WebSphere MQ 5.3

6. A default installation of GLUE 4.1.2 Professional

Note: You must install a valid license file into Glue.jar. For information about how to do this, see the GLUE documentation.

Installing WebSphere Application Server 5.0

To install IBM WebSphere Application Server 5.0, make sure you have downloaded the following files from the IBM Web site (*http://www7b.software.ibm.com/wsdd /downloads/*):

- Ibmwas5_trial_for_nt.zip
- Messaging_trial_for_nt.zip

Note: You must add the messaging component from the Messaging_trial_for_nt.zip file as described in steps 3 and 4 in the following procedure.

After you download these components, complete the following steps.

▶ **To install IBM WebSphere Application Server 5.0**

1. Expand the Ibmwas5_trial_for_nt.zip archive into the C:\Ibmwas5_trial_for_nt folder.

2. After the IBM WebSphere Application Server 5.0 installation files extract, unzip Messaging_trial_for_nt.zip to a folder of your choice.

3. Copy the Messaging folder from where you unzipped Messaging_trial_for_nt.zip and make it a subdirectory of the WebSphere installation folder, C:\Ibmwas5_trial_for_nt. (The Ibmwas5_trial_for_nt folder now contains seven subdirectories, one of which is Messaging.)

4. In the Ibmwas5_trial_for_nt folder, double-click **Install.exe**.

5. In the **Installation Wizard** dialog box, click **English**, and then click **OK**.

6. In the **Installation Wizard** introduction screen, click **Next**.

7. Click **Custom setup**, and then click **Next**.

8. On the **Select the features for "IBM WebSphere Application Server for Developers, Version 5" you would like to install** screen, make sure the check boxes for the following components are selected or not selected, as specified:

   - **Application Server**—Selected
   - **Application Server Samples**—Not selected
   - **Administration**—Selected (including all subcomponents)
   - **Application Assembly and Deployment Tools**—Selected (including all subcomponents)
   - **Embedded Messaging**—Selected
     - **Server and Client**—Not selected
     - **Client Only**—Selected
     - **Message-driven Bean Samples**—Not selected
   - **Web Server Plugins**—Selected
     - **IBM HTTP Server**—Not selected
     - **Apache, Microsoft IIS and IPlanet**—Not selected
     - **Lotus Domino Web Server**—Not selected
   - **Performance and Analysis Tools**—Not selected
   - **Javadocs**—Not selected

9. Click **Next**.

10. Do not install to the default location. In the target path for the program files, enter **C:\WAS\WebSphere\AppServer**, and then click **Next**.

11. Accept the default settings for **Node Name**, enter your computer's IP address in the **Host Name or IP Address** field, click **Next**.

12. Clear the **Run WebSphere Application Server as a service** check box, and then click **Next**.

13. In the installation summary screen, make sure the details are correct, and then click **Next**.

14. When the installation is complete, click **Finish**.

15. If a WebSphere Application Server **First Steps Version 5.0** page appears, click **Exit**.

Installing and Configuring IBM WebSphere MQ 5.3

To install and configure IBM WebSphere MQ 5.3, you have to do a custom installation of IBM WebSphere MQ, adding support for Java messaging. To do this, complete the following steps.

▶ **To install IBM WebSphere MQ**

1. Open Windows Explorer, and then double-click **WebSphereMQ_t_en_us.exe**.

2. In the **WebSphere MQ (Evaluation Copy)** dialog box, click **Next**.

3. The **Location to Save Files** page prompts you for a folder that you want to extract the installation files to. Note that this is not the directory into which you install IBM WebSphere MQ. The default folder is C:\Program Files\IBM\Source \WebSphere MQ t_en_us. Either accept the default value, enter a new directory, or click the **Change** button to browse for a directory, and then click **Next** to continue. The installation process extracts the WebSphere MQ installation files into the directory you specified.

4. After the installation files extract, the **WebSphere MQ Installation** dialog box appears. Click **Yes**. The **WebSphere MQ Installation Launchpad** dialog box appears.

5. On the **WebSphere MQ Installation Launchpad** page, click **Software Prerequisites** in the list of steps on the left.

6. The Launchpad checks your system for prerequisite software. On the **Software Prerequisites** page, make sure that the check boxes for all required components are selected. However, note that the installation routine can fail to detect the presence of a supported Java Runtime Environment 1.3 or later.

7. Click **Network Prerequisites** from the list of steps on the left. The **Preparing for installation on networks that include Windows 2000 Servers** page appears. Make sure your computer meets the requirements displayed. If the computer is in Workgroup mode, you can click **No** under **Do both conditions apply?**.

8. On the list of steps on the left, click **WebSphere MQ Installation**. The **WebSphere MQ Installation** page appears. Check the pre-installation status. If you are certain you have already installed a Java Runtime Environment v 1.3 or later, you can ignore any warnings about that component.

9. Click the **Launch WebSphere MQ Installer** button.

10. On the first page of the **WebSphere MQ Installation Wizard**, click **Next**.

11. On the **Program Maintenance** page, select **Modify**, and then click **Next**.

12. Accept the default installation folder of C:\was\IBM\WebSphere MQ\log\ for the log files, and then click **Next**.

13. On the **Features** page, click the red cross next to **Server**, click **Install this feature**, and then click **Next**.

14. On the **Ready to Modify WebSphere MQ** page, make sure the settings are correct, and then click **Modify**.

15. The **IBM WebSphere MQ** dialog box appears. If you are using the evaluation version of WebSphere MQ, click **Yes**; otherwise ensure you have sufficient licenses to run the product.

16. After the installation process completes, click **Finish**.

17. On the first page of the **Prepare WebSphere MQ Wizard**, click **Next**.

18. On the **WebSphere MQ Network Configuration** page, click **No**. This assumes that your computer is a member of a Workgroup. Click **Next**. The WebSphere MQ Service starts.

19. On the **Prepare WebSphere MQ** page, click **Setup the Default Configuration**.

20. On the first page of the **Default Configuration Wizard**, click **Next**.

21. On the **Set up Default Configuration page**, click **Next**.

22. On the **Select Options** page, leave the **Allow remote administration of the queue manager** and **Join the queue manager to the default cluster** check boxes selected. Make a note of what the Queue Manager is named because you will need this when installing the XBikes application, and then click **Next**.

23. On the **Join Default Cluster** page, select the **Yes, make it the repository for the cluster** radio button, and then click **Next**.

> **Note:** If you are using a computer that gets its IP address dynamically, a message may appear that asks if another computer with a fixed IP address is available to hold the repository. If this message appears, click **No**.

24. On the **Repository Location** page, click **Next**.

25. On the **Default Configuration Summary** page, make sure the settings are correct, and then click **Finish**.

26. WebSphere MQ then sets up the default configuration. The **WebSphere MQ Default Configuration** dialog box appears, showing the **Queue Manager** and **Default Cluster Membership** details. Click **Close**.

27. On the **Prepare WebSphere MQ Wizard** page, click **Next**.

28. On the **Completing the Prepare WebSphere MQ Wizard** page, clear all the check boxes, and then click **Finish**. This completes the installation and configuration of IBM WebSphere MQ.

29. Restart your computer before continuing.

Creating the XBikesQ Queue

To create the message queue that XBikes uses, complete the following steps.

▶ **To create the XBikes message queue**

1. Start WebSphere MQ Explorer by clicking **Start**, pointing to **All Programs**, pointing to **IBM WebSphere MQ**, and then clicking **WebSphere MQ Explorer**.

2. Expand **WebSphere MQ**, expand **Queue Managers**, and then expand **QM_<machine name>** (where <machine name> is the name of your computer).

3. Right-click **Queues**, point to **New**, and then click **Local Queue**.

4. In the **Queue Name** box, enter **XBikesQ**, and then click **OK**.

5. In the **WebSphere MQ** dialog box, click **Don't Share in Cluster**. The dialog box closes.

6. Close WebSphere MQ Explorer.

Installing the XBikes Sample Code

To install the XBikes sample code for the J2EE platform, complete the following steps.

Note: Check again that your system meets the prerequisites listed at the beginning of this section. For example, failure to install a component such as Microsoft SQL Server results in the database tables not installing.

▶ **To install the XBikes application and the XBikes database**

1. Open Windows Explorer, and then double-click **xbikesj2ee.msi**.

2. On the **Welcome to the XBikes J2EE Setup Wizard** page, click **Next**.

3. In the **Installation Options** dialog box, make sure **Single Tier** is selected, and then click **Next**.

4. In the second **Installation Options** dialog box, make sure the **Install Source Code**, **Install Database**, and **Install to WebSphere Application Server 5.0 (uncheck for single tier WSAD only)** check boxes are selected.

Note: You do not need to install the source code unless you want to look at the code.

Click **Next** to continue.

5. In the **Confirm Installation** dialog box, click **Next** to begin the installation.

6. In the **MQ Configuration** dialog box, enter the correct queue manager name, and then click **OK**. Note that this name is case sensitive. You should have made a note of this when installing WebSphere MQ. If not, you can find the name of the queue manager in WebSphere MQ Explorer.

7. The installation copies the XBikes sample code, configures the application server, and installs the XBikes database.

8. When the installation is complete, click **Close**.

Running the XBikes Application

You are now ready to run the XBikes application. To do this, open a browser window and enter http://localhost:9080/XBikesWeb.

Note: XBikesWeb is case sensitive.

The XBikes Web application allows you to browse bikes by type, order bikes, change quantities, and check out your order.

Deploying XBikes on WebSphere Application Server 5.0 on Multiple Computers

To install XBikes in a multi-computer configuration, you need three computers for the Presentation tier, Business tier, and Data tier respectively. All three computers need the following setup:

- Windows 2000 Server with Service Pack 3 or later in Workgroup mode
- A default installation of GLUE 4.1.2 Professional

Note: You must install a valid GLUE license file into Glue.jar. See the GLUE documentation for help.

Data Tier Computer Setup

The Data tier computer requires the following components to be installed:

- Microsoft SQL Server 2000 with mixed mode security and Service Pack 3
- Microsoft JDBC Driver for Microsoft SQL Server 2000
- A custom installation of IBM WebSphere MQ 5.3, as described in the "Configuring IBM WebSphere MQ 5.3" section earlier in this appendix.
- The **XBikesQ** message queue, as described in the "Creating the XBikesQ Queue" section earlier in this appendix.
- A custom installation of IBM WebSphere Application Server 5.0, as described in the "Installing WebSphere Application Server 5.0" section earlier in this appendix, including the messaging client installation in steps 3 and 4.

Installing XBikes into the Data Tier

To install the XBikes sample code and XBikes database for the J2EE platform, complete the following steps.

Note: Check again that your system meets the prerequisites listed at the beginning of this section.

▶ **To install the XBikes application into the Data tier**

1. Open Windows Explorer, and then double-click **xbikesj2ee.msi**.
2. On the **Welcome to the XBikes J2EE Setup Wizard** page, click **Next**.
3. In the **Installation Options** dialog box, make sure **Data Access Layer Only** is selected, and then click **Next**.
4. In the second **Installation Options** dialog box, make sure the **Install Source Code**, **Install Database**, and **Install to WebSphere Application Server 5.0 (uncheck for single tier WSAD only)** check boxes are selected.

   Note: You do not need to install the source code unless you want to look at the code.

   Click **Next** to continue.
5. In the **Confirm Installation** dialog box, click **Next** to begin the installation.
6. In the **MQ Configuration** dialog box, enter the correct queue manager name, and then click **OK**. Note that this name is case sensitive. You should have made a note of this when installing WebSphere MQ. If not, you can find the name of the queue manager in WebSphere MQ Explorer.
7. The installation copies the XBikes sample code, installs the XBikes database, and configures the application server.
8. When the installation is complete, click **Close**.

Business Tier Computer Setup

The Business tier computer requires a custom installation of IBM WebSphere Application Server 5.0. Follow the instructions in the "Installing WebSphere Application Server 5.0" section earlier in this appendix, except instead of choosing **Client Only**, choose **Server and Client** for the **Embedded Messaging**.

To install the XBikes sample code for the J2EE platform, complete the following steps.

Note: Check again that your system meets the prerequisites listed at the beginning of this section.

▶ **To install the XBikes application into the Business tier**

1. Open Windows Explorer, and then double-click **xbikesj2ee.msi**.

2. On the **Welcome to the XBikes J2EE Setup Wizard** page, click **Next**.

3. In the **Installation Options** dialog box, make sure **Business Logic Layer Only** is selected, and then click **Next**.

4. In the second **Installation Options** dialog box, make sure the **Install Source Code** check box is selected, the **Install Database** check box is not selected, and the **Install to WebSphere Application Server 5.0 (uncheck for single tier WSAD only)** check box is selected.

> **Note:** You do not need to install the source code unless you want to look at the code.

Click **Next** to continue.

5. In the **Confirm Installation** dialog box, click **Next**.

6. In the **MQ Configuration** dialog box, enter the correct queue manager name, and click **OK**. Note that this the name of the queue manager installed on the Data tier and the name is case sensitive. You should have made a note of this when installing WebSphere MQ on the Data tier. If not, you can find the name of the queue manager in WebSphere MQ Explorer.

7. In the next **MQ** Configuration dialog box, enter the host name of the computer running WebSphere MQ. This should be the name of the Data tier computer. The installation routine makes a best guess based upon the queue manager name you entered earlier.

8. The installation copies the XBikes sample code and configures the application server.

9. When the installation is complete, click **Close**.

Presentation Tier Computer Setup

The Presentation tier computer requires a custom installation of IBM WebSphere Application Server 5.0. Follow the instructions in the "Installing WebSphere Application Server 5.0" section earlier in this appendix, excluding the messaging client installation in steps 3 and 4.

To install the XBikes sample code for the J2EE platform, complete the following steps.

> **Note:** Check again that your system meets the prerequisites listed at the beginning of this section.

► **To install the XBikes application into the Presentation tier**

1. Open Windows Explorer, and then double-click **xbikesj2ee.msi**.

2. On the **Welcome to the XBikes J2EE Setup Wizard** page, click **Next**.

3. In the **Installation Options** dialog box, make sure **Web Tier** is selected, and then click **Next**.

4. In the second **Installation Options** dialog box, make sure the **Install Source Code** check box is selected, the **Install Database** check box is not selected, and the **Install to WebSphere Application Server 5.0 (uncheck for single tier WSAD only)** check box is selected.

Note: You do not need to install the source code unless you want to look at the code.

Click **Next** to continue.

5. In the **Confirm Installation** dialog box, click **Next**. The installation copies the XBikes sample code and configures the application server.

6. When the installation is complete, click **Close**.

Configuring the XBikes Application

Now that you have installed XBikes, you must configure the Web tier and the Business tier to use the correct JNDI servers.

► **To configure the Web tier for JNDI lookups**

1. On the Web tier computer, open the C:\Xbikes\Config\Webconfig.xml configuration file in Notepad.

2. Locate the **<iiop>** tag.

3. Change **localhost** in the **iiop** entry to the IP address of the server containing the business tier.

4. Save the file.

► **To configure the Business tier for JNDI lookups**

1. On the Business tier computer, open the C:\Xbikes\Config\Bllconfig.xml configuration file in Notepad.

2. Locate the **<iiop>** tag.

3. Change **localhost** in the **iiop** entry to the IP address of the server containing the data tier.

4. Save the file.

Running the XBikes Application

You are now ready to run the XBikes application. Make sure you start the computers in the following order: Data tier, Business tier, and then Presentation tier. After all the computers start, open a browser window on the Presentation tier computer, and then enter http://localhost:9080/XBikesWeb.

Note: XBikesWeb is case sensitive.

Changing Interoperability Methods

When you have the XBikes Web application operating correctly, you can change the interoperability methods so that XBikes uses different use case adapters or resource interoperability adapters. This section describes the possible options in the following topics:

- Using Web Services Adapters
- Using Ja.NET Adapters
- Using Message Queue Adapters

The following sections describe how to use each kind of adapter.

Using Web Services Adapters

You can use Web services adapters in the following scenarios:

- Using Web Service Adapters between the Web and Business Tiers
- Using Web Service Adapters between the Business and Data Tiers

To change XBikes to use Web services adapters, you must modify the application configuration to use the Web services adapters, update the application configuration with the URLs of the Web services, and then restart the application server. The following sections describe how to perform these tasks in each scenario.

Using Web Service Adapters between the Web and Business Tiers

This section describes how to use Web services between the Web and Business tiers. You can either use J2EE Web services or .NET Framework Web services; complete the steps in one of the following procedures.

▶ **To use J2EE Web services between the Web and Business tiers**

1. Open Windows Explorer and navigate to the C:\Xbikes\Config folder.
2. In Notepad, open WebConfig.xml.

   This file contains six entries for interoperability, one for each use case.

3. Locate the tag associated with the use case you want to change.

   For example, if you want to change the **GetCategories** use case, locate the \<GetCategories\> XML tag.

4. Change the class name defined in the use case tag to **xbikes.usecaseinteropadapters.j2ee.ws.XXXX**, where **XXXX** is the name of the use case you want to change. (You can change all the use cases if you want.)

5. Locate the **\<j2eews\>** tag, and change the URL to the location of the J2EE Web services.

   For example, if the J2EE Web services reside on a computer named **J2EEBLL**, the **\<j2eews\>** tag would look like the following.

   ```
   <j2eews>http://J2EEBLL:9080/XBikesBLLServiceInterface/services/BLLWSServiceInte
   rface.wsdl</j2eews>
   ```

6. Save WebConfig.xml.

7. Restart the application server that contains the Web tier to flush out the cached adapter configuration file.

▶ **To use .NET Web services between the Web and Business tiers**

1. Open Windows Explorer and navigate to the C:\Xbikes\Config folder.

2. In Notepad, open WebConfig.xml.

   This file contains six entries for interoperability, one for each use case.

3. Locate the tag associated with the use case you want to change.

   For example, if you want to change the **GetCategories** use case, locate the \<GetCategories\> XML tag.

4. Change the class name defined in the use case tag to **xbikes.usecaseinteropadapters.net.ws.XXXX**, where **XXXX** is the name of the use case you want to change. (You can change all the use cases if you want.)

5. Locate the **\<netws\>** tag, and change the URL to the location of the .NET Framework Web services.

   For example, if the .NET Framework Web services reside on a computer named **NETBLL**, the **\<netws\>** tag would look like the following.

   ```
   <netws>http://NETBLL/XBikes-BLL-
   WSServiceInterface/BLLWSServiceInterface.asmx?WSDL</netws>
   ```

6. Save WebConfig.xml.

7. Restart the application server that contains the Web tier to flush out the cached adapter configuration file.

Using Web Service Adapters between the Business and Data Tiers

This section describes how to use Web services between the Business and Data tiers. You can either use J2EE Web services or .NET Framework Web services; follow the steps in one of the following procedures.

▶ **To use J2EE Web services between the Business and Data tiers**

1. Open Windows Explorer and navigate to the C:\Xbikes\Config folder.
2. In Notepad, open BLLConfig.xml.

   This file contains two entries, one for the resource adapters and one for the **POResourceAdapter**. The **ResourceAdapter** tag is used for all data access except for placing an order, which is configured using the **POResourceAdapter** tag.

3. Locate the tag that you want to change.
4. Change the class name defined in the **ResourceAdapter** tag to **xbikes.resourceinteropadapters.dal.j2ee.ws.DALServiceFacadeAdapter**.
5. Locate the **<j2eews>** tag, and change the URL to the location of the J2EE Web services.

   For example, if the J2EE Web services reside on a computer named **J2EEDAL**, the **<j2eews>** tag would look like the following.

   ```
   <j2eews>http://J2EEDAL:9080/
   XBikesResWS/services/DALWSServiceInterface.wsdl</j2eews>
   ```

6. Save BLLConfig.xml.
7. Restart the application server that contains the Business tier to flush out the cached adapter configuration file.

▶ **To use .NET Framework Web services between the Business and Data tiers**

1. Open Windows Explorer and navigate to the C:\Xbikes\Config folder.
2. In Notepad, open BLLConfig.xml.

   This file contains two entries, one for the resource adapters and one for the **POResourceAdapter**. The **ResourceAdapter** tag is used for all data access except for placing an order, which is configured using the **POResourceAdapter** tag.

3. Locate the tag that you want to change.
4. Change the class name defined in the **ResourceAdapter** tag to **xbikes.resourceinteropadapters.dal.net.ws.DALServiceFacadeAdapter**.

5. Locate the **<netws>** tag, and change the URL to the location of the .NET Framework Web services.

   For example, if the .NET Framework Web services reside on a computer named **NETDAL**, the **<netws>** tag would look like the following.

   ```
   <netws>http://NETDAL/ XBikes-DAL-
   WSServiceInterface/DALWSServiceInterface.asmx?WSDL</netws>
   ```

6. Save BLLConfig.xml.
7. Restart the application server that contains the Business tier to flush out the cached adapter configuration file.

Note: If you want to change the Place Order functionality to use Web services, repeat one of the preceding procedures for the **POResourceAdapter** tag, using the class name **xbikes.resourceinteropadapters.dal.net.ws.PlaceOrderResourceAdapter**.

Using Ja.NET Adapters

You can use Ja.NET adapters in the following scenarios:

- Using Ja.NET Adapters between the J2EE Web Tier and the .NET Framework Business Tier
- Using Ja.NET Adapters between the J2EE Business Tier and the .NET Framework Data Tier

To change XBikes to use Ja.NET adapters, you must modify the application configuration to use the Ja.NET adapters, update the server configuration file to load the correct Ja.NET configuration file, and then restart the application server. The following sections describe how to perform these tasks in each scenario.

Using Ja.NET Adapters between the J2EE Web Tier and the .NET Framework Business Tier

This section describes how to use Ja.NET adapters between the J2EE Web tier and the .NET Framework Business tier.

▶ **Using Ja.NET adapters between the J2EE Web tier and the .NET Framework Business tier**

1. Open Windows Explorer and navigate to the C:\Xbikes\Config folder.
2. In Notepad, open WebConfig.xml. This file contains six entries for interoperability, one for each use case.
3. Locate the tag associated with the use case you want to change. For example, if you want to change the **GetCategories** use case, locate the **<GetCategories>** XML tag.

4. Change the class name defined in the use case tag to **xbikes.usecaseinteropadapters.net.janet.XXXX**, where **XXXX** is the name of the use case you want to change. (You can change all the use cases if you want.)

5. Save WebConfig.xml.

6. In Notepad, open the C:\Xbikes\Config\Janet_bll.xml file.

7. Locate the **JaNETConfiguration** element, followed by the **ClientMap** child element, followed by the **default** child element, followed by the **URI** child element. Make sure the **URI** element contains the correct URL to the XBikes-BLL-JaNetServiceInterface Web project.

8. Save the Janet_bll.xml file.

9. Copy the Janet_bll.xml file in the C:\Xbikes\Config folder to Janet_config.xml in the same folder.

Note: The Janet_config.xml file already exists, so overwrite it with the Janet_bll.xml file.

10. Restart the Web tier application server.

Using Ja.NET Adapters between the J2EE Business Tier and the .NET Framework Data Tier

This section describes how to use Ja.NET adapters between the J2EE Business tier and the .NET Framework Data tier.

▶ **Using Ja.NET adapters between the J2EE Business tier and the .NET Framework Data tier**

1. Open Windows Explorer and navigate to the C:\Xbikes\Config folder.

2. In Notepad, open BLLConfig.xml.

   This file contains two entries, one for the resource adapters and one for the **POResourceAdapter**. The **ResourceAdapter** tag is used for all data access except for placing an order, which is configured using the **POResourceAdapter** tag.

3. Change the class name defined in the **ResourceAdapter** tag to **xbikes.resourceinteropadapters.dal.net.janet.JaNetDALServiceFacadeAdapter**.

4. Save BLLConfig.xml.

5. In Notepad, open the C:\Xbikes\Config\Janet_dal.xml file.

6. Locate the **JaNETConfiguration** element, followed by the **ClientMap** child element, followed by the **default** child element, followed by the **URI** child element. Make sure the **URI** element contains the correct URL to the XBikes-DAL-JaNetServiceInterface Web project.

7. Save the Janet_dal.xml file.

8. Copy the Janet_dal.xml file in the C:\Xbikes\Config folder to Janet_config.xml in the same folder.

Note: The Janet_config.xml file already exists, so overwrite it with the Janet_dal.xml file.

---

9. Restart the Business tier application server.

Using Message Queue Adapters

XBikes allows you to use a message queue to place orders. To configure the XBikes application to use the message queue, complete the following steps.

▶ **To configure the "Place Order" functionality to use message queues**

1. Open Windows Explorer and navigate to the C:\Xbikes\Config folder.
2. In Notepad, open BLLConfig.xml.
3. Change the **POResourceAdapter** entry to **xbikes.resourceinteropadapters.queue.wsmq.PlaceOrderResourceAdapter**.
4. Save the BLLConfig.xml file.
5. Restart the application server.

The J2EE XBikes application contains a Web application on the Data tier to read orders from the queue and insert them into the database. If you have configured XBikes to use message queuing, and you have successfully placed an order, you can complete the following steps to view and process the orders.

▶ **To view and process orders from the message queue**

1. Open a Web browser window and enter http://localhost:9080/MQTestClient.
2. Click the **Check MQ for Orders** button to display orders in the Web browser window.

Manual Installation Instructions

The following section describes how to deploy the J2EE version of XBikes without using the automated setup.

Manually Configuring XBikes on IBM Application Server

After IBM WebSphere Application Server and WebSphere MQ are installed, you can configure XBikes.

▶ **To manually configure XBikes on WebSphere application server**

1. Create the XBikes Enterprise Archive (EAR) file.
2. Configure WebSphere Application Server:
   a. Configure the SQL Server login.
   b. Configure the XBikes data source.
   c. Add the licensed Glue.jar file.
   d. Add the EJB bindings.
3. Install the XBikes EAR file.
4. Configure WebSphere MQ support.
5. Restart WebSphere Application Server.

After you complete these procedures, you can test that you have successfully deployed the XBikes Web site.

Note: Make sure you install the XBikes sample code by following the instructions in the "Installing the XBikes Sample Code" section.

The XBikes EAR file contains the components, assemblies, and configuration information to run XBikes on a single computer.

▶ **To create the single computer XBikes EAR file**

1. Start WebSphere Application Developer Studio 5.0 by clicking **Start**, pointing to **All Programs**, pointing to **IBM WebSphere Studio**, and then clicking **Application Developer 5.0**.
2. In the **WebSphere Studio** dialog box, change the workspace to **C:\Xbikes\J2ee-Ibm**, and then click **OK**. The J2EE–IBM WebSphere Studio Application Developer window appears.
3. Switch to the **J2EE Perspective** view by clicking the **Window** menu, pointing to **Open Perspective**, and then clicking **J2EE**.
4. In the lower left pane, click the **J2EE Hierarchy** tab.
5. Expand **Enterprise Applications**, right-click **SingleTierXBikes**, and then click **Export EAR File**. The **Export** dialog box appears.
6. Under **Where do you want to export resources to**, enter **c:\xbikes\SingleTierXBikes.ear**.
7. Under **Options**, ensure that all three check boxes are selected, and then click **Finish**.
8. After the export process takes place, exit WebSphere Application Developer Studio 5.0.

► **To configure WebSphere Application Server**

1. Open a command prompt and navigate to the C:\Was\WebSphere\AppServer \Bin folder.
2. Type **startserver server1**, and then press **Enter**.
3. After a few seconds a message displays, indicating that server1 is open for e-business.
4. Open a Web browser window and navigate to http://localhost:9090/admin. For convenience, add this URL to your favorites.
5. In the **User ID** field, enter **admin**, and then click **OK**.

► **To configure the SQL Server login**

1. In the left pane, expand **Security**, expand **JAAS Configuration**, and then click **J2C Authentication Data**.
2. The right pane changes to **J2C Authentication Data Entries**. Click the **New** button.
3. Click the **Configuration** tab, enter **dhb** in the **alias** field, **dhb** in the **User ID** field, **bikes** in the **password** field, and then click **OK**.
4. The **Messages** section appears at the top of the right pane. Click the **Save** link.
5. In the **Save** pane, click the **Save** button. The right pane reverts to the **WebSphere Application Server** home page.

► **To configure the XBikes data source**

1. In the left pane, expand **Environment**, and then click the **Manage WebSphere Variables** link. The WebSphere Variables window appears in the right pane.
2. Click the **MSSQLSERVER_JDBC_DRIVER_PATH** link. The MSSQLSERVER_JDBC_DRIVER_PATH window appears in the right pane.
3. In the **Value** field, enter **C:\Program Files\Microsoft SQL Server 2000 Driver for JDBC\lib**, and then click **OK**.
4. The **Messages** section appears at the top of the right pane. Click the **Save** link.
5. In the **Save** pane, click the **Save** button. The right pane reverts to the **WebSphere Application Server** home page.
6. In the left pane, expand **Resources**, and then click **JDBC Providers**. The right pane changes to **JDBC Providers**.
7. Under **Scope**, select the **Server** option, and then click **Apply**.
8. Click **New**.
9. In the **JDBC Providers** list, click **Microsoft JDBC driver for MSSQLServer 2000**, and then click **OK**. The Microsoft JDBC driver for MSSQLServer 2000 window appears in the right pane.
10. Under **Configuration**, change the value of the **Name** field to **XBikesDB**.

11. Make sure the value of the **Implementation Classname** field is set to **com.microsoft.jdbcx.sqlserver.SQLServerDataSource**, and then click **OK**.

12. The **Messages** section appears at the top of the right pane. Click the **Save** link.

13. In the **Save** pane, click **Save**. The right pane reverts to the **WebSphere Application Server** home page.

14. In the left pane, click **JDBC Providers** again. The right pane changes to **JDBC Providers**.

15. Click the **XBikesDB** link. The right pane changes to **XBikesDB**.

16. At the bottom of the page under **Additional Properties**, click the **Data Sources** link. The right pane changes to the **Data Sources** page. Click the **New** button.

17. The right pane changes to **New**. In the **name** and **JNDI Name** fields, type **XBikesDB**. Select the **Use this Data Source in Container Managed Persistence (CMP)** option.

18. Next to **Component-managed Authentication Alias**, select the only option available from the drop down list box, which is in the form **servername/dhb**. Do the same for the **Container-managed Authentication Alias** field, and then click **OK**.

19. On the **Data Sources** page, click the **XBikesDB** link. The **XBikesDB** page appears.

20. At the bottom of the page under **Additional Properties**, click the **Custom Properties** link.

21. Select the **databaseName** option, and then click the **databaseName** link. The **databaseName** page appears.

22. In the **Value** field, enter **XBikes**, and then click **OK**.

23. Click the **serverName** link. The **serverName** page appears.

24. In the **Value** field, enter **localhost**, and then click **OK**.

25. In the **Messages** section, click the **Save** link.

26. In the **Save** pane, click the **Save** button. The right pane reverts to the **WebSphere Application Server** home page.

► To add the licensed Glue.jar file

1. In the left pane, expand **Environment**, and then click the **Shared Libraries** link.

2. Under **Scope**, select the **Server** option, and then click the **Apply** button.

3. Click the **New** button. The **New** page appears.

4. In the **Name** field, enter **GLUE.jar**.

5. In the **Classpath** field, enter **c:\tme\glue\lib\GLUE.jar**, and then click **OK**.

6. In the **Messages** section, click the **Save** link.

7. In the **Save** pane, click the **Save** button. The right pane reverts to the **WebSphere Application Server** home page.

▶ **To add the EJB bindings**

1. In the left pane, expand **Environment**, and then expand **Naming**.
2. Click the **Name Space Bindings** link. The right pane changes to the **Name Space Bindings** page.
3. Under **Scope**, select the **Server** option, and then click **Apply**.
4. Click **New**. The **New** page appears.
5. In the **Binding Type** options, select **EJB** and click **Next**.
6. In the **Binding Identifier** field, enter **BusinessServiceFacade**.
7. In the **Name in Name Space** field, enter **BusinessServiceFacade**.
8. In the **Enterprise Bean Location** field, type your WebSphere host name. This name is displayed at the top of the left pane in the administration console.
9. In the **Server** field, enter **server1**.
10. In the **JNDI Name** field, **enter ejb/xbikes/bll/facade /BusinessServiceFacadeHome**, click **Next**, and then click **Finish**.
11. Click the **New** button. The **New** page appears.
12. In the **Binding Type** options, select **EJB** and click **Next**.
13. In the **Binding Identifier** field, enter **DalServiceFacadeHome**.
14. In the **Name in Name Space** field, enter **DalServiceFacadeHome**.
15. In the **Enterprise Bean Location** field, type your WebSphere host name. This name is displayed at the top of the left pane in the administration console.
16. In the **Server** field, enter **server1**.
17. In the **JNDI Name** field, enter **ejb/xbikes/dal/façade/DalServiceFacadeHome**, click **Next**, and then click **Finish**.
18. In the **Messages** section, click the **Save** link.
19. In the **Save** pane, click the **Save** button. The right pane reverts to the **WebSphere Application Server** home page.

▶ **To Install the SingleTierApp enterprise archive file**

1. In the left pane, expand **Applications**.
2. Click the **Enterprise Applications** link. The **Enterprise Applications** page displays in the right pane.
3. Click **Install**, and then click **Browse** next to the **Local Path** field.
4. Navigate to C:\Xbikes, select the **singletierxbikes.ear** file, and then click **Open**. The full path to the singletierxbikes.ear file displays in the **Local Path** field. Click **Next** to continue.
5. On the **Preparing for the application installation** page, click **Next**.
6. On the **Step 1** page, select the **Deploy EJBs** option, and then click **Next**.

7. On the **Step 2** page, select **MSSQLServer_2000** in the **Database Type** list box, and then click **Next**.

8. On the **Step 3** page, click **Next**.

9. On the **Step 4** page, enter **XBikesDB** in the **JNDI name** field next to **XBikesDal**, and then click **Next**.

10. Steps 5, 6, 7, 8 and 9 do not require any changes. Click **Next** on the page for each of these steps, and then click **Finish** on the **Step 10** page. A command prompt window appears and messages display on the **Installing** page in the right pane.

Note: Do not do anything else until the deployment process completes and the command prompt window disappears.

11. Click the **Save to Master Configuration** link.

12. In the **Save** pane, click the **Save** button. The right pane reverts to the **WebSphere Application Server** home page.

13. In the left pane, expand **Applications**.

14. Click the **Enterprise Applications** link. The **Enterprise Applications** page displays in the right pane.

15. Click the **SingleTierXBikes** link. The **SingleTierXBikes** page displays in the right pane.

16. In the **Additional Properties** section, click the **Libraries** link. The **Library Ref** page displays in the right pane.

17. Click the **Add** button. The **New** page displays.

18. Ensure that **GLUE.jar** appears next to the **Library Name** field, and then click **OK**.

19. In the **Messages** section, click the **Save** link.

20. In the **Save** pane, click the **Save** button. The right pane reverts to the **WebSphere Application Server** home page.

► **To configure WebSphere MQ support**

1. In the left pane, expand **Resources**, and then select **WebSphere MQ JMS Provider**.

2. Under **Scope**, select the **Server** option, and then click **Apply**.

3. Under **Additional Properties**, select the **WebSphere MQ Queue Connection Factories** link. The **WebSphere MQ Queue Connection Factories** page appears.

4. Click the **New** button. Next to the **Name** and **JNDI Name** fields, enter **XBikesQCF**.

Note: JNDI Name is case sensitive.

5. In the **Queue Manager** field, enter the name of your Queue Manager. Typically, this is *QM_YourComputerName*.

6. In the **Host** field, enter **localhost**, and then click **OK** to create the connection factory.

7. Under **Resources** in the left pane, click the **WebSphere MQ JMS Provider** link. The **WebSphere MQ JMS Provider** page displays.

8. Under **Additional Properties**, click the **WebSphere Queue Destinations** link. The **WebSphere MQ Queue Destinations** page displays.

9. Click the **New** button. In the **Name, JNDI Name**, and **Base Queue Name** fields, enter **XBikesQ**.

Note: These fields are case sensitive.

---

10. In the **Base Queue Manager** field, enter the name of your Queue Manager, and then click **OK**.

11. In the **Messages** section, click the **Save** link.

12. In the **Save** pane, click the **Save** button. The right pane reverts to the **WebSphere Application Server** home page.

13. Click the **Logout** link at the top of the page to leave the Web Admin tool, and then close your browser window.

Restarting WebSphere Application Server

Before you can test the application, you need to restart WebSphere application server.

▶ **To restart WebSphere application server**

1. Open a command prompt and navigate to the C:\Was\WebSphere\AppServer \Bin folder.

2. Type **stopserver server1**, and then press **Enter**. Wait for the prompt indicating that server1 has stopped.

3. Type **startserver server1**, and then press **Enter**.

4. After a few seconds a message displays, indicating that server1 is open for e-business.

Testing the XBikes Application

You are now ready to test the XBikes application. To do this, open a browser window and enter http://localhost:9080/XBikesWeb.

Note: XBikesWeb is case sensitive.

After the XBikes Web site displays, you can change the configuration files to test Web Service, Message Queuing, and Interoperability functionality just as you did in the previous section.

Preparing XBikes for Multi-Tier Deployment

To deploy the J2EE XBikes to multiple computers, you need to export the enterprise archive files from the XBikes application. If you installed IBM Application Developer Studio 5.0 on the Presentation tier computer, complete the following steps on that computer.

▶ **To export the enterprise archive files**

1. Start WebSphere Application Developer Studio 5.0 by clicking **Start**, pointing to **All Programs**, pointing to **IBM WebSphere Studio**, and then clicking **Application Developer 5.0**.

2. A **WebSphere Studio** dialog box appears. Change the workspace to **C:\Xbikes\J2ee-Ibm**, and then click **OK**. The J2EE–IBM WebSphere Studio Application Developer window appears.

3. Switch to the **J2EE Perspective** view by clicking the **Window** menu, pointing to **Open Perspective**, and then clicking **J2EE**.

4. Click the **J2EE Hierarchy** tab at the bottom of the left pane, and then expand **Enterprise Applications**.

5. Right-click **SingleTierXBikes**, and then click **Delete**. The **Delete Enterprise Applications Options** dialog box appears.

6. Make sure **Delete Selected Enterprise Application Project(s) only** is selected, and then click **OK**. The **Confirm Project Delete** dialog box appears.

7. Make sure **Also delete contents under c:\xbikes\j2ee-ibm\SingleTierXBikes** is selected, and then click **Yes**. This removes the application and the **Repair Server Configuration** dialog box appears.

8. Click **OK**.

9. Click the **J2EE Navigator** tab at the bottom of the left pane, right-click **XBikesWeb**, and then click **Properties**. The **Properties for XBikes Web** dialog box appears.

10. In the left pane, click **Web Library Projects**, and then click **Add**. The **Add a Library Project** dialog appears.

11. Click **Browse**. The **Select a Java Project** dialog box appears.

12. Click **XBikesBiz**, and then click **OK**. The **Select a Java Project** dialog box closes. The **Add a Library Project** dialog box now shows **XBikesBiz.jar** as the **JAR Name** and **XBikesBiz** as the **Java Project**.

13. Click **OK**. The **XBikesBiz.jar (XBikesBiz)** is now listed as a **Web Library Project**.

14. Click **OK** to close the dialog box.

15. In the **Navigator** view, right-click **XBikesBiz**, and then click **Properties**. The **Properties for XBikesBiz** dialog box appears.

16. In the left pane, click **Java JAR Dependencies**, and then make sure **XBikesDALUtility.jar** is selected. Click **OK**.

17. At the bottom of the left pane, click the **J2EE Hierarchy** tab.

18. Right-click **XBikesWebApp**, and then click **Export EAR File**. The **Export** dialog box appears.

19. Under **Where do you want to export resources to**, enter **c:\xbikes\XBikesWebApp.ear**.

20. Under **Options**, make sure that all three check boxes are selected, and then click **Finish**.

21. Repeat steps 18 to 20 for XBikesBLL and XBikesDAL, naming the exported files **XBikesBLL.ear** and **XBikesDAL.ear** respectively.

22. After you complete exporting the three EAR files, exit WebSphere Application Developer Studio 5.0.

23. Copy the **XBikesBLL.ear** file to the **C:\xbikes** directory on the Business tier computer.

24. Copy the **XBikesDAL.ear** file to the **C:\xbikes** directory on the Data tier computer.

Deploying XBikes on the Presentation Tier Computer

To deploy XBikes on the Presentation tier computer, complete the following procedures:

1. Configure the WebSphere server.
2. Install the XBikesWebApp enterprise archive file.
3. Start the XBikes Presentation tier component.

▶ **To configure the WebSphere server**

1. Open a command prompt and navigate to the C:\Was\WebSphere\AppServer\Bin folder.

2. Type **startserver server1**, and then press **Enter**.

3. After a few seconds a message displays that indicates that server1 is open for e-business.

4. In Notepad or another text editor, open the C:\Xbikes\Config\WebConfig.xml file.

5. Change the **localhost** entry within the **<iiop>** and **<j2eews>** tags to the name of the Business tier computer. This entry should now read as follows.

```
<iiop>iiop://BusinessTierComputerName</iiop>
<j2eews>http://BusinessTierComputerName:9080/XBikesBLLServiceInterface/services
/BLLWSServiceInterface.wsdl</j2eews>
```

6. Open a Web browser window and navigate to http://localhost:9090/admin. For convenience, add this URL to your favorites.

7. In the **User ID** field, enter **admin**, and then click **OK**.

8. In the left pane, expand **Environment**, and then click the **Shared Libraries** link. The **Shared Libraries** page appears in the right pane.

9. Under **Scope**, select the **Server** option, and then click **Apply**.

10. Click the **New** button. The **New** page appears.

11. In the **Name** field, enter **GLUE.jar** in the **Name** field.

12. In the **Classpath** field, enter **c:\tme\glue\lib\GLUE.jar**, and then click **OK**.

13. The **Messages** section appears at the top of the right pane. Click the **Save** link.

14. In the **Save** pane, click the **Save** button. The right pane reverts to the **WebSphere Application Server** home page.

► **To install the XBikesWebApp enterprise archive file**

1. In the left pane of the Admin console, expand **Applications**, and then click the **Install New Application** link.

2. Ensure the **Local Path** is selected, and then click **Browse**.

3. In the C:\Xbikes folder, click **XBikesWebApp.ear**, and then click **Next**.

4. On the **Preparing for the application installation page**, click **Next**.

5. On each page for **Steps 1–3**, accept the default settings by clicking **Next**.

6. On the **Step 4** page, click **Finish**.

7. After the application installs, click the **Manage Applications** link in the right pane.

8. On the **Enterprise Applications** page, click the **XBikesWebApp** link.

9. In **Additional Properties** box at the bottom of the page, click the **Libraries** link.

10. Click the **Add** button. The **New** page appears in the right pane.

11. The **GLUE** library should already be selected next to **Library Name**. Click **OK**.

12. The **Messages** section appears at the top of the right pane. Click the **Save** link.

13. In the **Save** pane, click the **Save** button. The right pane reverts to the **WebSphere Application Server** home page.

► **To start the XBikes Presentation tier component**

1. In the left pane, click **Enterprise Applications**.

2. Select the **XBikesWebApp** check box, and then click **Start**. The XBikes Presentation Tier component should start.

3. Close the administration console.

Deploying the Business Tier Components

To install the XBikes Business tier components on the Business tier computer, complete the following procedures:

1. Configure the WebSphere server.
2. Install the XBikesBLL enterprise archive file.
3. Start the XBikes Business tier component.

▶ **To configure the WebSphere server**

1. Open a command prompt and navigate to the C:\Was\WebSphere\AppServer \Bin folder.
2. Type **startserver server1**, and then press **Enter**.
3. After a few seconds a message displays that indicates that server1 is open for e-business.
4. In Notepad or another text editor, open the C:\Xbikes\Config\BLLConfig.xml file.
5. Change the **localhost** entry within the **<iiop>**, **<j2eews>**, and **<netws>** tags to the name of the Data tier computer. This entry should now read as follows.

```
<iiop>iiop://DataTierComputerName</iiop>
<j2eews>http://DataTierComputerName:9080/XBikesResWS/services/DALWSServiceInter
face.wsdl</j2eews>
<netws>http://DataTierComputerName/XBikes-DAL-
WSServiceInterface/DALWSServiceInterface.asmx?WSDL</netws>
```

6. Open a Web browser window and navigate to http://localhost:9090/admin. For convenience, add this URL to your favorites.
7. In the **User ID** field, enter **admin**, and then click **OK**.
8. In the left pane, expand **Environment**, and then click the **Shared Libraries** link. The **Shared Libraries** page appears in the right pane.
9. Under **Scope**, select the **Server** option, and then click **Apply**.
10. Click the **New** button. The **New** page appears.
11. In the **Name** field, enter **GLUE.jar**.
12. In the **Classpath** field, enter **c:\tme\glue\lib\GLUE.jar**, and then click **OK**.
13. The **Messages** section appears at the top of the right pane. Click the **Save** link.
14. In the **Save** pane, click the **Save** button. The right pane reverts to the **WebSphere Application Server** home page.
15. In the left pane, expand **Naming**, and then click the **Name Space Bindings** link.
16. Under **Scope**, select the **Server** option, and then click **Apply**.
17. Click the **New** button. The **New** page appears.

18. Click **EJB**, and then click **Next**. The **New Name Space Binding** page appears.

19. In the **Binding Identifier** field, enter **BusinessServiceFacade**.

20. In the **Name in Name Space** field, enter **BusinessServiceFacade**.

21. In the **Enterprise Bean Location** enter, the name of your WebSphere host. This should appear at the top of the navigation tree in the left pane of the Administrative console.

22. In the **Server** field, enter **server1**.

23. In the **JNDI name** field, enter **ejb/xbikes/bll/façade /BusinessServiceFacadeHome**, and then click **Next**.

24. On the **Summary** page, click **Finish**.

25. The **Messages** section appears at the top of the right pane. Click the **Save** link.

26. In the **Save** pane, click the **Save** button. The right pane reverts to the **WebSphere Application Server** home page.

▶ **To configure WebSphere MQ support**

1. In the left pane, expand **Resources**, and then click **WebSphere MQ JMS Provider**.

2. Under **Scope**, select the **Server** option, and then click **Apply**.

3. Under **Additional Properties**, click the **WebSphere MQ Queue Connection Factories** link. The **WebSphere MQ Queue Connection Factories** page appears.

4. Click the **New** button. Next to the **Name** and **JNDI Name** fields, enter **XBikesQCF**.

Note: JNDI Name is case sensitive.

---

5. In the **Queue Manager** field, enter the name of your Queue Manager. Typically this is *QM_DataTierComputerName*.

6. In the **Host** field, enter the name of the Data tier server.

7. In the **Port** field, enter **1414**.

8. In the **Transport Type** field, choose **CLIENT**, and then click **OK**.

9. Under **Resources** in the left pane, click the **WebSphere MQ JMS Provider** link. The **WebSphere MQ JMS Provider** page displays.

10. Under **Additional Properties**, click the **WebSphere Queue Destinations** link. The **WebSphere MQ Queue Destinations** page displays.

11. Click the **New** button. In the **Name**, **JNDI Name**, and **Base Queue Name** fields, enter **XBikesQ**.

Note: These fields are case sensitive.

---

12. In the **Base Queue Manager** field, enter the name of your Queue Manager, and then click **OK**.

13. In the **Messages** section, click the **Save** link.

14. In the **Save** pane, click the **Save** button. The right pane reverts to the **WebSphere Application Server** home page.

15. Click the **Logout** link at the top of the page to leave the Web Admin tool, and then close your browser window.

► To install the XBikesBLL enterprise archive file

1. In the left pane of the Admin console, expand **Applications**, and then click the **Install New Application** link.

2. Ensure the **Local Path** option is selected, and then click **Browse**.

3. In the C:\Xbikes folder, click **XBikesBLL.ear**, and then click **Next**.

4. On the **Preparing for the application installation** page, click **Next**.

5. On the **Step 1** page, select the **Deploy EJBs** check box, and then click **Next**.

6. On each page for **Steps 2–7**, accept the default settings by clicking **Next**.

7. On the **Step 8** page, click **Finish**. The application then installs and a blank command window displays.

8. After the application installs, click the **Manage Applications** link in the right pane.

9. On the **Enterprise Applications** page, click the **XBikesBLL** link.

10. In **Additional Properties** box at the bottom of the page, click the **Libraries** link. The **Library Ref** page appears.

11. Click the **Add** button. The **New** page appears in the right pane.

12. The **GLUE.JAR** library should already be selected next to **Library Name**. Click **OK**.

13. The **Messages** section appears at the top of the right pane. Click the **Save** link.

14. In the **Save** pane, click the **Save** button. The right pane reverts to the **WebSphere Application Server** home page.

► To start the XBikes Business tier component

1. In the left pane, click **Enterprise Applications**.

2. Select the **XBikesWebApp** check box, and then click **Start**. The XBikes Business tier component should start and a message in the **Messages** section at the top of the right pane should confirm this.

3. Close the administration console.

Configuring the Data Tier Computer

To set up the Data tier computer, complete the following procedures:

1. Configure the WebSphere server.
2. Configure the EJB bindings.
3. Configure the paths for the Microsoft JDBC driver.
4. Configure the SQL Server login.
5. Configure the XBikes JDBC data source.
6. Install the XBikesDAL enterprise archive file.
7. Start the XBikes Data tier component.

After you complete these procedures, you should be able to test the XBikes application.

Note: Ensure you have installed the XBikes database tables.

▶ **To configure the WebSphere server**

1. Open a command prompt and navigate to the C:\Was\WebSphere\AppServer\Bin folder.
2. Type **startserver server1**, and press **Enter**.
3. After a few seconds a message displays that indicates that server1 is open for e-business.
4. Open a Web browser window and navigate to http://localhost:9090/admin. For convenience, add this URL to your favorites.
5. In the **User ID** field, enter **admin**, and then click **OK**.
6. In the left pane, expand **Environment**, and then click the **Shared Libraries** link. The **Shared Libraries** page appears in the right pane.
7. Under **Scope**, select the **Server** option, and then click **Apply**.
8. Click the **New** button. The **New** page appears.
9. In the **Name** field, enter **GLUE.jar**.
10. In the **Classpath** field, enter **c:\tme\glue\lib\GLUE.jar**, and then click **OK**.
11. The **Messages** section appears at the top of the right pane. Click the **Save** link.
12. In the **Save** pane, click the **Save** button. The right pane reverts to the **WebSphere Application Server** home page.

▶ **To configure the EJB bindings**

1. In the left pane, expand **Environment**, expand **Naming**, and then click the **Name Space Bindings** link.
2. Under **Scope**, select the **Server** option, and then click **Apply**.

3. Click the **New** button. The **New** page appears.

4. Click **EJB**, and then click **Next**.

5. In the **Binding Identifier** field, enter **DalServiceFacadeHome**.

6. In the **Name in Name Space** field, enter **DalServiceFacadeHome**.

7. In the **Enterprise Bean Location** field, enter the name of your WebSphere host name. This should appear at the top of the navigation tree in the left pane of the Administrative console.

8. In the **Server** field, enter **server1**.

9. In the **JNDI name** field, enter **ejb/xbikes/dal/façade/DalServiceFacadeHome**, and then click **Next**.

10. On the **Summary** page, click **Finish**.

11. The **Messages** section appears at the top of the right pane. Click the **Save** link.

12. In the **Save** pane, click the **Save** button. The right pane reverts to the **WebSphere Application Server** home page.

► **To configure the paths for the Microsoft JDBC driver**

1. In the left pane, expand **Environment**, and then click the **Manage WebSphere Variables** link. The WebSphere Variables window appears in the right pane.

2. Click the **MSSQLSERVER_JDBC_DRIVER_PATH** link. The MSSQLSERVER_JDBC_DRIVER_PATH window appears in the right pane.

3. In the **Value** field, enter **C:\Program Files\Microsoft SQL Server 2000 Driver for JDBC\lib**, and then click **OK**.

4. The **Messages** section appears at the top of the right pane. Click the **Save** link.

5. In the **Save** pane, click the **Save** button. The right pane reverts to the **WebSphere Application Server** home page.

► **To configure the SQL Server login**

1. In the left pane, expand **Security**, expand **JAAS Configuration**, and then click **J2C Authentication Data**.

2. The right pane changes to **J2C Authentication Data Entries**. Click the **New** button.

3. Click the **Configuration** tab.

4. Enter **dhb** in the **alias** field, enter **dhb** in the **User ID** field, enter **bikes** in the **password** field, and then click **OK**.

5. The **Messages** section appears at the top of the right pane. Click the **Save** link.

6. In the **Save** pane, click the **Save** button. The right pane reverts to the **WebSphere Application Server** home page.

▶ **To configure the XBikes JDBC data source**

1. In the left pane, expand **Resources**, and then click **JDBC Providers**. The right pane changes to **JDBC Providers**.

2. Under **Scope**, select the **Server** option, and then click **Apply**.

3. Click the **New** button.

4. In the **JDBC Providers** list, click **Microsoft JDBC driver for MSSQLServer 2000**, and then click **OK**. The Microsoft JDBC driver for MSSQLServer 2000 window appears in the right pane.

5. Under **Configuration**, change the value of the **Name** field to **XBikesDB**.

6. Make sure the value of the **Implementation Classname** field is set to **com.microsoft.jdbcx.sqlserver.SQLServerDataSource**, and then click **OK**.

7. The **Messages** section appears at the top of the right pane. Click the **Save** link.

8. In the **Save** pane, click the **Save** button. The right pane reverts to the **WebSphere Application Server** home page.

9. In the left pane, click **JDBC Providers** again. The right pane changes to **JDBC Providers**.

10. Click the **XBikesDB** link. The right pane changes to **XBikesDB**.

11. At the bottom of the page under **Additional Properties** box, click the **Data Sources** link. The right pane changes to the **Data Sources** page. Click the **New** button.

12. The right pane changes to **New**. In the **name** and **JNDI Name** fields, type **XBikesDB**. Select the **Use this Data Source in Container Managed Persistence (CMP)** check box.

13. Next to **Component-managed Authentication Alias**, select the only option available from the drop down list box, which is in the form **servername/dhb**. Do the same for the **Container-managed Authentication Alias** field, and then click **OK**.

14. On the **Data Sources** page, click the **XBikesDB** link. The **XBikesDB** page appears.

15. At the bottom of the page under **Additional Properties**, click the **Custom Properties** link.

16. Click the **databaseName** link. The **databaseName** page appears.

17. In the **Value** field, enter **XBikes**, and then click **OK**.

18. Click the **serverName** link. The **serverName** page appears.

19. In the **Value** field, enter **localhost**, and then click **OK**.

20. In the **Messages** section, click the **Save** link.

21. In the **Save** pane, click the **Save** button. The right pane reverts to the **WebSphere Application Server** home page.

▶ **To configure WebSphere MQ support**

1. In the left pane, expand **Resources**, and then click **WebSphere MQ JMS Provider**.

2. Under **Scope**, select the **Server** option, and then click **Apply**.

3. Under **Additional Properties**, click the **WebSphere MQ Queue Connection Factories** link. The **WebSphere MQ Queue Connection Factories** page appears.

4. Click the **New** button. Next to the **Name** and **JNDI Name** fields, enter **XBikesQCF**.

Note: JNDI Name is case sensitive.

---

5. In the **Queue Manager** field, enter the name of your Queue Manager. Typically this is *QM_YourComputerName*.

6. In the **Host** field, enter **localhost**, and then click **OK**.

7. In the left pane under **Resources**, click the **WebSphere MQ JMS Provider** link. The **WebSphere MQ JMS Provider** page displays.

8. Under **Additional Properties**, click the **WebSphere Queue Destinations** link. The **WebSphere MQ Queue Destinations** page displays.

9. Click the **New** button. In the **Name**, **JNDI Name**, and **Base Queue Name** fields, enter **XBikesQ**.

Note: These fields are case sensitive.

---

10. In the **Base Queue Manager** field, enter the name of your Queue Manager, and then click **OK**.

11. In the **Messages** section, click the **Save** link.

12. In the **Save** pane, click the **Save** button. The right pane reverts to the **WebSphere Application Server** home page.

13. Click the **Logout** link at the top of the page to leave the Web Admin tool and then close your browser window.

▶ **To install the XBikesDAL enterprise archive file**

1. In the left pane, expand **Applications**, and then click the **Enterprise Applications** link. The **Enterprise Applications** page displays in the right pane.

2. Click the **Install** button, and then click **Browse** next to **Local Path**.

3. Navigate to C:\Xbikes and select the XBikesDAL.ear file. Click **Open** and the full path to the **XBikesDAL.ear** file displays in the **Local Path** field. Click **Next**.

4. On the **Preparing for the application installation** page, click **Next**.

5. On the **Step 1** page, select the **Deploy EJBs** check box, and then click **Next**.

6. On the **Step 2** page, select **MSSQLServer_2000** in the **Database Type** list box, and then click **Next**.

7. On the **Step 3** page, click **Next**.

8. On the **Step 4** page, enter **XBikesDB** in the **JNDI name** field next to **XBikesDal**, and then click **Next**.

9. Steps 5, 6, 7, 8 and 9 do not require any changes. Click **Next** on each of these steps, and then click **Finish** on the **Step 10** page. A command prompt window appears and messages display on the **Installing** page in the right pane.

Note: Do not do anything else until the deployment process completes and the command prompt window disappears.

10. Click the Save to Master Configuration link.

11. In the **Save** pane, click the **Save** button. The right pane reverts to the **WebSphere Application Server** home page.

12. In the left pane, expand **Applications**.

13. Click the **Enterprise Applications** link. The **Enterprise Applications** page displays in the right pane.

14. Click the **XBikesDal** link. The **XBikesDal** page displays in the right pane.

15. In the **Additional Properties** section, click the **Libraries** link. The **Library Ref** page displays in the right pane.

16. Click the **Add** button. The **New** page displays.

17. Ensure that **GLUE.jar** appears next to the **Library Name** field, and then click **OK**.

18. In the **Messages** section, click the **Save** link.

19. In the **Save** pane, click the **Save** button. The right pane reverts to the **WebSphere Application Server** home page.

▶ **To start the XBikes Data tier component**

1. In the left pane, click **Enterprise Applications**.

2. Select the **XBikesDal** check box, and then click **Start**. The XBikes Business Tier component should start and a message in the **Messages** section at the top of the right pane should confirm this.

3. Close the administration console.

Testing the XBikes Application

You are now ready to test the XBikes application. To do this, open a browser window and enter http://localhost:9080/XBikesWeb.

Note: XBikesWeb is case sensitive.

After the XBikes Web site displays, you can change the configuration files to test Web service, message queuing, and interoperability functionality just as you did in the single tier section.

Appendix B

Installing XBikes on .NET

Introduction

There are two ways in which you can deploy the .NET Framework version of the XBikes sample application using Microsoft Windows Installer (.msi). This appendix describes the following deployment scenarios

- Deploying XBikes on a Single Computer
- Deploying XBikes on Multiple Computers

This appendix also describes how to configure the various XML files that control configuration and interoperability choices. There are also sections on how to execute and uninstall the application.

Deploying XBikes on a Single Computer

Using the XBikes .NET sample code on a single computer requires the following software to be installed:

- Windows Server 2003 or Windows 2000 Server with Service Pack 3 or later in Workgroup mode
- .NET Framework 1.1 (Windows 2000 only; included in Windows 2003)
- .NET Framework 1.1 SDK or Visual Studio 2003
- Internet Information Services—World Wide Web Server
- ASP.NET Application Server component (Windows 2003 only)
- Microsoft Enterprise Instrumentation Framework (EIF)
- Microsoft Message Queuing (also known as MSMQ)
- Microsoft SQL Server 2000 with mixed mode security and Service Pack 3
- JNBridgePro version 1.4 Enterprise Edition (run time only)

Note: ASP.NET Session State Service should be running and its startup type should be set to automatic.

Installing the XBikes Application

To install the XBikes application for the .NET platform on a single computer, complete the following steps.

▶ **To install XBikes for the .NET platform**

1. Open Windows Explorer, and then double-click **xbikes3tier.msi**.
2. On the **xbikes3tier** wizard page, click **Next**.
3. On the **Select Installation Folder** page, make sure C:\Xbikes is the installation path, select the **Everyone** option to install XBikes for all users on the computer, and then click **Next**.
4. On the **Confirm Installation** page, click **Next**.
5. On the **Install Options** page, make sure **Single Tier** is selected, and then click **Next**.
6. In the **Winzip Self Extractor** dialog box, make sure **Unzip to folder** is set to **C:\xbikes**, and then click **Unzip**.
7. The dialog box shows that files were unzipped successfully, click **OK**.
8. In the **Winzip Self-Extractor** dialog box, click **Close**.
9. The installation program continues the setup process for a few seconds.
10. On the **Installation Complete** page, click **Close**.

Configuring the XBikes Web Application

The XBikes application is now installed. Before you execute the application, you will need to modify the identity of the COM+ to Network Service to allow the application to execute without the need for someone to be logged in.

▶ **To configure the COM+ Application**

1. In Control Panel, double-click **Administrative Tools**, and then double-click **Component Services**. The Component Services Manager loads.
2. In the tree on the left, expand **Component Services**, expand **Computers**, and then expand **My Computer**.
3. Expand **COM+ Applications**. A list of installed COM+ applications is shown in the tree view.
4. Right-click **XBikes**, and then click **Properties**. The **XBikes Properties** dialog box appears.

5. Click the **Identity** tab, and then click the **Network Service** option.

6. Click **OK**. The **XBikes Properties** dialog box closes.

7. Close Component Services Manager.

Now you have the COM+ Application configured, the next task is to check the database connection string is correct for your system.

▶ To configure the database connection string

1. In Notepad, open the Dllhost.exe.config file from the C:\Windows\System32 folder.

2. Find the start tag of the **<SqlServer>** element.

3. Check to make sure the connection string includes the correct server name. The server name is shown in bold below to help you.

```
<SqlServer>
  <connection>
    <add
      key="connectionString"
      value="server=localhost;database=xbikes;user id=dhb; password=bikes"
    />
  </connection>
</SqlServer>
```

If you need to change the connection string, modify the **value** attribute appropriately.

4. Locate the **<QueueNames>** tag. Change the **NET-MSMQ** value to include the correct IP address of your computer.

```
<Queue>
    <QueueNames>
        <add key="NET-MSMQ"
value="FormatName:DIRECT=TCP:192.168.0.5\Private$\XBikes-OrderQueue" />
```

5. Save Dllhost.exe.config.

6. Using Notepad, open XBikes-DAL-MSMQServiceInterface.exe.config from the C:\Xbikes\Net\Xbikes-Dal-Msmqserviceinterface\Bin\Debug folder.

7. Repeat steps 2 through 4, and then save the file.

This completes the configuration of the XBikes Web application.

Running XBikes on a Single Tier

To test the installation and execute XBikes complete the following steps.

▶ **To execute XBikes**

1. Load Internet Explorer.
2. In the **Address** field, enter the URL **http://localhost/XBikes-Web**.

The XBikes Web application allows you to browse bikes by type, order bikes, change quantities and check out your order.

When orders are written, they go to the message queue. To move orders from the .NET Message Queue into the SQL Server database, you must run a DOS console application. Complete the following steps on the .NET computer.

▶ **To run the DOS console application**

1. Open a command prompt.
2. Type **cd /D C:\xbikes\net\xbikes-dal-msmqserviceinterface\bin\Debug**, and then press ENTER.
3. Execute **XBikes-DAL-MSMQServiceInterface.exe**. One message is read from the queue. The XML representation of the Order is displayed.
4. If there are more messages on the queue press **Y;** otherwise press any other key to exit the application.

Deploying XBikes on Multiple Computers

This section describes how to install XBikes in a distributed environment, so that the Presentation tier, Business tier, and Data tier are installed on different computers.

Another configuration option is to set up the database on a separate computer. In this case, the configuration settings for the Data tier connection string must to be set appropriately to point to this computer.

Note: In a distributed setup, none of the in-memory adapters work. This is by design because they can work only when all three tier processes run on the same computer. For a .NET Framework-only setup, use the .NET Remoting adapters instead.

Identifying Requirements for Each Computer

This section describes the components that must be installed on each computer in a distributed environment before you install the XBikes application.

Presentation Tier Computer Setup

The Presentation tier computer requires the following components:

- Windows Server 2003 or Windows 2000 Server with Service Pack 3 or later in Workgroup mode
- .NET Framework 1.1
- .NET Framework 1.1 SDK or Visual Studio 2003
- Internet Information Service — World Wide Web Server
- ASP.NET Application Server component (Windows 2003 only)
- Microsoft Enterprise Instrumentation Framework (EIF)
- JNBridgePro v1.4 Enterprise Edition (run time only)

Note: ASP.NET Session State Service should be running and its startup type should be set to automatic.

Installing XBikes on the Presentation Tier

To install XBikes on the presentation tier computer, complete the following steps.

▶ **To install XBikes on the Presentation tier computer**

1. Open Windows Explorer, and then double-click **xbikes3tier.msi**.
2. On the **xbikes3tier** wizard page, click **Next**.
3. On the **Select Installation Folder** page, make sure C:\Xbikes is the installation path, select the **Everyone** option to install XBikes for all users on the computer, and then click **Next**.
4. On the **Confirm Installation** page, click **Next**.
5. On the **Install Options** page, select **Web Tier Only**, and then click **Next** to continue.
6. In the **Winzip Self Extractor** dialog box, make sure **Unzip to folder** is set to **C:\xbikes**, and then click **Unzip**.
7. In the dialog box that shows how many files were unzipped successfully, click **OK**.
8. In the **Winzip Self-Extractor** dialog box, click **Close**.

   The installation program continues the setup process for a few seconds.
9. On the **Installation Complete** page, click **Close**.

Configuring XBikes on the Presentation Tier

The XBikes Web application uses .NET Remoting to communicate between the tiers when deployed across multiple machines. Before executing the application, you must change the configuration for .NET Remoting to point to the correct machine.

▶ **To configure the .NET Remoting on the Presentation tier**

1. Using Notepad, open the **Remoting.config** from the C:\Xbikes\Net\Xbikes-Web folder.

2. Find the **<wellknown>** element, and then set its **url** attribute to the URL of the .NET Remoting Business tier service interface. You must set the server name to the name of the computer where the Business tier components are installed as shown in the following example.

```
<wellknown
  url="http://BusinessTierComputer/XBikes-BLL-
RemotingServiceInterface/BLLRemotingServiceInterface.rem"
  type="XBikes.BLL.ServiceInterface.Net.Remoting.BLLRemotingServiceInterface,
XBikes-BLL-RemotingServiceInterface"
/>
```

3. Save Remoting.config.

This completes the configuration of the Presentation tier computer.

Business Tier Computer Setup

The Business tier computer requires the following components:

- Windows Server 2003 or Windows 2000 Server with Service Pack 3 or later in Workgroup mode
- .NET Framework 1.1
- .NET Framework 1.1 SDK or Visual Studio 2003
- Internet Information Service—World Wide Web Server
- ASP.NET Application Server component (Windows 2003 only)
- Microsoft Enterprise Instrumentation Framework (EIF)
- JNBridgePro v1.4 Enterprise Edition (run time only)

Installing XBikes on the Business Tier

To install XBikes on the Business tier computer complete the following steps.

▶ **To install XBikes on the Business tier computer**

1. Open Windows Explorer, and then double-click **xbikes3tier.msi**.
2. On the **xbikes3tier** wizard page, click **Next**.
3. On the **Select Installation Folder** page, make sure **c:\xbikes** is the installation path, select the **Everyone** option to install XBikes for all users on the computer, and then click **Next**.
4. On the **Confirm Installation** page, click **Next**.
5. On the **Install Options** page, select **Business Logic Layer Only**. Click **Next**.

6. In the **Winzip Self Extractor** dialog box, make sure **Unzip to folder** is set to **C:\xbikes**, and then click **Unzip**.

7. In the dialog box that shows how many files were unzipped successfully, click **OK**.

8. In the **Winzip Self-Extractor** dialog box, click **Close**.

   The installation program continues the setup process for a few seconds.

9. On the **Installation Complete** page, click **Close**.

Configuring XBikes on the Business Tier

The XBikes application is now installed on the Business tier computer. Before you execute the application, you will need to modify the identity of the COM+ to Network Service to allow the application to execute without the need for someone to be logged in. You will also have to configure .NET Remoting.

▶ **To configure the COM+ application on the Business tier**

1. In Control Panel, double-click **Administrative Tools**, and then double-click **Component Services**. The Component Services Manager loads.

2. In the tree on the left, expand **Component Services**, expand **Computers**, and then expand **My Computer**.

3. Expand **COM+ Applications**. A list of installed COM+ applications is shown in the tree view.

4. Right-click **XBikes**, and then click **Properties**. The **XBikes Properties** dialog box appears.

5. Click the **Identity** tab, and then click the **Network Service** option.

6. Click **OK**. The **XBikes Properties** dialog box closes.

7. Close Component Services Manager.

▶ **To configure .NET Remoting on the Business tier**

1. In Notepad, open the **Remoting.config** file. This file is located in the System32 directory located under the system folder, such as C:\Windows, of the computer hosting the Business tier components.

2. Find the **<wellknown>** element, and set its **url** attribute to the URL of the .NET Remoting Data tier service interface. You must set the server name to the name of the computer where the Data tier components are installed as shown in the following example.

```
<wellknown
  url="http://DataTierComputer/XBikes-DAL-
RemotingServiceInterface/DALRemotingServiceInterface.rem"
  type="XBikes.DAL.ServiceInterface.Net.Remoting.DALRemotingServiceInterface,
XBikes-DAL-RemotingServiceInterface"
/>
```

3. Save Remoting.config.

This completes the configuration of the Business tier computer.

Data Tier Computer Setup

The Data tier computer requires the following components:

- Windows Server 2003 or Windows 2000 Server with Service Pack 3 or later in Workgroup mode
- .NET Framework 1.1
- .NET Framework 1.1 SDK or Visual Studio 2003
- Microsoft Message Queuing (also known as MSMQ)
- Microsoft SQL Server 2000 with mixed mode security and Service Pack 3
- Internet Information Service — World Wide Web Server
- ASP.NET Application Server component (Windows 2003 only)
- Microsoft Enterprise Instrumentation Framework (EIF)

Installing XBikes on the Data Tier

To install XBikes on the Data tier computer, complete the following steps.

▶ **To install XBikes on the Data tier computer**

1. Open Windows Explorer, and then double-click **xbikes3tier.msi**.
2. On the **xbikes3tier** wizard page, click **Next**.
3. On the **Select Installation Folder** page, make sure C:\Xbikes is the installation path, select the **Everyone** option to install XBikes for all users on the computer, and then click **Next**.
4. On the **Confirm Installation** page, click **Next**.
5. On the **Install Options** page, select **Data Access Layer Only**. Click **Next**.
6. In the **Winzip Self Extractor** dialog box, make sure **Unzip to folder** is set to **C:\xbikes**, and then click **Unzip**.
7. In the dialog box that shows how many files were unzipped successfully, click **OK**.
8. In the **Winzip Self-Extractor** dialog box, click **Close**.

   The installation program continues the setup process for a few seconds.
9. On the **Installation Complete** page, click **Close**.

Configuring XBikes on the Data Tier

The XBikes application is now installed on the Data tier. Before you can execute the application you must configure the queue and database connection settings. To perform the configuration, complete the following steps.

► **To configure the database connection string**

1. In Notepad, open the Dllhost.exe.config file from the C:\Windows\System32 folder.

2. Find the start tag of the **<SqlServer>** element.

3. Check to make sure the connection string includes the correct server name. The server name is shown in bold below to help you.

```
<SqlServer>
  <connection>
    <add
      key="connectionString"
      value="server=localhost;database=xbikes;user id=dhb; password=bikes"
    />
  </connection>
</SqlServer>
```

If you need to change the connection string, modify the **value** attribute appropriately.

4. Locate the **<QueueNames>** tag. Change the **NET-MSMQ** value to include the correct IP address of your computer.

```
<Queue>
    <QueueNames>
        <add key="NET-MSMQ"
 value="FormatName:DIRECT=TCP:192.168.0.5\Private$\XBikes-OrderQueue" />
```

5. Save Dllhost.exe.config.

6. Using Notepad, open **XBikes-DAL-MSMQServiceInterface.exe.config** from the C:\Xbikes\Net\Xbikes-Dal-Msmqserviceinterface\Bin\Debug folder.

7. Repeat steps 2 through 4, and then save the file.

Running XBikes on Multiple Computers

To test the installation and execute XBikes complete the following steps on the Presentation tier computer.

► **To execute XBikes**

1. Load Internet Explorer.

2. In the **Address** field, enter the URL **http://localhost/XBikes-Web**.

The XBikes Web application allows you to browse bikes by type, order bikes, change quantities, and check out your order.

When orders are written, they go to the message queue. To move orders from the .NET Message Queue into the SQL Server database, you must run a DOS console application. Complete the following steps on the Data tier computer.

▶ **To run the DOS console application**

1. Open a command prompt.

2. Type **cd /D C:\xbikes\net\xbikes-dal-msmqserviceinterface\bin\Debug**, and then press ENTER.

3. Execute **XBikes-DAL-MSMQServiceInterface.exe**. One message is read from the queue. The XML representation of the Order is displayed.

4. If there are more messages on the queue press **Y**; otherwise press any other key to exit the application.

Changing Interoperability Methods

When you have the XBikes application operating correctly, you can change the interoperability methods so that XBikes uses different use case adapters or resource interoperability adapters. This section describes the possible options in the following topics:

- Using Web Services Adapters
- Using Ja.Net Adapters
- Using JNBridgePro Adapters

The following sections describe how to use each kind of adapter.

Using Web Service Adapters

You can use Web services adapters in the following scenarios.

- Using Web Service Adapters between the Web and Business Tiers
- Using Web Service Adapters between the Business and Data Tiers

To change XBikes to use Web services adapters, you must modify the application configuration to use the Web services adapters, update the application configuration with the URLs of the Web services, and then restart the application. The following sections describe how to perform these tasks.

Using Web Service Adapters between the Web and Business Tiers

This section describes how to use Web services between the Web and Business tiers. You can either use .NET Web services or J2EE Web services; complete the steps in one of the following procedures.

▶ **To use .NET Framework Web services between the Web and Business tiers**

1. In Notepad, open the Web.config file for the XBikes application. This file is located in the C:\Xbikes\Net\XBikes-Web folder.

2. Find the start tag of the **<appSettings>** element in the **Web.config** file.

3. Find the **<add>** child element that specifies the URL of the .NET Framework Web service Business tier service interface. Set the **value** attribute to the correct URL as show in the following example.

```
<add
   key="XBikes-UseCaseInteropAdapters.Net.BLLWSSI.BLLWSServiceInterface"
   value="http://localhost/XBikes-BLL-
WSServiceInterface/BLLWSServiceInterface.asmx"
/>
```

4. Locate the **<adapters>** tag. Locate the <!-- .NET WS Adapters --> comment and remove the comments from configuration information located immediately below this comment.

5. Within the **<adapters>** section. Locate an existing group of tags that have not been commented out. Wrap the section with comments.

6. Save Web.config.

▶ **To use J2EE Web services between the Web and Business tiers**

1. In Notepad, open the Web.config file for the XBikes application. This file is located in the C:\Xbikes\Net\XBikes-Web folder.

2. Find the start tag of the **<appSettings>** element in the **Web.config** file.

3. Find the **<add>** child element that specifies the URL of the J2EE Web service Business tier service interface. Set the **value** attribute to the correct URL as shown in the following example.

```
<add
   key="XBikes-UseCaseInteropAdapters.J2EE.BLLWSSI.BLLWSServiceInterface"
   value="http://192.168.99.199:9080/XBikesBLLServiceInterface/
services/BLLWSServiceInterface"
/>
```

4. Locate the **<adapters>** tag. Locate the <!-- J2EE WS Adapters --> comment and remove the comments from configuration information located immediately below this comment.

5. Within the **<adapters>** section. Locate an existing group of tags that have not been commented out. Wrap the section with comments.

6. Save Web.config.

Using Web Service Adapters between the Business and Data Tiers

This section describes how to use Web services between the Business and Data tiers. You can either use .NET Web services or J2EE Web services; complete the steps in one of the following procedures.

▶ **To use .NET Framework Web services between the Business and Data tiers**

1. In Notepad, open the Dllhost.exe.config file from the C:\Windows\System32 folder.

2. Find the start tag of the **<appSettings>** element in the file.

3. Find the **<add>** child element that specifies the URL of the .NET Framework Web service Data tier service interface. Set the **value** attribute to the correct URL as shown in the following example.

```
<add
  key="XBikes-ResourceInteropAdapters.Net.DALWSSI.DALWSServiceInterface"
  value="http://localhost/XBikes-DAL-WSServiceInterface/
DALWSServiceInterface.asmx"
/>
```

4. Locate the **<adapters>** tag. Locate the <!-- .NET WS Adapters --> comment and remove the comments from configuration information located immediately below this comment.

5. Within the **<adapters>** section. Locate an existing group of tags that have not been commented out. Wrap the section with comments.

6. Save Web.config.

▶ **To use .NET Framework Web services between the Business and Data Tiers**

1. In Notepad, open the Dllhost.exe.config file from the C:\Windows\System32 folder.

2. Find the start tag of the **<appSettings>** element in the file.

3. Find the **<add>** child element that specifies the URL of the J2EE Web service Data tier service interface. Set the **value** attribute to the correct URL as shown in the following example.

```
<add
  key="XBikes-ResourceInteropAdapters.J2EE.DALWSSI.DALWSServiceInterface"
  value="http://192.168.99.199:9080/XBikesResWS/services/
DALWSServiceInterface"
/>
```

4. Locate the **<adapters>** tag. Locate the <!-- J2EE WS Adapters --> comment and remove the comments from configuration information located immediately below this comment.

5. Within the **<adapters>** section. Locate an existing group of tags that have not been commented out. Wrap the section with comments.

6. Save Web.config.

Using Ja.NET Adapters

You can use Ja.NET adapters in the following scenarios:

- Using Ja.NET Adapters between the Web and Business Tiers
- Using Ja.NET Adapters between the Business and Data Tiers

To change XBikes to use Ja.NET adapters, you must modify the application configuration to use the Ja.NET adapters, update the application configuration with the URLs of the Ja.NET service, and then restart the application. You must also reconfigure the J2EE application to allow Ja.NET to function, because out of the box, the J2EE application is configured for J2EE to .NET interoperability. The following sections describe how to perform these tasks.

Reconfiguring the J2EE Application for Ja.NET

To enable the Ja.NET adapters to communicate with the J2EE version of XBikes, you must complete one of the following tasks depending upon your configuration.

▶ **To change the WebSphere Studio Application Developer 5.0 configuration**

1. Start WebSphere Application Developer Studio 5.0 by clicking **Start**, pointing to **All Programs**, pointing to **IBM WebSphere Studio**, and clicking **Application Developer 5.0**.

2. A **WebSphere Studio** dialog box appears. Change the workspace to **c:\xbikes \j2ee-ibm** and then click **OK**.

3. The J2EE–IBM WebSphere Studio Application Developer window appears.

4. In the left window, click the **J2EE Hierarchy** tab. The J2EE Hierarchy window appears.

5. Expand **Server Configurations**, and then double-click **WebSphere v5.0 Server Configuration**. The **WebSphere v5.0 Server Configuration** appears in the main window.

6. Click the **Paths** tab from the bottom of the main window. The **Paths** configuration screen appears.

7. Click **c:\xbikes\J2EE-IBM\janet_libs\janetNetDalProxies.jar**, and then click **Remove**.

8. Repeat step 7 for **c:\xbikes\J2EE-IBM\janet_libs\JanetNetBllProxies.jar** and **c:\xbikes\J2EE-IBM\janet_libs\janet.jar**.

9. Click the **Environment** tab from the bottom of the main window. The **Environment Options** configuration screen appears.

10. Remove all the entries from the **Java VM Arguments** field.

11. Close the **WebSphere v5.0 Server Configuration** window. The **Save Resource** dialog box appears. Click **Yes** to save your changes.

12. Switch to the **J2EE Navigator** view in the left pane.

13. Expand **JaNetBLL**, expand **Java Source**, and then expand **com.intrinsyc.janet**.

14. Open **JaNet.xml**.

15. Locate the **<URI>** tag and replace **http://192.168.0.200:9080/JaNetBLL** with **http://<ipaddress>/JaNetBLL**, where **<ipaddress>** is the IP address of the computer hosting the JaNetBLL.

16. Repeat steps 13–15 for both **JaNetDAL** and **JaNetJMS**.

17. You may now restart or start your server.

▶ **To change the WebSphere application server configuration**

1. On the computer hosting the Ja.NET service interfaces, open a command prompt and navigate to the C:\Was\Websphere\Appserver\Bin folder.

2. Type **startserver server1**, and then press ENTER. After a short period of time, a message displays indicating that server1 is open for e-business.

3. Open a Web browser window and navigate to http://localhost:9080/admin.

4. In the **User ID** field, enter **admin**, and then click **OK**.

5. In the left pane, expand **Servers**, and then click **Application Servers**. The Application Servers window appears in the right pane.

6. In the right pane, click **server1**. The server1 window appears.

7. In the right pane, click **Process Definition**. The Process Definition window appears.

8. In the right pane, click **Java Virtual Machine**. The Java Virtual Machine window appears.

9. Remove all entries from the **Classpath** field **EXCEPT** the entry **c:\tme\glue\lib \GLUE.jar**.

10. Remove the entry from the **Generic JVM arguments** field. The field should be empty.

11. Click **OK**. The **Messages** section appears at the top of the right pane. Click the **Save** link.

12. In the **Save** pane, click the **Save** button. The right pane reverts to the **WebSphere Application Server** home page.

13. Close your browser and restart the server for the changes to take effect.

You must now update the EAR that contains the Ja.NET adapters you want to access. To do this you must have access to the source code.

▶ **To update the EAR that contains the Ja.NET adapters you want to access**

1. Start WebSphere Application Developer Studio 5.0 by clicking **Start**, pointing to **All Programs**, pointing to **IBM WebSphere Studio**, and then clicking **Application Developer 5.0**.

2. A **WebSphere Studio** dialog box appears. Change the workspace to **c:\xbikes \j2ee-ibm** and then click **OK**.

3. The J2EE–IBM WebSphere Studio Application Developer window appears.

4. Close the WebSphere v5.0 Server Configuration window. In the **Save Resource** dialog box, click **Yes** to save your changes.

5. Switch to the **J2EE Navigator** view in the left pane.

6. Expand **JaNetBLL**, expand **Java Source**, and then expand **com.intrinsyc.janet**.

7. Open **JaNet.xml**.

8. Locate the **<URI>** tag and replace **http://192.168.0.200:9080/JaNetBLL** with **http://<ipaddress>/JaNetBLL**, where **<ipaddress>** is the IP address of the machine hosting the JaNetBLL.

9. Repeat steps 13–15 for both **JaNetDAL** and **JaNetJMS**.

You must now recreate the EARs. To do this, follow the steps for manual deployment in Appendix A, and then deploy the EAR to the server. If you have already installed the EARs using the installer, or if you manually installed the EARs, you must uninstall the EARs. This can be done using the Web-based Administrative Console.

Note: To revert back to the original J2EE configuration, you must add the entries you removed in the previous steps. The quickest way to do this is to uninstall, and then reinstall, the J2EE version of XBikes.

Using Ja.NET Adapters between the Web and Business Tiers

This section describes how to use Ja.NET between the Business and Data tiers. To enable the Ja.NET adapters, complete the following steps.

▶ **To configure the Ja.NET use case interoperability adapters**

1. In Notepad, open the Remoting.config file for the XBikes application. This file is located in the C:\Xbikes\Net\XBikes-Web folder.

2. Find the **<client url="..."">** element, and then set its **url** attribute to the URL of the Ja.NET BLL service interface as shown in the following example.

```
<client url="http://192.168.99.199:9080/JaNetBLL">
```

3. Save Remoting.config.

4. In Notepad, open the Web.config file for the XBikes application. This file is located in the C:\Xbikes\Net\XBikes-Web folder.

5. Locate the **<adapters>** tag. Locate the <!-- JaNET Adapters --> comment and remove the comments from configuration information located immediately below this comment.

6. Within the **<adapters>** section. Locate an existing group of tags that have not been commented out. Wrap the section with comments.

7. Save Web.config.

Using Ja.NET Adapters between the Business and Data Tiers

This section describes how to use Ja.NET between the Business and Data tiers. To enable the Ja.NET adapters, complete the following steps.

▶ **To configure the Ja.NET resource interoperability adapters**

1. In Notepad, open the Remoting.config file. This file is located in the System32 directory located under the system folder, such as C:\Windows, of the computer hosting the Business tier components.

2. Find the **<client url="...">** element that sets the URL for the Ja.NET Data tier service interface, and set its **url** attribute to the correct URL as shown in the following example.

```
<client url="http://192.168.99.199:9080/JaNetDAL">
```

3. Find the **<client url="...">** element that sets the URL for the Ja.NET queue service interface, and then set its **url** attribute to the correct URL as shown in the following example.

```
<client url="http://192.168.99.199:9080/JaNetJms">
```

4. Save Remoting.config.

5. In Notepad, open the Dllhost.exe.config file for the XBikes application. This file is located in the C:\Windows\System32 folder.

6. Locate the **<adapters>** tag. Locate the <!-- JaNET Adapters --> comment and remove the comments from configuration information located immediately below this comment.

7. Within the **<adapters>** section. Locate an existing group of tags that have not been commented out. Wrap the section with comments.

8. Save Dllhost.exe.config.

► **To configure the queue name**

1. In Notepad, open the Dllhost.exe.config file. This file is located in the System32 directory located under the system folder, such as C:\Windows, of the computer hosting the Business tier components.

2. Find the **<QueueNames>** element. If the name of the MQSeries queue or queue factory has been changed in the J2EE application, define **<add>** elements to specify the MQSeries queue name and queue factory name for the Ja.NET queue resource interoperability adapter as shown in the following example.

```
<add key="JaNET-MQSeries-QName" value="XBikesQ" />
<add key="JaNET-MQSeries-QFactoryName" value="XBikesQCF" />
```

3. Save Dllhost.exe.config.

Using JNBridgePro Adapters

You can use JNBridgePro adapters in the following scenarios.

- Using JNBridgePro Adapters between the Web and Business Tiers
- Using JNBridgePro Adapters between the Business and Data Tiers

To change XBikes to use JNBridgePro adapters, you must modify the application configuration to use the JNBridgePro adapters, update the application configuration with the URLs of the JNBridgePro, and then restart the application. The following sections describe how to perform these tasks.

Using JNBridgePro Adapters between the Web and Business Tiers

This section describes how to use JNBridgePro between the Business and Data tiers. To enabled the JNBridgePro adapters, complete the following steps.

► **To configure the JNBridge use case interoperability adapters**

1. In Notepad, open the JNBProxy.config from the C:\Inetpub\Wwwroot folder.

2. Find the **<wellknown>** element, and then set its **url** attribute to the URL of the JNBridge BLL service interface as shown in the following example.

```
<wellknown
  url="jtcp://192.168.99.199:8085/JNBDispatcher"
  type="com.jnbridge.jnbcore.JNBDispatcher, JNBShare"
/>
```

3. Save JNBProxy.config.

4. In Notepad, open the Web.config file for the XBikes application. This file is located in the C:\Xbikes\Net\XBikes-Web folder.

5. Locate the **<adapters>** tag. Locate the <!-- JNBridge Adapters --> comment and remove the comments from configuration information located immediately below this comment.

6. Within the **<adapters>** section. Locate an existing group of tags that have not been commented out. Wrap the section with comments.

7. Save Web.config.

Using JNBridgePro Adapters between the Business and Data Tiers

This section describes how to use Web services between the Business and Data tiers. To enabled the JNBridgePro adapters, complete the following steps.

▶ **To configure the JNBridge resource interoperability adapters**

1. In Notepad, open the Dllhost.exe.config file from the C:\Windows\System32 folder.

2. Find the **<jnbridge>** element.

3. Make sure the **<add>** child element specifies the URL for the JNBridge Data tier service interface as shown in the following example.

```
<add
  key="DAL_PrimaryURL"
  value="jtcp://javabox:8086/JNBDispatcher"
/>
```

4. Find the **<QueueNames>** element. If the name of the MQSeries queue or queue factory has been changed in the J2EE application, define **<add>** elements to specify the MQSeries queue name and queue factory name for the JNBridge queue resource Interoperability adapter as shown in the following example.

```
<add key="JNBridge-MQSeries-QName" value="XBikesQ" />
<add key="JNBridge-MQSeries-QFactoryName" value="XBikesQCF" />
```

5. Locate the **<adapters>** tag. Locate the <!-- JNBridge Adapters --> comment and remove the comments from configuration information located immediately below this comment.

6. Within the **<adapters>** section. Locate an existing group of tags that have not been commented out. Wrap the section with comments.

7. Save Dllhost.exe.config.

Uninstalling XBikes

To uninstall the .NET XBikes Web application, complete the following steps.

► **To uninstall XBikes**

1. In Control Panel, double-click **Add or Remove Programs**.

2. In the Add or Remove Programs window, click **xbikes3tier** in the list of currently installed programs, and then click **Remove**.

3. Click **Yes** to confirm that you want to remove this program from your computer.

Next, the following items must be removed manually.

► **To delete additional items on a single computer**

1. Delete the Com+ application named XBikes:

   a. In Control Panel, double-click **Administrative Tools**, and then double-click **Component Services**.

   b. In the Component Services node, expand the tree until you see My Computer.

   c. Expand **COM+ Applications**, right-click **XBIKES**, and then click **Delete**.

2. Delete the following virtual directories:

   - XBikes-Web
   - XBikes-BLL-RemotingServiceInterface
   - XBikes-BLL-WSServiceInterface
   - XBikes-DAL-WSServiceInterface
   - XBikes-DAL-RemotingServiceInterface
   - xbikes-bll-janetserviceinterface
   - xbikes-dal-janetserviceinterface

3. In Control Panel, double-click **Administrative Tools**, and then double-click **Internet Information Services**. Expand the tree for your computer, click **Web sites**, and then click **Default Web site**. Right-click each entry listed in step 2, and click **Delete** for each one.

4. Delete the following from the global assembly cache:

   - xbikes-common
   - jnbridgebllproxies
   - jnbridgeDALProxies
   - jnbshare
   - janetBllEjb
   - janetDalEjb
   - JaNetJms

5. In Control Panel, double-click **Administrative Tools**, and then double-click **Microsoft .NET Framework 1.1 Configuration**. Click **Assembly Cache** in the left pane, and then click **Assembly Cache** or **View List of Assemblies** in the right pane. Right-click each entry in step 4, and click **Delete** for each one.

6. In Windows Explorer, delete the following folders:

   - C:\Xbikes
   - C:\Windows\System32\Dllhost.exe.config
   - C:\Windows\System32\Dllhost.exe.config.xsd
   - C:\Windows\System32\EnterpriseInstrumentation.config
   - C:\Windows\System32\Remoting.config
   - C:\Inetpub\Wwwroot\Jnbproxy.config

7. Delete the SQL database named XBIKES:

   a. Click **Start**, point to **All Programs**, point to **Microsoft SQL Server**, and then click **Enterprise Manager**.

   b. Expand **Console Root**, expand **Microsoft SQL Servers**, and then expand **SQL Server Group**. You should see your computer—if not, you need to register your SQL instance. For information about how to do this, see the article "How to register a server (Enterprise Manager)" on MSDN.

   c. Expand your computer, and then expand **databases**.

   d. Right-click **XBikes**, and then click **Delete**.

8. Delete the private message queue named XBikes-orderqueue:

   a. In Control Panel, double-click **Administrative Tools**, and then double-click **Computer Management**.

   b. Expand **Services and Applications**, expand **Message Queuing**, and then expand **Private Queue**.

   c. Right-click **XBikes-orderqueue**, and then click **Delete**.

▶ **To delete additional items on a Web tier computer**

1. Delete the virtual directory named XBikes-Web:

   a. In Control Panel, double-click **Administrative Tools**, and then double-click **Internet Information Services**.

   b. Expand the tree for your computer, expand **Web sites**, and then click **Default Web site**.

   c. Right-click each entry listed in step 2 of the preceding procedure, and click **Delete** for each one.

2. Delete the following from the global assembly cache:
   - xbikes-common
   - jnbridgebllproxies
   - jnbshare
   - janetBllEjb

3. In Control Panel, double-click **Administrative Tools**, and then double-click **Microsoft .NET Framework 1.1 Configuration**. Click **Assembly Cache** in the left pane, and then click **Assembly Cache** or **View List of Assemblies** in the right pane. Right-click each entry listed in step 2 (of this procedure), and click **Delete** for each one.

4. In Windows Explorer, delete the C:\Xbikes folder and the file C:\Inetpub \Wwwroot\Jnbproxy.config.

▶ **To delete additional items on a Business tier computer**

1. Delete the Com+ application named XBikes:
   a. In Control Panel, double-click **Administrative Tools**, and then double-click **Component Services**.
   b. In the Component Services node, expand the tree until you see **My Computer**.
   c. Expand **COM+ Applications**.
   d. Right-click **XBIKES**, and then click **Delete**.

2. Delete the following virtual directories:
   - XBikes-BLL-RemotingServiceInterface
   - XBikes-BLL-WSServiceInterface
   - xbikes-bll-janetserviceinterface

3. In Control Panel, double-click **Administrative Tools**, and then double-click **Internet Information Services**. Expand the tree for your computer, expand **Web sites**, and then click **Default Web site**. Right-click each entry listed in step 2, and click **Delete** for each one.

4. Delete the following from the global assembly cache:
   - xbikes-common
   - jnbridgeDALProxies
   - jnbshare
   - janetDalEjb
   - JaNetJms.dll

5. In Control Panel, double-click **Administrative Tools**, and then double-click **Microsoft .NET Framework 1.1 Configuration**. Click **Assembly Cache** in the left pane, and then click **Assembly Cache** or **View List of Assemblies** in the right pane. Right-click each entry listed in step 4, and click **Delete** for each one.

6. In Windows Explorer, delete the following folders:

- C:\Xbikes.
- C:\Windows\System32\Dllhost.exe.config.
- C:\Windows\System32\Dllhost.exe.config.xsd.
- C:\Windows\System32\EnterpriseInstrumentation.config.
- C:\Windows\System32\Remoting.config.
- C:\Inetpub\Wwwroot\Jnbproxy.config.

▶ **To delete additional items on a Data tier computer**

1. Delete the following virtual directories:

- XBikes-DAL-WSServiceInterface
- XBikes-DAL-RemotingServiceInterface
- xbikes-dal-janetserviceinterface

2. In Control Panel, double-click **Administrative Tools**, and then double-click **Internet Information Services**. Expand the tree for your computer, expand **Web sites**, and then click **Default Web site**. Right-click each entry listed in step 1, and click **Delete** for each one.

3. Delete the following from the global assembly cache:

- xbikes-common
- jnbshare

4. In Control Panel, double-click **Administrative Tools**, and then double-click **Microsoft .NET Framework 1.1 Configuration**. Click **Assembly Cache** in the left pane, and then click **Assembly Cache** or **View List of Assemblies** in the right pane. Right-click each entry listed in step 3, and click **Delete** for each one.

5. In Windows Explorer, delete C:\Xbikes.

6. Delete the SQL database named XBIKES:

a. Click **Start**, point to **All Programs**, point to **Microsoft SQL Server**, and then click **Enterprise Manager**.

b. Expand **Console Root** then **Microsoft SQL Servers** and then **SQL Server Group**. You should see your computer—if not, you need to register your SQL instance. For information about how to do this, see the article "How to register a server (Enterprise Manager)" on MSDN.

c. Expand the tree under your computer, and then expand the tree under **databases**.

d. Right-click **XBikes**, and then click **Delete**.

7. Delete the private message queue named XBikes-orderqueue:

   a. In Control Panel, double-click **Administrative Tools**, and then double-click **Computer Management**.

   b. Expand **Services and Applications**, expand **Message Queuing**, and then expand **Private Queue**.

   c. Right-click **XBikes-orderqueue**, and then click **Delete**.

Index

N

Contributors

The team that produced Application Interoperability: Microsoft .NET and J2EE came from a wide range of areas within Microsoft and from many of our partner organizations.

The following people made a substantial contribution to the writing, developing, and testing of this content.

Development

Peter Laudati, Microsoft Consulting Services
William Loeffler, Microsoft Platform Architecture Group
David Aiken, Arkitec Ltd.
Keith Organ, Arkitec Ltd.
Anthony Steven, Content Master Ltd.
Mike Preradovic, Intrinsyc Software
Wayne Citrin, JNBridge, LLC
Peter Clift, VMC Consulting Corporation

Test

Chris Sfanos, Microsoft Platform Architecture Group
Sameer Tarey, Infosys Technologies Ltd.
Prashant Bansode, Infosys Technologies Ltd.
Manish Mendiratta, Infosys Technologies Ltd.
Rohit Sharma, Infosys Technologies Ltd.
Nancy Fabiana K., Infosys Technologies Ltd.
Paresh Gujar, Infosys Technologies Ltd.
Sameer Aras, Infosys Technologies Ltd.

Edit

RoAnn Corbisier, Microsoft Platform Architecture Group
Tina Burden, Entirenet

Review

Gianpaolo Carraro, Microsoft Corporation
Simon Guest, Microsoft Corporation
Sandy Khaund, Microsoft Corporation
Arvindra Sehmi, Microsoft Corporation